CHURCHILL AND EDEN

PARTNERS THROUGH WAR AND PEACE

CHURCHILL AND EDEN

PARTNERS THROUGH WAR AND PEACE

DAVID CHARLWOOD

PEN & SWORD **HISTORY**

AN IMPRINT OF PEN & SWORD BOOKS LTD.
YORKSHIRE – PHILADELPHIA

First published in Great Britain in 2020 by
PEN AND SWORD HISTORY
An imprint of
Pen & Sword Books Ltd
Yorkshire – Philadelphia

ISBN 978 1 52674 489 0

Typeset in Times New Roman 11.5/14 by
SJmagic DESIGN SERVICES, India.
Printed and bound in the UK by TJ International Ltd.

Pen & Sword Books Limited incorporates the imprints of Atlas, Archaeology,
Aviation, Discovery, Family History, Fiction, History, Maritime, Military, Military
Classics, Politics, Select, Transport, True Crime, Air World, Frontline Publishing,
Leo Cooper, Remember When, Seaforth Publishing, The Praetorian Press,
Wharncliffe Local History, Wharncliffe Transport, Wharncliffe True Crime and
White Owl.

For a complete list of Pen & Sword titles please contact
PEN & SWORD BOOKS LIMITED
47 Church Street, Barnsley, South Yorkshire, S70 2AS, England
E-mail: enquiries@pen-and-sword.co.uk
Website: www.pen-and-sword.co.uk

Or
PEN AND SWORD BOOKS
1950 Lawrence Rd, Havertown, PA 19083, USA
E-mail: Uspen-and-sword@casematepublishers.com
Website: www.penandswordbooks.com

Contents

Introduction..vii

PART ONE

Chapter 1   Sun, sand and Fascism 2
Chapter 2   'The complete gangster'..6
Chapter 3   Going quietly 11
Chapter 4   Wars and rumours of wars 16

PART TWO

Chapter 5   Downing Street, De Gaulle and Dunkirk..........................22
Chapter 6   The home front 27
Chapter 7   Priorities...32
Chapter 8   The dark hour..37
Chapter 9   'The Prime Minister's compliments'..................................41
Chapter 10   Uncle Joe and FDR 47
Chapter 11   Avoiding losses 53
Chapter 12   To Moscow..58
Chapter 13   Churchill, Eden and the Holocaust 64
Chapter 14   Casablanca 68
Chapter 15   East to west 73
Chapter 16   Second-in-command 79
Chapter 17   Visiting friends..84
Chapter 18   A very small country 90
Chapter 19   Maladies..95
Chapter 20   D-Day, De Gaulle and Doodlebugs 100
Chapter 21   'A deathless memory' 106
Chapter 22   The post-war world 110
Chapter 23   Vive la France 115
Chapter 24   Hands off the British Empire 119

Chapter 25   A Greek Christmas 123
Chapter 26   To Yalta 127
Chapter 27   'We have been deceived'... 131
Chapter 28   The final act 137
Chapter 29   The worst form of government 141

PART THREE

Chapter 30   Licking wounds... 148
Chapter 31   Old friends, new enemies....................................... 152
Chapter 32   A changed world 158
Chapter 33   The road back to power.. 163

PART FOUR

Chapter 34   Side by side... 170
Chapter 35   Commitments 175
Chapter 36   Frailties 181
Chapter 37   Bermuda and Berlin.. 188
Chapter 38   Eden's finest hour... 193
Chapter 39   The end of the road 200
Chapter 40   'I am going'.. 204

PART FIVE

Chapter 41   Flying solo 210
Chapter 42   Dark horizons.. 215
Chapter 43   Suez... 220
Chapter 44   'A slow bleeding to death'....................................... 225
Chapter 45   A premature end 230

PART SIX

Chapter 46   Out of office.. 238
Chapter 47   Old men 242

Epilogue 248
Acknowledgements.. 252
Endnotes.. 253
Select Bibliography.. 276
Index 281

Introduction

Churchill and Eden presided over Britain's foreign policy through a period of momentous change. When Anthony Eden died in 1977, *The Times* wrote, 'He was the last prime minister to believe Britain was a great power and the first to confront a crisis which proved she was not.' It was a harsh judgement, but reflected the realities of a new world order. Churchill and Eden's close, sometimes fractious, but enduring working relationship began as Hitler's armies swept through France in 1940 and continued through the early part of the Cold War to the decline of Britain's Empire in the Middle East nearly two decades later. Few politicians in history have played such a prominent part in shaping a nation's destiny.

The attention of historians and biographers is usually drawn to the vibrant, iconic figure of Winston Churchill, but for nearly a decade Anthony Eden served as his foreign secretary, confidant and, at times, his voice of reason. Far from being simply a supplicant to the whims of Britain's most popular prime minister, Eden played a key role in the outworking of policy. His strengths, however, were very different. He was not a decisive man of ideas; he was a man of intelligence, charm and principle. But for all their differences, the two leaders largely shared an outlook on the world and Britain's place in it. Eden was not just Churchill's heir apparent, he was his anointed successor. But the years Eden waited in Churchill's shadow stretched their relationship to breaking point.

This book is not a dual biography; several historians have produced deeply researched accounts of Eden's life and Churchill is one of the most analysed figures in history. Neither is it an attempt to reveal new 'secrets' about their lives. Instead, it is a new perspective: to tell the story of events and how Churchill's and Eden's actions and relationship shaped them.

The narrative ranges from the sunny south of France to the deserts of Africa and the jungles of Vietnam, covering the eras of the

Second World War, the decline of Britain's Empire and the coming of the Cold War. It also encompasses the wider relationships between Churchill, Eden and other statesmen, including Roosevelt, Stalin, De Gaulle, Eisenhower and Nasser. Because the focus of the book is on world events, it primarily covers foreign policy. This is, in part, also due to the fact that when Eden eventually became prime minister, he continued to focus on foreign rather than domestic affairs. The book also centres on the relationship between Churchill and Eden themselves; to do justice to the roles of the key advisors and friends would simply be beyond the scope of this narrative.

Despite the fact that their destinies were closely aligned for so much of their political careers, Winston Churchill is consistently ranked in public polls as Britain's best prime minister, while Anthony Eden is frequently listed as one of the worst. His entire time in office has been eclipsed in most people's minds by the Suez Crisis, the fatal mistake that brought about his downfall and became a deeply embarrassing episode in modern British history. Perhaps the truism that 'you are only as good as your last performance' holds for actors on the world's stage, as well as those in the West End. To some degree this book is therefore an effort to encourage a reappraisal of Eden, or at least to place his greatest failure in the context of the achievements of his earlier career, which typically go unnoticed.

When both men entered politics, the world had only endured one global conflict and the sun never set on the British Empire. By the time they departed, Britain had given up India – once the 'jewel' of the Crown's overseas possessions – and the tattered remnants of Britain's prestige in the Middle East lay trampled in the Egyptian desert. Instead of ruling the world, Britain was a junior partner in the Western alliance against the great Soviet threat. It can be argued that Churchill and Eden never reconciled themselves to the changing circumstances of the nation they led: both believed that Britain should be 'great'.

The events that transpired were not simply the inexorable march of history, as they are so often portrayed. A second world war was not guaranteed to happen and almost no one – Churchill and Eden included – could have envisaged the decline and fall of Britain's Empire, or a Cold War between East and West that would last half a century and outlive them both.

PART ONE

Chapter 1

Sun, sand and Fascism

On 5 January 1938 three holidaying British politicians rendezvoused at a restaurant on the French Riviera for lunch. David Lloyd George was early, Anthony Eden was on time and Winston Churchill was late. It was bad form on the part of Churchill, who had invited the former wartime prime minister and the young foreign secretary to join him at *La Bonne Auberge*. Eden asked, 'Where's our host?' to which Lloyd George laughed and responded, 'Have you ever known Winston in time for a meal yet?'[1]

When Eden lunched with Lloyd George and Churchill on the Riviera he was forty years old and had already been foreign secretary for nearly three years (at the time of his appointment he was the youngest man to hold the post since before the Crimean War). He was tall, with an engaging smile and a charming manner, and he was always immaculately attired; a French newspaper once gave him the title of best-dressed Englishman. He walked with a languid stride and spoke with eloquence and clarity, but his debonair exterior masked deep self-doubt, which plagued him throughout his life and affected his health. The great Shakespearean actor Anthony Quayle remarked, on meeting Eden for the first time, that he 'seemed like an actor playing the part of Anthony Eden.'

Before going to Oxford University, Eden had volunteered to join the King's Royal Rifle Corps, serving on the Western Front and fighting at the Somme, where he was awarded the Military Cross. In 1918 he became the youngest Brigade Major in the army. (His subsequent account of his wartime experiences made no mention of his award for bravery.) After the war he studied Oriental Languages – Persian and Arabic – at Christ Church College and it was on one Christmas break from university that Eden first met Churchill. The young student accompanied his mother and family friends to a political rally in Sunderland, where Churchill was speaking. Eden later vividly remembered the crowded hall and a line from Churchill's speech on Russia. When he met him afterwards, Churchill asked Eden whether he intended to go into politics.[2] Some fifteen years later, Eden was sitting with him at lunch as foreign secretary.

Over their meal, the trio around the table discussed 'the state of Europe and the threats of the two dictators', Adolf Hitler and Benito Mussolini. Hitler had been appointed German chancellor five years previously and within three months had bullied the German parliament into amending the constitution to grant him powers that made the Reichstag and its members irrelevant. On the afternoon of 5 November 1937 Hitler had held a secret meeting in the Reich Chancellery in Berlin, in which he asserted that the future of the 'German race' depended on the acquisition of greater living space: '*lebensraum*'. He informed the chiefs of the army, navy and Luftwaffe that the problem could only be solved by the use of force and that such action would have to take place before 1943 to maintain the technical superiority of the German armed forces. In several of the scenarios outlined, Germany's first action would be to annex Czechoslovakia and Austria.[3] Unbeknown to the British politicians sitting in the French sunshine perusing the lunch menu at *La Bonne Auberge* nine weeks later, Hitler had already set a deadline for war.

Mussolini, who prided himself on being the son of an impoverished blacksmith, had been dictator of Italy since 1925. After coming to power he annexed Abyssinia (Ethiopia), in part justifying his actions by connecting the ideology of Italian Fascism with the idea of ancient Rome: he intended to restore Italy to its historic greatness. One of Eden's biographers claims that *Il Duce* was the cause of personal embarrassment to Eden when the junior Foreign Office minister visited Italy in 1934. The story goes that, when entering Mussolini's vast study in the Palazzo Venezia, Eden tripped over a rug, at which the Fascist dictator laughed uproariously. According to another report, during the same meeting Mussolini thumped his desk to emphasise his point so violently that he splashed ink onto Eden's waistcoat.[4] Whether either event is true is a matter of conjecture – Eden insisted they were not – but Eden certainly felt no personal warmth towards the Italian leader. Churchill, on the other hand, had been rather complimentary of Mussolini when he first came to power, a fact largely air-brushed from many biographies. He made an unofficial visit to Rome in 1927 and told the press, 'I could not help being charmed, like so many other people have been, by Signor

Mussolini's gentle and simple bearing and by his calm detached poise in spite of so many burdens and dangers … anyone could see that he thought of nothing but the lasting good, as he understands it, of the Italian people.'[5] Churchill's admiration was not just confined to Mussolini, but also extended to Fascism itself, which he described as a movement that had 'rendered a service to the whole world' by countering the spread of Communism. Italian Fascism, he claimed, 'provided the necessary antidote to the Russian poison.'[6] A decade later, as Hitler morphed from an angry agitator to a strident dictator, Churchill had rather changed his tune about Fascism. Along with Communism, he now equated it as being 'totalitarian', but right up until the outbreak of war he clung to an undimmed personal admiration for Mussolini.[7]

Other than the two dictators, the primary issue affecting 'the state of Europe' was that Spain was in the midst of a bitter civil war; a prelude to the total war that would engulf Europe in the years that followed. The conflict pitted Franco's fascist Nationalists against socialist Republicans, roughly dividing the country between those who supported the monarchy, the army, landowners and the Catholic Church, and those who supported the socialist cause, represented by trade unions, agricultural labourers and many of the educated middle class. The conflict lured in idealistic Communist supporters, some of whom joined 'international brigades' to fight for the Republican side, as well as those keen to watch a war, among them the American writer Ernest Hemingway, who reported for the *Alliance* newspaper. His experiences inspired his novel *For Whom the Bell Tolls*, which tells the story of a young American who joins the international brigades. As Churchill, Eden and Lloyd George ate lunch, Hemingway was less than 500 miles to the south-west, reporting on the battle raging in the Spanish city of Teruel.

The Spanish Civil War was also a proxy war, as Europe's 'two dictators' aided the Nationalist side, while the Soviet government supported the Republicans. Money, men and arms flowed into Spain, turning the country into a killing field. Hemingway made little secret of his support for the Republican cause and was especially critical of the involvement of German and Italian air support for the Nationalists. In an article he penned for the Russian newspaper *Pravda* later in 1938, he wrote, 'During the last 15 months I saw murder done in Spain by the fascist invaders.' Commenting on German and Italian air attacks, he stated, '[they] try the effect of their various bombs in preparation for the war that Italy and Germany expect to make. Their bombs are very good. They have learned much in their experimenting in Spain and their bombing is getting better every time.'[8]

Fascist support was not just confined to the air. Italian submarines had also engaged in torpedo attacks on ships approaching Republican-held ports, action which caused alarm in France and Britain. When a number of neutral vessels, including a British-registered tanker, were sunk, the French pushed for action. Eden was equally keen and exchanged a series of telephone calls with his French opposite number to organise an international conference to deal with what was officially being described as 'piracy', as none of the submarines had formally identified themselves and Italy was not officially at war. Eden's intention was to secure international agreement that neutral powers would not allow their submarines to operate off the Spanish coast and that any found 'would be liable to be sunk'.[9] Neville Chamberlain, who had been appointed prime minister only five months previously, was wary of upsetting Mussolini, as he had begun pursuing a policy of appeasement that included potential recognition of Abyssinia as Italian. But he eventually acquiesced to Eden's desire for a robust response, admitting, 'Mussolini must not think he has a free hand to do what he liked just because we had made some friendly remarks to him.'[10] However, the two men were not in step. Their difference of opinion led to open argument in Cabinet, a harbinger of what would become a widening division between the prime minister and his foreign secretary. The Nyon Conference convened in Switzerland in the autumn of 1937 and the final agreement provided for the sinking of any submarine which attacked neutral shipping, or any found in the vicinity of a recent attack deemed to be responsible. In a sham but inspired piece of diplomacy, Italy was invited to be one of the naval powers to police the Mediterranean, although Britain and France would patrol the coast of Spain.

Over their lunch a few months later, Lloyd George and Churchill expressed to Eden their 'warm approval' of the outcome of the Nyon Conference, which had brought a halt to the threat of submarine attacks on shipping. For now, it seemed war in Europe was being contained.

Chapter 2

'The complete gangster'

At the start of 1938 the sixty-three-year-old Winston Churchill was still a political pariah, shunned by many as old-fashioned and belligerently militaristic. He had resigned from the shadow cabinet in 1931, in protest at proposed Conservative support for the idea of granting dominion status to India, and spent much of the early 1930s travelling, painting and writing. In the process of researching a biography of the first Duke of Marlborough, he stayed in Munich for three days in the summer of 1932, where he met a friend of Hitler's who attempted to arrange a meeting. Hitler, whose party had just secured thirty-seven percent of the vote in the German general election, but who himself was still not in power, turned down the invitation. He told his friend, 'In any case, what part does Churchill play? He is in opposition and no one pays attention to him.'[1] It was a brutal and largely accurate observation.

Winston Churchill had already packed a lifetime's worth of experiences into his threescore years. In his early adult life he was a soldier and war correspondent and travelled to India, Sudan, South Africa and Egypt, before becoming a Conservative Member of Parliament in 1900, then later defecting to the Liberal Party. He rose to the position of First Lord of the Admiralty by 1911, but his championing of the disastrous Gallipoli campaign during the First World War, which Churchill himself had proposed, eventually forced his resignation. After briefly serving on the Western Front, he returned to politics and began rehabilitating his reputation. He 'crossed the floor' once more, returning to the Conservative Party to take the position of Chancellor of the Exchequer in Stanley Baldwin's 1924 government. His tenure as chancellor was controversial: one of his first actions was to return Britain to the Gold Standard, pegging sterling at the pre-war rate of £1 to $4.85, an action which prolonged the post-war depression and was one of the triggers for the 1926 General Strike, the first in Britain's history.

Despite controversy, Churchill remained as chancellor until the 1929 election, when the Conservatives were swept from power. Churchill held his parliamentary seat, although in opposition he became an increasingly isolated figure in his own party. But he still had a few trusted friends, among them Anthony Eden.

Before Christmas 1937 Churchill had spoken several times in the House of Commons in support of Eden's foreign policy position and throughout Eden's tenure at the Foreign Office the two exchanged occasional letters. They were in many ways an unlikely pairing: the portly, balding and slack-jowled former minister and the stylish and precise foreign secretary.

In public speaking style the two were almost the exact opposite: while at the Foreign Office, Eden gained a reputation among his staff for taking out the more melodramatic lines written for him in speeches, while Churchill was notorious for his hyperbole. But in Eden, Churchill sensed he had found a like-minded soul, later writing, 'He felt and feared the Hitler peril. It might almost be said that there was not much difference of view between him and me, except, of course, that he was in harness [i.e. restrained by his official position].'[2]

Eden and Churchill are often simplistically viewed as 'anti-appeasers' who pointed out the dangers of Hitler and Mussolini, but who, until the outbreak of war, were prophets unwelcome in their home town. However, their positions were not identical, despite Churchill's later suggestion that there was 'not much difference of view' between them. Eden's own perspective is perhaps best expressed in a memo he wrote in December 1937. He stated it would be a mistake to give in to any one member of the German-Italian-Japanese 'bloc', as 'The aims of all three are in varying degrees inimical to British interests and a surrender to one might well be the signal for further concerted action on the part of all three.'[3] Eden's view was that it would be 'safer and more in accordance with our honour and our interests, to tolerate for the time being at any rate, the present state of armed truce … [to] maintain some kind of equilibrium … For periods in the past, Europe has managed to exist, under armed truce, without a general settlement, but without war.' It was, he said, the price Britain and her allies might have to pay for 'our inability effectively to assert the principles of international order against the aggressor states since 1931.' He summarised his view as 'the unheroic policy of so-called "cunctation" [delay].'

Although Eden has been roundly criticised by several historians for this position – one particularly uncharitable description claims it demonstrated 'carping hesitation' – it would be unfair to claim his position was one of inaction. Eden's response to the threat of Italian submarine attacks on neutral shipping off Spain in 1937 was swift and decisive. When the French suggested combined action Eden immediately tried to get Chamberlain to return from holiday so they could move without delay. The position Eden devised with his French counterpart for the Nyon Conference was uncompromising, but it was also internationalist; Eden secured an end to Italian submarine attacks with the agreement of multiple states and left a face-saving compromise open to Mussolini. In contrast, Churchill's own suggestion to Eden of a solution for the problem of submarine attacks was devoid of any subtlety at all. He wrote to Eden, proposing that the British should secretly put Royal Naval personnel, along with 4-in guns, on tankers and merchant ships, which would then 'offer themselves' to unsuspecting submarines and give them a nasty surprise.[4]

Equilibrium, armed truce and cunctation may have been acceptable to Eden as a way of at least staving off another European war, but he was particularly unenthusiastic about direct negotiation with Mussolini, which Chamberlain seemed desperate to start. Eden confided in his private secretary in autumn 1937 that the prime minister, 'had a certain sympathy for dictators whose efficiency appealed to him … [and] really believed it would be possible to get an agreement with Muss[olini] by running after him.'[5]

In early 1938 there was a genuine belief among most British politicians that Hitler was not a completely unreasonable man. Eden, for all his personal dislike of Mussolini, did not oppose negotiating with Hitler, recommending on 1 January 1938, 'if we wish for a general settlement with Germany, it will be for us, and not for the German Government, to take the next step.'[6] The proposal on the table was to offer Hitler former German colonies in Africa (side-stepping the fact that they now officially belonged to Belgium and Portugal), while simultaneously agreeing concessions over the majority German-speaking Sudetenland in Czechoslovakia. While the Foreign Office prepared instructions for the British ambassador in Berlin, Chamberlain was also pursuing talks with Mussolini. The prime minister exchanged telegrams with his foreign secretary while Eden was on holiday in the Riviera, which disrupted

Eden's attempts to find time for swimming and tennis. Chamberlain wanted to include recognition of Abyssinia as part of what he called 'a general scheme for appeasement' towards Italy. Eden vehemently disagreed, noting, 'Mussolini is, I fear, the complete gangster and his pledged word means nothing. It would be most unfortunate to take any action at this time which gave Mussolini the appearance of a diplomatic triumph.'[7]

The 'state of Europe' was also exercising politicians on the other side of the Atlantic. A surprise telegram arrived from Washington on 12 January, with a message from the president of the United States. Franklin Delano Roosevelt proposed a conference to negotiate a 'new and comprehensive European settlement, based on the fundamental principles of international law.' He was keen to instruct US diplomats to begin making overtures in Europe, and the American Under Secretary of State insisted on utmost secrecy and on receiving a reply within seven days for the scheme to go ahead. Eden's senior aide at the Foreign Office telephoned him in France, cryptically calling Eden urgently back to London and cutting short his holiday. A diplomatic bag with the relevant papers was dispatched to meet his train in Marseilles, but it missed the connection and Eden's attempt to fly back from Paris was thwarted when all flights were cancelled due to high winds. Eden only found out the reason for the summons when he docked at Folkestone on 15 January after a rough crossing and was met by his staff. He learned that, with the deadline still two days away, Chamberlain had already replied, pouring cold water on the proposal, which the prime minister felt would receive a 'possibly hostile reception' in Germany and Italy and upset the appeasement applecart.[8] Eden dashed off an emolliating second reply to the now disgruntled American Under Secretary of State and confronted Chamberlain the following day (Sunday) at Chequers, the prime minister's private retreat. A livid Eden told Chamberlain that his choice was between Anglo-American cooperation or a dubious settlement with Mussolini. Recognition of Abyssinia would, Eden said, increase Mussolini's authority and 'make him more attractive [as an ally] to Hitler.'[9] Eden was not so much seized by the details of the US peace plan, which were vague anyway, but by the desire for America not to be dissuaded from taking a more active role in world affairs. Given the choice between a combined international effort to reduce tensions in Europe, or the British cutting a deal with the dictators out of what appeared to be desperation, Eden had no doubt which option he preferred. Chamberlain recorded in his diary that Eden was so upset that he 'had suggested resignation [over the matter] but I had pointed out the impossibility ... since [President] Roosevelt had enjoined complete secrecy upon us.'[10]

The government's Foreign Policy Committee met for nearly the entire day on 21 January. Eden's Cabinet colleagues, almost to a man, backed the prime minister, but Eden continued to argue his case. They agreed a compromise, in which Chamberlain sent two telegrams to Washington. The first was a personal message to Roosevelt stating that Chamberlain 'warmly welcomed' the initiative and would do his best to contribute to its success. The second was a contradictory message that laid out Chamberlain's argument for recognising Abyssinia, but stated that such action would only come as part of a general settlement with Italy. Eden was upset, but he appeared to have partially brought Chamberlain around to his point of view. What he did not know was that the prime minister was secretly making plans to do a deal with Italy behind his foreign secretary's back.

Chapter 3

Going quietly

Lady Ivy Chamberlain was the widow of the prime minister's half-brother. In December 1937, following the death of her considerably older husband, she took up permanent residence in Italy, ensconcing herself in the Grand Hotel in Rome. Officially, she was the gracefully ageing widow of a former politician, enjoying her later years in a more amenable climate, who happened occasionally to write to her brother-in-law, the prime minister. Unofficially, she was Chamberlain's secret envoy to Mussolini. She was less secret in her efforts to charm the higher-ups of the Fascist government, writing to Chamberlain not long after her arrival that she was becoming well acquainted with 'the people who count', adding, 'If nothing else, I have put the British Embassy on the map here.'[1]

On 31 December 1937, when Eden was already on holiday in France, she held a private audience with the Italian foreign minister, Count Galeazzo Ciano. She shared a personal letter from Chamberlain, which affirmed the prime minister's determination to open talks with Italy. A secret meeting was arranged between Chamberlain and the Italian ambassador, Dino Grandi, in London for 17 January, but it had to be cancelled at the last minute, when the senior civil servant at the Foreign Office recalled Eden back from his holidays on his own initiative to deal with the Roosevelt peace proposal. Following the lengthy meeting of the Foreign Policy Committee on 21 January, Eden departed for a pre-arranged trip to Geneva. Upon his return, Chamberlain announced that the Italian ambassador had asked to hold preliminary talks about an agreement. On 9 February the *Daily Mail* ran the headline, 'Britain to hasten new talks with Italy – all issues to be discussed, Count Ciano [bound] for London?' The Foreign Office news department confirmed to Eden the story had nothing to do with them: Number 10 was leaking to the press, for the benefit of the Italians. Eden was flatly insistent that no meeting should take place between the Italian ambassador and the prime minister, as it would in the first instance appear desperate. Eden summoned Grandi to the Foreign Office, but in an extraordinary snub, the ambassador claimed he was too busy golfing to attend, fully aware that the foreign secretary was at cross-purposes with his prime minister. Grandi messaged Ciano in Rome that he had put Eden off, 'bringing up as a pure excuse that I had a golfing engagement (I hate golf, but pretend to play it when necessary).'[2] Around the same time, Eden learned that Ivy Chamberlain had been engaged in private conversations with Ciano. He confided in a colleague that he felt 'double crossed' and wrote a bitter letter to Chamberlain, stating, 'Without wishing to be unduly punctilious, I am sure you will understand that this kind of unofficial diplomacy does place me in a most difficult position.'[3]

Chamberlain and Grandi finally met on 18 February, with an angry Eden in attendance. Eden later admitted privately that the Italian ambassador was 'a very skilful diplomat', and at the meeting at Downing Street, Grandi played Chamberlain beautifully. He told the prime minister that 'if it was impossible to improve relations with Great Britain, then it would be necessary for Italy to draw still closer to Germany.'[4] The divisions between the two men in the room were so obvious that Grandi relayed to Rome afterwards, 'Chamberlain and Eden were not Prime Minister and Foreign Secretary discussing with the Ambassador of a foreign Power a delicate situation ... They were – and revealed themselves as such to me ... two enemies confronting each other.'[5] When Grandi left, having been told to return on Monday to receive an answer, Chamberlain and Eden got into an open row. The prime minister paced up and down shouting at his foreign secretary. At Chamberlain's assertion that he wanted to announce negotiations would open at once, in Rome, Eden replied it would 'look like capitulation to blackmail or panic.' Eden demanded an emergency Cabinet meeting.

Cabinet met on the Saturday, an almost unheard-of occurrence since the war. News of the extraordinary meeting had reached the press and a crowd gathered outside. Chamberlain opened the meeting with what one member described as a 'lecture on history', outlining the background to negotiations and painting his support for them as an attempt to avert the risks of war and draw Mussolini away from Hitler. Chamberlain told his colleagues that his own view of Italy was that 'the country represented a hysterical woman': the implication was that starting negotiations would calm everyone down.[6] In sum, he stated it was 'an opportunity to show Signor Mussolini that he might have other friends besides Herr Hitler,' adding, 'not to embrace it would be not only unwise but criminal.' Eden responded that in his view the Italian offer was 'political blackmail' and that suggestions that the announcement of official negotiations would produce an immediate détente in Europe were wrong: 'the conversations would have to include *de jure* recognition [of Abyssinia] and it would be regarded as another surrender to the Dictators.'

One by one, the Cabinet shared their own views. They were divided between a majority who supported the prime minister and a few who sided with the foreign secretary. After they had spoken, Eden calmly informed the room that he could not recommend to parliament a course of action he did not believe in, adding that if his colleagues decided against his view 'he hoped they would find someone else to help them carry through this decision.' At Eden's understated announcement of his intention to resign 'there was a gasp of horror.'[7] It was a complete shock to most of the Cabinet, who had had no previous idea how deep the division was between the foreign secretary and his prime minister. Chamberlain implored Eden to consider his decision overnight and hauled the entire Cabinet back on the Sunday. But more hours of discussion led nowhere. That afternoon Eden wrote his formal letter of resignation to Chamberlain. He noted that recent events had 'made plain a difference between us on a decision of great importance,' and that he had 'become increasingly conscious ... of a difference of outlook between us in respect to the international problems of the day and also as to the methods by which we should seek to resolve them.' He sombrely concluded, 'It cannot be in the country's interest that those who are called upon to direct its affairs should work in an uneasy partnership, fully conscious of differences in outlook yet hoping that they will not recur.' He tendered his resignation, but thanked Chamberlain for his advice, adding that he hoped their 'differences' would not influence their friendship. Eden went quietly, in a civilised manner, stating publicly that his departure was due to 'a divergence, not of aim, but of outlook and approach,' before going to stay with friends in the Yorkshire Dales to escape the media attention.

The British press was largely favourable to the prime minister, but the *Daily Herald* asserted, 'Mr. Chamberlain has come out stark and nakedly on the side of a system of power politics ... any concession, however ignoble and however humiliating will be made to the forces of International Fascism … make no mistake about it, Mr. Eden has been sacrificed to Mussolini.'[8]

The same day that Eden penned his resignation, Hitler addressed the Reichstag; his speech was also broadcast on the Austrian radio network. 'The German Reich is no longer willing to tolerate the suppression of ten million Germans across its borders … I am glad to say, however, that the Austrian chancellor has shown insight and satisfactory agreement has been reached with Austria.'[9]

The Austrian chancellor's 'insight' had been to cave to threats from Hitler. On 12 February Kurt von Schuschnigg accepted an invitation to visit Hitler at his Bavarian Alpine retreat. The bespectacled, polite Austrian premier arrived on a freezing morning – having been driven through multiple army checkpoints – to discover that Hitler had also invited most of his military top brass and that the Berghof was crawling with men in braided uniform. On meeting Hitler, Schuschnigg began by complimenting his surroundings, but was interrupted: 'Herr Schuschnigg, we did not gather here to speak of the fine view or the weather.'[10] Instead, Hitler presented him with an ultimatum to hand over control of nearly all senior government positions to Austrian Nazis (they had been banned from Austrian government positions in 1934, but allowed back in 1936 as part of a German-Austrian non-aggression pact, which Hitler was now ignoring). When Schuschnigg demurred from effectively handing over his government to Nazis, Hitler informed him, 'You will either sign it as it is and fulfil my demands within three days, or I will order the march into Austria.' Believing his options were capitulation or a German invasion, the Austrian chancellor gave in. Revealingly, in their two-hour meeting, which Schuschnigg later described as 'somewhat unilateral', Hitler affected that the Austrian chancellor was the one risking war: 'It is easy enough to talk of war while we are sitting here in our comfortable easy-chairs. But war means endless misery for millions. Do you want to take this responsibility upon yourself Herr Schuschnigg? Don't think for one moment that anybody on earth is going to thwart my decisions. Italy? I see eye to eye with Mussolini, the closest ties of friendship bind us. And England? England will not move one finger for Austria.'[11]

On 22 February Churchill joined others in the House of Commons criticising Eden's departure. In typical Churchill fashion, he spoke at length and with feeling. He began by referring to Eden as the 'late' foreign secretary, a turn of phrase also used by other members, but one which made it sound as if Eden had died. 'I must express my keen personal sympathy with the late Foreign Secretary, whose policy I admired and whose friendship I enjoy ... he is an irreparable loss to the Government ... and I feel personally, as an older man, the poignancy of his loss all the more because he seems to be the one fresh figure of first magnitude arising out of the generation which was ravaged by the War.' Churchill went on to echo the sentiments of the *Daily Herald*, that Eden had been sacrificed because of the desire to appease Mussolini, adding, 'The Cabinet, from the usual vague, well-intentioned desire for peace and friendship, enjoined the Foreign Secretary to have these talks. It is quite clear that he was reluctant to do so, and, in my opinion, he was right.' Churchill was unflinching in outlining what he saw as the repercussions of Eden's departure, claiming that it would give Mussolini and Hitler the upper hand:

> This last week has been a good week for dictators – one of the best they ever had. The German dictator has laid his heavy hand upon a small but historic country [Austria], and the Italian dictator has carried his vendetta to a victorious conclusion against my right hon. Friend [Eden] ... Let me remind hon. Members when they talk about Germany's desire for peace, that this small country has declared that it will resist, and if it resists that may well light up the flames of war ... I predict that the day will come when at some point or other on some issue or other you will have to make a stand, and I pray to God that when that day comes we may not find that through an unwise policy we are left to make that stand alone.'[12]

Chapter 4

Wars and rumours of wars

On 12 March 1938 the German army marched into Austria. Schuschnigg had tried to row back on the agreement he had been forced to sign in February, announcing he would offer the Austrian people a referendum on unification with Germany. Hitler was outraged and manufactured a 'request' for German troops to enter Austria before the referendum could be held. The former Austrian chancellor spent the rest of the war in Nazi concentration camps, although he survived and later emigrated to America. Hitler was met by cheering crowds on his arrival into Vienna and conclusively won a carefully controlled referendum the following month. Austria was now part of the Third Reich, although it was a development that much of the Austrian population warmly welcomed.

The following month Chamberlain concluded the Anglo-Italian Agreement with Mussolini. The agreement was technically conditional on the withdrawal of Italian 'volunteers' fighting for Franco's Fascists in Spain, but what mattered was that Britain granted recognition to Italian Abyssinia. The upbeat Pathé newsreel of the signing on 16 April shows a beaming Ciano firmly shaking hands with the British representative, while in clipped tones the voiceover states, 'So from now on we're all good friends and good neighbours.'[1] Two days after the agreement was announced Churchill wrote to Eden: 'The Italian pact is of course a complete triumph for Mussolini, who gains our cordial acceptance … for his conquest of Abyssinia, and for his violence in Spain.' He went on to state, however, that he felt caution was needed in opposing the agreement, 'It is called a move toward peace,' but added, 'Before making up my mind, I should like to know your views.' Eden replied ten days later, agreeing that strong opposition would be counterproductive, and adding, 'The most anxious feature of the international situation, as I see it, is that temporary relaxation of tension may be taken as a pretext for the relaxation of national effort, which is already inadequate to the times.'[2] If war came, Eden was concerned Britain would not be prepared.

Chamberlain continued his efforts to appease. As Hitler railed against Czechoslovakia and threatened the Sudetenland over the summer and into the autumn of 1938, European conflict appeared closer than at any time before. Czechoslovakia's alliance with France meant that France was duty-bound to come to her aid if attacked, and if France declared war, Britain, as France's ally, was expected to follow. Eden maintained a low public profile, but did have a letter published in *The Times* on 12 September which stated that it was 'a dangerous illusion to assume that once a conflict had broken out in Central Europe it could be localised.'[3] A few days later Chamberlain travelled to Germany for the first of several talks with Hitler. In collusion with the French, Chamberlain negotiated the Munich Agreement, which granted the Sudetenland to Germany. The proposal was presented to the Czech government, who agreed to it after being informed that neither France nor Britain would come to their aid if Germany annexed the Sudetenland by force. When his plane landed in London, Chamberlain was met by jubilant supporters. Speaking later from the steps of 10 Downing Street, he claimed the agreement was 'symbolic of the desire of our two peoples never to go to war with one another again … I believe it is peace for our time.'

A week later the House of Commons voted overwhelmingly in support of Chamberlain and the Munich Agreement, although Churchill and Eden were among thirty Conservatives who abstained. As the other MPs lined up to vote, both men pointedly remained seated in the chamber. But while Eden and Churchill publicly opposed the Munich Agreement, Eden shared the majority view that conflict had been averted because of it. Speaking in Parliament ahead of the vote, he said, 'for the moment we can breathe again, and it is the duty of each one of us to devote what time we can to stocktaking and to considering how it was that Europe came thus to the very edge of the abyss … There is throughout the world at this time an immense sense of relief and thankfulness that war has been averted.'[4]

Although Eden's words and actions seem almost contradictory, it demonstrates on two counts his personal approach to foreign policy: firstly, his gentleman's view that diplomatic agreements, once made, should be strictly adhered to; secondly, a certain pragmatism that once something was a *fait accompli*, it was better to try to make the best of it.

Unlike Hitler, who had already boasted to the Czechs that Britain would not come to their aid if Germany invaded, Eden was firmly, and naively, of the opinion that Britain would stick to the agreements she had made. In the same speech, he noted, 'the appearance in the Press of this country [Britain] on Tuesday last of this statement: "It was authoritatively stated in London last night that should Germany, in spite of all efforts made by the British Prime Minister, attack Czechoslovakia, France would be compelled immediately to go to the Czechs' assistance and Britain ... would certainly stand by France." I believe that the historian of the future will give that statement an important place among the deterrents to war a week ago.' In the event, historians have instead found themselves recounting how Hitler invaded Czechoslovakia and Britain stood by and did nothing.

In sharp contrast, when Churchill spoke in Parliament before he and Eden abstained from the vote he referred to the Munich Agreement as a 'total and unmitigated defeat'. Prophetically, he said, 'I venture to think that in future the Czechoslovak state cannot be maintained as an independent entity. You will find that in a period of time which may be measured by years, but may be measured only by months, Czechoslovakia will be engulfed in the Nazi regime.' He was understanding of what he described as the 'spontaneous outburst of joy and relief' among the public, but concluded, 'they should know the truth ... that we have sustained a defeat without a war, the consequences of which will travel far with us along our road.'[5]

Churchill's prediction came true five months later, in March 1939. Czechoslovakia was absorbed into the Third Reich, greeted by little more than the collective wringing of hands. Churchill and Eden were sitting together in the House of Commons' smoking room when the evening papers arrived bearing the news that German troops had marched into Prague. Churchill later recalled, 'Even those who like us had no illusions ... were surprised at the sudden violence of this outrage.'[6] Not for the first time, Hitler had broken his word. For Eden, the Nazi invasion and annexation of Czechoslovakia finally eclipsed any notions that Hitler could be negotiated with. A few days later the Spanish Civil War ended in a victory for Franco's Fascists. As one historian has remarked, 'Eden came from a world where diplomacy was conducted between gentlemen and agreements, once made, were honoured. Hitler and Mussolini, however, were a new breed who were neither honourable nor gentlemen and Eden could not conceal his perplexity at, and his distaste for, their methods.'[7]

The uneasy spring of 1939 gave way to a false calm over the summer, shattered by the announcement in late August of the Nazi-Soviet pact. Instead of joining Britain and France in defending Poland, the Soviet Union had, secretly, agreed to help Germany invade. As war in Europe loomed once more, Parliament was recalled. Churchill and Eden were photographed walking side by side to the House of Commons: Churchill looking austere in a dark suit and hat, a stick in his right hand, with Eden striding alongside him in a three-piece suit and striped tie. The caption to the image published in *The Tatler* magazine read, 'if we are to have an inner War Cabinet, it is difficult to see how either of them can be left out of it.'

On 1 September 1939 Hitler invaded Poland. That afternoon the prime minister asked Churchill to visit him at Downing Street. A dejected Chamberlain told Churchill that he saw no way of averting war with Germany and that he intended to form a special War Cabinet, as had been done during the Great War. He invited Churchill to be a member. Churchill agreed, returning to the post of First Lord of the Admiralty, which he had held during the Great War. The following day, Churchill wrote to Chamberlain, suggesting that Eden be included, as 'Eden's influence with the section of Conservatives who are associated with him … seems to me to be a very necessary reinforcement.' He also pointed out that the men who were part of the War Cabinet were rather advanced in years: 'Aren't we a very old team? I make out the six you mentioned to me yesterday aggregate 386 years, or an average of over sixty-four … If however you added [Archibald] Sinclair (49) [leader of the Liberal Party, which now numbered only twenty MPs] and Eden (42) the average age comes down to 57 ½.'[8] Chamberlain did invite Eden back into government later that week, offering him the position of Dominion Secretary, which at least gave him a seat at the table of the War Cabinet, although not as an official member. After debating whether he should instead rejoin his old unit to serve in uniform, Eden accepted.

Eden listened to Chamberlain's radio statement of the declaration of war on 3 September, sitting with a group of friends. The prime minister told the listeners that, earlier that morning, the British ambassador in Berlin had delivered a final note of warning to Hitler that 'unless we heard from them by 11 o'clock that they were prepared at once to withdraw their troops from Poland, a state of war would exist between us.' Chamberlain solemnly added, 'I have to tell you now that no such undertaking has been received, and that consequently this country is at war with Germany.'[9] It was, Chamberlain said, a 'bitter blow', admitting, 'my long struggle to win peace has failed.' Eden was less charitable in his description of the prime minister's statement, remarking, 'It seemed the lament of a man deploring his own failure, rather than the call of a nation to arms.' Churchill was also listening to the broadcast, at his London home with his wife. When Chamberlain finished speaking the couple went up on the flat roof to look out over the capital: 'Around us on every side, in the clear cool September light, rose the roofs and spires of London,' Churchill later wrote, 'Above them were already slowly rising thirty or forty cylindrical [barrage] balloons.'[10] Britain was again at war.

PART TWO

Chapter 5

Downing Street, De Gaulle and Dunkirk

Churchill's moment of destiny came in May 1940. After months of 'phoney war' following the German conquest of Poland, the German invasion of neutral Norway finally led to open warfare between British and German forces. Even though the Royal Navy was superior to the *Kriegsmarine*, German airpower proved the decisive factor and the British were forced into an embarrassing withdrawal, having suffered the loss of an aircraft carrier, two cruisers and seven destroyers. Although Churchill was culpable in the Norway fiasco, it was the moment Chamberlain's opponents had been waiting for. After a two-day debate in Parliament, he resigned on 10 May 1940 and Winston Churchill was invited to form a National Government, with representatives from all political parties. After years in the wilderness, Churchill had completed a remarkable turnaround to become prime minister. The same day, Hitler's armies invaded Holland and Belgium and swept towards France. In Churchill's famous first speech as prime minister, he told the nation, 'We have before us an ordeal of the most grievous kind.' But he asserted that the only aim was 'victory at all costs; victory in spite of all terror; victory, however long and hard the road may be. For without victory, there is no survival.'[1] Churchill appointed Eden as his Secretary of State for War, placing him in a pivotal position of responsibility. Eden gladly accepted what he viewed as a crucial role, but recorded in his diary, '[The] Position will be [a] very difficult one, for [the] state of [the] army is inglorious, and it will not be easy to maintain harmony with W.[inston]'[2]

One of Eden's first actions was to announce the formation of the Local Defence Volunteers. He broadcast on the BBC, giving a call to arms for those ineligible for normal service who would be invited to provide the nation's last line of defence in the event of a German invasion. He told 'men of all ages who wish to do something for the defence of their country ... Here, then, is the opportunity for which so many of you have been waiting.'[3] There was a swift and positive response, but one element of Eden's announcement resulted in his first wartime spat with Churchill. The new prime minister wrote to his recently appointed Secretary of State for War, 'I don't think much of the name LOCAL DEFENCE VOLUNTEERS … The word "local" is uninspiring … I think "Home Guard" would be better.'[4] Eden protested, with the support of the government's information minister, who thought Home Guard was too confusingly close to Horse Guards, but Churchill's stubbornness won out and 600,000 armbands that had been manufactured and distributed had to be recalled. It was an early demonstration of how keenly and spiritedly Churchill could involve himself in even minor matters if it took his fancy.

As the German blitzkrieg scythed through France, it seemed that Eden's Home Guard might be called into action sooner than anyone had anticipated. At the end of May the War Cabinet ordered the 'tactical withdrawal' of the British Expeditionary Force, which in truth meant a headlong retreat to the Channel ports. Churchill telegrammed Roosevelt with a personal message, outlining his worst fear: 'If necessary, we shall continue the war alone, and we are not afraid of that. But I trust you realise, Mr President, that the voice and force of the United States may count for nothing if they are withheld too long. You may have a completely subjugated Nazified Europe established with astonishing swiftness, and the weight may be more than we can bear.'[5]

By 9 June German forces were just fifty miles from Paris. Two days later Churchill and Eden flew to Briare in central France, escorted by Hurricane fighters, for a conference at the Château du Muguet. Churchill had left England in a bad temper but recovered by the time he arrived to listen to the French Supreme Commander, Maxime Weygand, describe the disastrous military situation. Among the others seated at the dining room table in the château was the famous Great War general Philippe Pétain and the French Under Secretary for War, Charles De Gaulle. Although none of the audience had requested it, Churchill took the opportunity of the conference to give a long speech in his trademark mangle of French and English. Recalling the disasters from the Great War from which the Allies had recovered, he stated they would 'fight on and on – *toujours*, all the time – everywhere.' He advocated guerrilla warfare in the streets of Paris, a proposal that appalled Pétain, who violently responded that such a policy would result in 'the destruction of the country'.[6] For the rest of the discussions, Pétain sat, Eden recorded, 'mockingly incredulous'. Churchill was blissfully unaware that the French high command had already decided to abandon Paris to the advancing Germans, who marched into the French capital unopposed later that week. The conference demonstrated to both Churchill and Eden that the military defeat of France was already inevitable. On their return to London, their conversations shifted to how, not when, the French would capitulate. Eden wrote to Churchill, 'You will keep in mind the vital distinction between armistice and peace. The former is military, the latter political. We could consent to France asking for the former under military duress. We could never agree to her making peace.'[7]

The immediate concern was the evacuation of British soldiers from the European mainland. Dunkirk is now a legend of British fighting spirit, immortalised by Hollywood. In one sense the collective memory has bought into the propaganda myth that would portray the ignominious withdrawal of tens of thousands of soldiers, many of whom had discarded their weapons, as a form of victory. In the final week of May, 200,000 British and 160,000 French troops were encircled at Dunkirk: by the end of the month, 100,000 had been safely evacuated to Britain, with the assistance of an armada of small civilian vessels that had made the perilous Channel crossing. On 13 May Churchill had already taken the decision not to send any more RAF squadrons to France. The apparent lack of intervention by British fighters against the incessant German air attacks on soldiers on the beaches would forever be seared into the memories of many of the men in uniform who were easy targets on the open sand. In reality, the RAF fought hard over Dunkirk, downing 394 German planes for the loss of 114. The evacuation ended on 3 June, with a total of 224,318 British and 111,172 French troops rescued. Churchill did not overstate what had happened at Dunkirk, telling the House of Commons on the day after that, while the evacuation was 'a miracle of deliverance', Britain 'must be very careful not to assign to this deliverance the attributes of victory. Wars are not won by evacuations.' Three weeks later the French signed an armistice. Italy had by now also declared war, despite Churchill sending an imploring personal message to Mussolini, which read, 'Is it too late to stop a river of blood from flowing between the British and Italian peoples?'[8]

Eden's earlier warning of the 'vital distinction' between armistice and peace proved to be a relevant one, as the terms of the armistice divided France in two, creating a northern zone under German military occupation alongside a nominally independent southern zone. General Pétain became head of the French Vichy government, while a disgusted De Gaulle fled to Britain and declared himself the head of a new French National Committee. After a brief moment of indecision, Churchill agreed to stand by him, and on 28 June the British government released a statement affirming that 'His Majesty's Government recognise General De Gaulle as the leader of all free Frenchmen, wherever they may be, who rally to him in support of the Allied cause.'[9] Key to the British recognition was the idea that De Gaulle might rally to him some of France's overseas territories, which officially remained under the control of the Vichy government, and indeed French Equatorial Africa did declare its allegiance to De Gaulle a few months later. But the passionate, patriotic De Gaulle would come to infuriate Churchill as the war progressed, although Eden would often defend the Frenchman and his actions.

The summer of 1940 was the moment when the country fought for its life. Uniquely, the population watched the battle unfold. Britain's summer-blue skies were the setting for the duel between the Luftwaffe and the RAF, a fight Churchill would later describe as the 'finest hour' and the battle upon which 'the survival of Christian civilisation' depended. Churchill himself prepared for an invasion, practising shooting with a revolver at Chequers. On 16 August Churchill visited the headquarters of 11 Group, Fighter Command, responsible for coordinating the defence of London and the South-East. It was a bad day for the RAF, as forty-seven aircraft were destroyed on the ground. The experience was a deeply moving one for the prime minister, who refused to speak for some time afterwards during the car journey back to London. Eventually, he leant forward and said to his staff officer, 'Never in the field of human conflict has so much been owed by so many to so few.'[10]

Eden had rented a small house on the Downs, a few miles from Dover, and therefore had a front-row seat to watch the deadly dogfights that eventually halted Hitler's invasion plans. The Battle of Britain came especially close to home one August day, when an RAF fighter and a German Messerschmitt engaged in a dogfight in the skies above the garden. Eden was in the bath at the moment when the German plane headed toward the ground, at one point looking like it might hit the house. In the event it crashed in nearby woods, the pilot bailing out just in time. On 22 September Eden was again staying at the Dover house when

Churchill telephoned with an urgent message. The Germans were planning to invade that afternoon. The information came from US intelligence reports Churchill had received via Roosevelt himself. Although Churchill suggested Eden return to London, Eden told him he would rather stay where he was. The weather was filthy, with a wet and windy autumn gale blowing, and Eden tramped up to the top of a hill overlooking the Channel and returned to message Churchill that 'any German who attempted to cross the Channel would be very sea-sick.'[11] It later transpired that the message had been decoded incorrectly. The American president had attempted to forewarn the British about the invasion of Indochina.

Indochina was the name given to the geographical area encompassing modern-day Vietnam, Cambodia and Laos. In 1940, as part of the French empire, Indochina was still under the control of the Vichy French government. On 22 September, Japanese forces briefly invaded northern Vietnam, to dissuade French authorities from permitting the transit of arms and raw materials to China, with whom Japan had been at war since 1937. In the face of overwhelming forces, the French agreed to the Japanese demands after only four days of fighting. The situation in the Far East came up again two days later. Churchill was sceptical of the Japanese threat and objected to the keeping of two brigades in readiness to defend Singapore. Eden disagreed, writing to him, 'It seems difficult to maintain now that the Japanese threat to Malaya is not serious ... There is every indication that Germany has made some deal with Japan.'[12] Eden's hunch was correct, and Japan signed the Tripartite Pact with Germany and Italy a few days later. Britain was not yet at war with Japan, but it seemed only a matter of time.

At the end of September Churchill and Eden spent the evening together. The Blitz was claiming the lives of almost a thousand Londoners a week, but the immediate threat of invasion was lessening; in fact, Hitler had ordered the indefinite postponement of Operation Sealion the week before. Churchill was in a reflective mood that night, telling Eden that, at sixty-five, he was 'an old man' and would not repeat the mistake of Lloyd George, who had led the wartime coalition government during the First World War and then carried on as prime minister afterwards. Eden recorded in his diary that Churchill told him, 'the succession must be mine.' It was a promise Eden would cling to, but one that Churchill would not fulfil. They ended their evening on cheery terms, Churchill telling his friend, 'we shall win this war together.'

Chapter 6

The home front

Churchill and Eden both had complicated private lives and endured personal struggles. Churchill is said to have been hounded by the 'black dog' of depression – although the extent of his battles with mental health is disputed – while stress left Eden intermittently bedridden with gastric ulcers. For both, escaping to their houses in the country gave them solace, although the Eden family home in Surrey never represented the place of sanctuary that Chartwell – Winston and Clementine's country house in Kent – became to Churchill.

Eden had married Beatrice just prior to his election to parliament in 1923. At the time, she was only eighteen years of age and seen as a rather wayward child. The twenty-six-year-old Eden, with his Military Cross, good Oxford degree and political prospects seemed the perfect match. Eden was equally pleased, writing on the day she accepted his proposal, 'I have indeed won a treasure.' The couple's first boy, Simon, was born in 1924, but their second son tragically died only fifteen minutes after being born by caesarean section. The funeral of 'the sweetest little baby' was, Eden noted, the most wretched day of his life. Beatrice travelled to the West Indies to convalesce, but, although they went on to have another boy, Nicholas, the death of their second son would prove, according to one of Eden's biographers, a turning point in the marriage. Both went on to have affairs throughout the war, Eden more discreetly than Beatrice. Their situation was an open secret among their social circles but a cause of concern for the secret service, who were aware that as the couple's marital troubles were not known publicly they left Eden potentially open to blackmail. In a culture where divorce was still anathema for public figures – marriage to a divorcee had only recently forced the abdication of the British monarch – such an 'understanding' was a far more common, albeit risky arrangement. Their marriage, which by the end of the war was one of primarily political convenience, would finally be shattered by a shared personal tragedy and the two would go on to divorce in 1950. But events following the end of Eden's first marriage would serve to draw Eden even closer to Churchill.

Although Eden was troubled by ill-health, the newspaper cartoonists' characterisation of him as a sickly man was not always true, despite the fact it has now become the received wisdom. For his age and despite the hours required of his work, Eden was remarkably fit in middle age. He had always enjoyed swimming and playing tennis but stepped up his physical exercise in 1940 when he rejoined the government, primarily in response to Churchill's working habits. Churchill's indefatigable energy and seemingly minimal requirement for sleep meant he had a penchant for late-night meetings and even later phone calls. A summons from bed was not unusual. Churchill appears to have been almost blissfully unaware of the inconvenience of his working methods: staff and colleagues were simply expected to appear at his beck and call for whatever issue was deemed urgent at that particular moment, with the late shift at Downing Street seldom released to their beds before 3am. In August 1940 Eden began going on early-morning runs, sometimes with his eldest son, Simon. On 5 August he noted in his diary, 'Simon and I went for a run at 6am I left him to rest half way. Not bad for 43!'

While Eden was extremely close to Simon, Churchill's tempestuous relationship with his only son, Randolph, who was thirteen years Simon's senior, was almost the exact opposite. At the age of twenty-one, Randolph admitted in a newspaper article that his two main ambitions in life were to 'make an immense fortune and to be Prime Minister.'[1] Churchill initially had great plans for his son, telling a friend that same year, 'Naturally I have high hopes for Randolph. He has a gift and a power of presentation which I have not seen equalled in his age. Whether he will be noble and diligent has yet to be proved.' As it transpired, diligence of the type required to persevere in politics was not to be one of Randolph's traits. His attitude toward his father appalled Eden and greatly saddened Churchill. On one occasion Eden made a surprise visit to Churchill's house to deliver some late-night telegrams and found a drunk Randolph engaged in a blazing row with Churchill. Eden's arrival broke up the argument and Churchill and Eden discussed the newly arrived messages. When they were done, Churchill walked Eden to the door. Eden later remembered, 'He stopped, looked at me and with tears in his eyes said: "I hope that your Simon will never cause you the pain Randolph has caused me.'" Eden added that, in his own view, he 'thought it a crime that Randolph should debauch himself and distress his father.'[2] Historians have been equally unkind. Max Hastings, in his book on Churchill's war years, writes, 'Posterity owes little to Churchill's wayward son Randolph.'[3]

But Churchill himself had a combative personality. When, during the height of the Battle of Britain, a close friend commented to Churchill's wife, Clementine, that the prime minister's 'obstinate and barky' nature was worsening, it prompted her to write to him. Her letter, adorned with a sketch of a cat, began, 'My Darling, I hope you will forgive me if I tell you something that I feel you ought to know.' She said that a 'devoted friend' had told her that there was 'a danger of your becoming generally disliked by your colleagues ... because of your rough sarcastic and overbearing manner.' She put it down to the strain, noting, 'you are not so kind as you used to be ... you won't get the best results by irascibility and rudeness.' She ended, 'your loving, devoted and watchful Clemmie.'[4]

Clementine and Churchill had married in 1908. She had broken off two engagements prior to agreeing to marry Churchill and wavered a few weeks before their wedding day, aware of the impact Churchill's political ambitions might have. She went through with the union and a delighted Churchill wrote to his mother from their Italian honeymoon that his bride was 'very happy and beautiful', reporting that they were having a relaxing time away: 'We have only loitered and loved. A good and serious occupation for which the histories furnish respectable precedents.'[5]

Far from being in awe of her husband, Clementine was intelligent and opinionated and could equal Churchill's passionate rages. The two frequently had noisy arguments, but in public she was unflinching in her backing of her husband and in private they adored each other. When the war was over, Churchill left Clementine a small gift at the house accompanied by a note which read, 'I send this token, but how little it can express my gratitude to you for making my life and any work I have done possible.' As well as Randolph, the couple had four daughters, but the Churchills, like Eden and Beatrice, experienced family tragedy. Marigold, their third daughter, born in 1918, contracted septicaemia when she and her elder brother and sister were spending a holiday in Scotland under the care of an inexperienced French governess. Clementine and Churchill were unaware that she was ill for a fortnight and by the time they had rushed to her bedside there was little they could do. She died the next day, three months before her third birthday. Churchill wept and for days was unable to speak. Their daughter's untimely death did not fracture their marriage, but following the funeral, Churchill and Clementine barely spoke of her again, although Marigold's framed picture remained on her mother's dressing table.

Churchill and Eden shared a love of art, but Eden's enthusiasm was for collecting it, while Churchill preferred to make it himself. During his lifetime Eden would acquire paintings or sketches by Constable, Monet and Picasso, although when he and Beatrice divorced he was forced to divide up his collection. When he finally became prime minister, he hung some of his treasures in the upstairs flat at Downing Street, among them a Degas painting he had inherited from his father. His interest in art was for pleasure rather than profit, and following a visit to an exhibition of John Singer Sargent's work at the Royal Academy in 1926, he wrote in his diary: 'Brilliant painting, no subtlety, little sense of colour ... It is never "I must have that picture, I cannot live without it" – but, "how brilliant, how damnably clever."'

For Churchill, painting was a form of therapy as much as it was a hobby. After the war, when his political fortunes had turned for the worse again, Churchill took a holiday abroad and wrote to Clementine, 'The painting has been a great pleasure to me, and I have really forgotten all my vexations. It is a wonderful cure, because you cannot really think of anything else.'[6] Churchill had only taken up painting at the age of forty-one, at the suggestion of his sister-in-law, as something that might alleviate his doldrums as the disaster at Gallipoli unfolded. Time-consuming, absorbing, and a world removed from the stresses of political life, an aide once remarked that it was 'a distraction and a sedative that brought [to Churchill] a measure of ease to his frustrated spirit.'

Eden's escape was literature. He read voraciously, and was particularly fond of the works of Dickens, but his first love was Shakespeare. He frequently attended theatre performances and his diary contains many direct and subtle references to different works. He read plays to the family after dinner and, much to his personal delight, succeeded in passing on to Simon his passion. He also read political biographies, inscribing pencil notes in the margins, and maintained his fluency in the Persian and Arabic he had studied at university. His semi-celebrity status also resulted in him being the recipient of complimentary books:

Dale Carnegie sent him a signed copy of his now-legendary work, *How to Win Friends and Influence People*, writing inside, 'To Anthony, who doesn't need to read this book. He lives it.'[7]

The significant political positions that Churchill and Eden held were, much of the time, all-consuming. Churchill seldom questioned what he thought was the hand of destiny, but, on more than occasion, Eden debated whether he wanted to continue in politics. After his resignation in 1938, when Eden escaped to the Yorkshire Dales, he wrote to a friend, 'The moors in this glorious [spring] weather do not exactly encourage me to contemplate a return to political life, ever.'[8] When the end of the war with Hitler finally came, the vagaries of democracy would hand to both men another opportunity to ponder their political futures.

Chapter 7

Priorities

In autumn 1940 fighting on land in Western Europe had ended, but hostilities had opened on a new front in North Africa. In September Italian forces in Libya advanced east into British-controlled Egypt. Despite facing a numerically superior Italian force, British and Indian troops held them back.

On 11 October Eden began a trip to the Middle East and North Africa, taking a Sunderland flying boat first to Gibraltar, then Malta and on to Cairo. The aircrew had received detailed instructions for how to make their final approach: to arrive from the south, to not fly over the city, and to circle around the second tower on the Heliopolis road before landing. The flying boat's crew were Australians who had never been to Egypt before and neither they nor Eden had any idea how to find the Heliopolis road. 'We decided to bravely ignore all this,' Eden wrote in his diary that night, 'and we flew gaily over Cairo without being shot at and plomped down firmly but gracefully on the Nile.' The following morning he met with the two senior British commanders. Not content with holding off the Italians, they were quietly confident that, with sufficient reinforcements, they could defeat them. A delighted Eden immediately telegrammed Churchill, informing him that it was hoped a serious offensive could be launched in January 1941, noting that 'a fair prospect of success' would depend upon equipment being made available. Eden visited the army headquarters in the Western Desert, enjoying a dip in the Mediterranean, before flying to a forward base at Siwa to meet the commanders and men of the 7th Armoured Division. Eden's trips to meet front-line serving men were one of the things he most enjoyed. He wrote in his diary during the war, 'Nothing gives me more comfort than when a soldier's face lights up with pleasure when he recognises me. I suppose this is vanity, but I hope not entirely. The truth is I like our people and to be with them.' But Eden's joy at meeting and encouraging soldiers, a task he excelled at, was cut short.

Priorities

On 28 October Eden was woken early in the morning and informed that the Italians had invaded Greece from Albania. Eden confided in his diary, 'we are not in a position to give effective help by land or air, and another guaranteed nation looks like falling to the Axis.' Churchill emphatically took the opposing view, insisting that Britain should hold to a commitment made by Chamberlain in 1939, that it would support Greece against aggression. From Egypt, Eden cabled Churchill on 1 November to inform him of his strong objections: 'We cannot, from the Middle East resources, send sufficient air or land reinforcements to have any decisive influence upon [the] course of fighting in Greece … [it] would imperil our whole position in the Middle East and jeopardise plans for offensive operations now being laid.'[1] Churchill obdurately insisted on sending arms and men, telling the War Cabinet back in London that if Greece was overwhelmed, 'it would be said that in spite of our guarantees we had allowed one more small ally to be swallowed up.'[2] Churchill then dispatched a fiery reply to Eden, accusing him of passivity and negativity. Thousands of miles away, Eden was unable to change Churchill's mind, although he contemplated cutting short his trip to fly home when he discovered two fighter squadrons and a battalion were being sent as reinforcements. Privately, he wrote that Churchill's fixation on Greece was 'strategic folly.' The British Ambassador in Egypt was even less restrained, telegraphing London that sending military aid to Greece was 'completely crazy', for which he received a personal rebuke from Churchill.[3] When Eden did return to London to explain in detail the planned desert offensive, Churchill promptly changed his mind, and halted further support for the Greek army, which in any event was managing to beat back the Italians. The prospect of Britain going on the attack greatly pleased the prime minister, who remarked, 'At long last we are going to throw off the intolerable shackles of the defensive. Wars are won by superior willpower. Now we will wrest the initiative from the enemy and impose our will on him.'[4]

While preparations for the offensive in the Western Desert got underway, Britain continued to suffer under German bombing attacks. On the night of 3 November, for the first time since early September, no German bombers attacked London. But the quiet night was a false dawn. On 14 November 300 German bombers struck Coventry. It was the heaviest raid of the war so far. Munitions factories in the town were damaged and the bombing triggered a firestorm in the city centre that destroyed its historic cathedral. In total, 568 civilians were killed and 2,306 homes were destroyed. A young teenage girl later recounted that she emerged from the bomb shelter in which she had spent the night to an apocalyptic scene. 'I saw a dog running down the street with a child's arm in its mouth. There were lines of bodies stretched out on blankets. A poor fireman was watching helplessly while the buildings were still burning.'[5]

Popular myth has led to Churchill being widely criticised for the events that night. It has been claimed that through the efforts of Enigma code-breakers at Bletchley Park, Churchill was informed in advance of the Coventry raid, but took no action so as not to alert Hitler to the fact that the British were intercepting secret German communications. In fact, although Churchill may have been sent a message around 3pm, the evidence that he read it is circumstantial. When the RAF detected Luftwaffe radio navigation beams converging on Coventry, just before 4pm, a fighter patrol 100-strong was redirected to the city and anti-aircraft gunners were alerted in advance. Churchill himself was convinced that London was going to be heavily bombed and ordered his female staff to be sent home and two of his duty private secretaries to spend the night in a deep air-raid shelter in Piccadilly, telling them, 'You are too young to die.'[6]

Tom Harrisson, an anthropologist who visited Coventry after the raid, gave a short account after the 9pm news on BBC radio two days later:

> I've spent a good deal of my life listening to other people talk, but I've never heard people talk less than in Coventry yesterday. Many walked through the city rather blankly looking at the mess ... I've been chasing air raids in this country ever since they began: often I've heard awful stories of the damage and then arrived to find them grossly exaggerated. But at Coventry there hasn't been much exaggeration: in fact the centre of the town reminded me more than anything of the photos of Ypres in the last war.[7]

His sombre observation contrasted with the normal broadcasts of British pluck in the face of the Blitz and it was debated at the War Cabinet meeting on 18 November. Eden and Churchill were both strongly critical. Eden stated the broadcast was 'most depressing' and would 'have a deplorable effect on [the morale of soldiers in] Warwickshire units' concerned about loved ones back home. The result was that two 'government advisors' were appointed to monitor the BBC's output the following year. It was the closest the British wartime government ever came to banning the free press.

The BBC soon had some good news to report, however, as the offensive in the Western Desert began on 9 December, only a week after Churchill's sixty-sixth birthday. Among the greetings the prime minister received was one from Eden, which read, 'Many and happier returns of the day. Very few men in all history have had to bear such a burden as you have carried in the last six months … Bless you; thank you for all your kindness to me, and may we yet celebrate the last stage of a long hard road travelled.'[8] Churchill wrote back, 'I am very grateful to you for all your help and comfort.' Operation Compass transpired to be an even better birthday present than Churchill could ever have imagined. Within the first three days, 38,000 Italian prisoners were captured for the loss of only 624 Indian and British troops. Churchill messaged the overall commander, General Wavell, to 'maul the Italian Army and rip them off the African shore.'[9] The planned offensive was quickly upscaled, as British divisions hounded the remnant of the shattered Italian forces along the Libyan coast towards Tobruk, which was captured a few weeks later.

In the midst of the success in the desert came news that Lord Lothian, the British ambassador in Washington, had died suddenly. Churchill first offered the post to the seventy-seven-year-old former prime minister, David Lloyd George, who declined on the basis that his doctor had told him he was not well enough to accept. Churchill then summoned Eden to a midnight meeting, and proposed that the foreign secretary, Lord Halifax, should go to Washington and that Eden should take his place. Rather than grasping at a return to his former, more prominent, role, Eden recalled that he 'went home sad at the thought of leaving the soldiers.' He clearly relished the close contact with the fighting men that came with being Secretary of State for War. The position was further complicated the following day, when Churchill formally offered Halifax the ambassadorship and he declined. Halifax stated that both he and his wife preferred to live in their Yorkshire home rather than in Washington. Eventually, Churchill ordered him to accept the post. Meeting at Chequers on 20 December, a tired Churchill, who was nursing a headache, informed Eden that he had ordered Halifax to Washington.

He stated he was aware that Eden 'did not want to move' but that he was sure it was the right thing, confessing to Eden that he 'found personal matters between friends exhausting.' Eden reluctantly accepted, writing subsequently in his memoirs, 'Though my feelings were mixed, I knew that there could not really be any argument and that my responsibility must be greater as Churchill's colleague at the Foreign Office.'[10] For his part, Churchill was pleased to see Eden back heading up foreign affairs. He wrote that Eden was 'like a man going home'.[11]

On the first night of the New Year, Eden was summoned to Downing Street to debate a communication to Roosevelt. When other ministers had left, Churchill took Eden up on to the roof. It was raining that night, which seemed to have put off the German bombers, as the anti-aircraft barrage was light. Staring up at the London sky, darkened by the city's compulsory blackout against the Blitz, Eden pondered what fate would have in store in 1941. What neither could have imagined was that Hitler was preparing to make a decision that would ultimately lose him the war.

Chapter 8

The dark hour

The defeats inflicted on the Italians in North Africa and Greece had not gone unnoticed. Hitler's response was to order the invasion and occupation of Greece and the formation of the *Afrika Korps*. The special expeditionary force, under the command of the talismanic general, Erwin Rommel, would be sent to reverse the British successes in Libya.

Eden and Churchill had warning of the first of Hitler's plans and Eden's inaugural trip as foreign secretary was to Greece, to reassure the government of Britain's support. The wild success of Operation Compass had, for the second time, changed the prime minister's mind and he now wanted to defend the Balkans against the Italian and German threat. Eden left on 14 February, again taking a Sunderland to Gibraltar. The Australian co-pilot from his previous trip was in command. They took off in rough weather, but it transpired that the Met Office forecast that flying conditions would improve was completely wrong. The plane found itself fighting a violent storm. Eden and the other passengers sat in their life jackets, many being sick. Eden managed to sleep and was roused to be told that the plane, which had been completely lost for a time, might not have enough fuel to reach Gibraltar. The pilot stated he could put into Cadiz, in neutral Spain, but in all likelihood the aircraft and its passengers would be interned by Franco's government for the remainder of the war. Eden went up to the cockpit to chat with the pilot and the navigator and they agreed to press on. They reached Gibraltar having almost exhausted the Sunderland's reserve tank, with only enough fuel for ten more minutes' flying time. Eden's aircraft was one of three flying to Gibraltar that day, the one following his Sunderland never made it. It was one of Eden's closest shaves of the war.

By the time Eden arrived in Athens, the Germans had already assembled twenty-three divisions in Romania. The King of Greece put on an impressive show of defiance, but, as Eden wrote to Churchill, the military problem was 'essentially one of time and space'. In the event, the four divisions Churchill insisted on sending to Greece were woefully insufficient. German forces invaded on 6 April, in greater strength than had been anticipated, and before the British reinforcements were even in place. Eighteen days later they were evacuating, although 3,000 were killed and a further 9,000 were captured. Athens fell on 27 April. Churchill was aware of the risks of his insistence on supporting Greece, admitting to one general while Eden was away, 'We have taken a grave and hazardous decision to sustain the Greeks and to try and make a Balkan front.'[1] It is not to Eden's credit that, having fought to not weaken the forces in North Africa, he then allowed four divisions to be sent to Greece. Either he thought it feasible that Greece could be defended – the view espoused in his memoirs, which state that none of the generals had anticipated the total Greek collapse – or he had decided to proceed with Churchill's wishes, against his better judgement. Worse, the debacle in Greece probably contributed to the simultaneous British military reversal in North Africa. Rommel's *Afrika Korps* advanced in Libya at the start of April. On 3 April the British retreated from Benghazi and by 11 April they had been pushed back to the start line of Operation Compass, while the 9th Australian Division was under siege at Tobruk. Churchill's fêted desert victory had been reversed and Greece had fallen to Hitler.

The war at sea was also going badly. In March 1941 German U-boats had sunk a record total of over 350,000 tonnes of Allied shipping. Submarines were not the only threat to the convoys that were Britain's lifeline: the *Kriegsmarine*'s expanding surface fleet was also a serious danger. Over an eight-week period from January 1941, the German battleships *Scharnhorst* and *Gneisenau* sank a total of 116,000 tonnes of shipping. The sighting of a German capital ship, and sometimes even just reports of their presence on the convoy routes, could cause convoys to scatter, leaving lone vessels vulnerable to U-boats. The only saving grace was that to reach the Atlantic, German vessels had to travel from the primary shipping yard of Wilhelmshaven and either navigate the narrow English Channel, or sail around Britain via the North Sea. On 21 May 1941 a British informant relayed to the Admiralty a message that two large warships had been sighted off the southern coast of Sweden. The *Kriegsmarine*'s newest battleship, the *Bismarck*, along with the heavy cruiser *Prinz Eugen*, was sailing to attack the convoys. The same day, the British battlecruiser HMS

Hood, along with the newly commissioned battleship HMS *Prince of Wales*, left the Navy's base at Scapa Flow in Scotland to try and intercept. Churchill's own experience as First Lord of the Admiralty had left him with a fascination regarding naval matters. He was acutely aware of the threat the *Bismarck* posed, noting in December 1940 that *Bismarck* and her sister ship, *Tirpitz*, were at least as capable as the Royal Navy's two latest battleships, *King George V* and *Prince of Wales*. On hearing *Bismarck* and *Prinz Eugen* had sailed, Churchill cabled Roosevelt, 'Should we fail to catch them going out, your Navy should surely be able to mark them down for us … Give us the news and we will finish the job.'[2]

The *Hood* was the darling of the Royal Navy. Commissioned in 1920, by 1941 she was a comparatively antiquated design and a planned refit had been indefinitely postponed at the start of the war, but the public and navy personnel had a real affection for her. In 1923-24 the flagship circumnavigated the globe, visiting South Africa, Australia, New Zealand and the United States. *Hood* had literally flown the flag around the entire world.

On the early morning of 24 May *Hood* and *Prince of Wales* engaged the German ships, which were being shadowed by two British cruisers in the Denmark Strait. After initially mistakenly firing on the *Prinz Eugen*, under the impression it was the *Bismarck*, *Hood* then steered to try and bring all her guns to bear. A shell from the *Bismarck* penetrated the deck and hit the ship's midships magazine. *Hood* exploded, sinking in three minutes. Only three of the 1,419 crew members survived. The *Prince of Wales* was forced to retreat. The dramatic sinking of the *Hood* shocked the nation. Eden wrote, 'The Navy must avenge her … Poor *Hood*, the loveliest ship to look at in all the Royal Navy and for many years to millions its emblem.' There was glee in Germany, with the *Essener Zeitung* newspaper declaring, 'The mightiest bulwark of British sea power was sunk and with it crumbles the last cornerstone of the British hope of victory.'[3]

What neither the press in Britain or Germany were aware of was that the *Prince of Wales* had managed to hit the *Bismarck*, causing sufficient damage to her fuel supply that the ship changed course to try and reach a port in occupied France. On 26 May, as a Royal Navy force including an aircraft carrier and the battleship *King George V* frantically hunted down the *Bismarck*, the German battleship managed to lose her shadowers. Eden recorded it was, 'A most gloomy day. *Bismarck* appears to have been lost … The worst Cabinet meeting we have had yet in [the] evening. Winston was nervy and unreasonable and everyone else on edge.' The sinking of HMS *Hood* was the first item on the agenda at the 5pm War Cabinet meeting at Downing Street, at which the First Sea Lord described to the men gathered around the table how the *Hood* had blown up twenty minutes into the engagement. It was a sombre moment.

That night, Churchill, not knowing that the *Bismarck* had already been crippled, determined that she should be sunk, whatever the risk. He drafted a signal to the admiral in charge of the chasing squadron: '*Bismarck* must be sunk at all costs and if to do this it is necessary for the *King George V* to remain on the scene, then she must do so, even if it subsequently means towing *King George V* [if she runs out of fuel]'.[4] It was a remarkable signal, demonstrating Churchill at his melodramatic worst. Concerned above all with the moral statement and the powerful image that would result from avenging the *Hood*, he was willing to overrule an admiral and order that the Royal Navy's most powerful warship be allowed to run out of fuel in an area of known U-boat activity. Thankfully, the signal was only dispatched mid-morning on 27 May, by which time the *Bismarck* had already been found and sunk by a combination of shellfire and torpedoes. The admiral later described it as 'the stupidest and most ill-considered signal ever made', stating that he would have disobeyed the order at the risk of court martial.[5] Churchill was in the House of Commons on 27 May and had just sat down when he was handed a note. He stood again, 'Mr Speaker, I do not know whether I might venture, with great respect, to intervene for one moment. I have just received news that the *Bismarck* is sunk.'[6] There was spontaneous rejoicing and MPs cheered and waved their order papers.

The sinking of the *Bismarck*, which went down with 2,090 German sailors, was only a momentary victory in a year that had so far almost entirely been one of military losses and reversals. The following month, an attempted counter-offensive against Rommel in North Africa began well and then deteriorated into failure, with the British losing more than a hundred tanks. On 18 June a dejected Churchill telephoned Eden and asked him to come to Downing Street for a discussion. As the two men talked, Churchill showed Eden a telegram from President Roosevelt, which stated that the recent decision to freeze the American assets of Germans and Italians and to close German consulates had received widespread public support. It seemed another indication that the US was edging towards finally entering the war. Eden noted the news was 'some comfort in a dark hour'.

Chapter 9

'The Prime Minister's compliments'

Eden regularly spent weekends at the prime ministerial country retreat of Chequers in Buckinghamshire, the leafy surrounds of the sixteenth-century manor providing a peaceful backdrop to late-night conversations over drinks. On one such weekend, Churchill personally lit the fire in Eden's bedroom after which Eden put down in his diary, 'I know no one with such perfect manners as host, especially when he feels like it!' Eden's Sunday lie-in on 22 June 1941 was disturbed by a knock on the door. It was Churchill's valet. On entering, he presented Eden with a large cigar on a silver tray and said, 'The Prime Minister's compliments, and the German armies have invaded Russia.'[1] Eden promptly donned a dressing gown and went along to Churchill's bedroom, although he left the cigar untouched as he was not keen to smoke that early in the morning. They discussed how to respond, Churchill deciding that he should address the nation, and state that Britain would treat the Russians as partners in the struggle against Hitler. It was a moment that changed the outcome of the war.

The German invasion of Soviet Russia was not the cataclysmic surprise that it is often portrayed to have been. The British government was aware at a fairly early stage of Hitler's preparations and had in fact warned the Russians in advance. As Operation Barbarossa began and Hitler's armoured columns rumbled across the Russian border, it came as more of a shock to Stalin than it did to Churchill or Eden. Legend has it that after several days of frantically giving orders that left him shattered and looking 'like a bag of bones in a grey tunic', the Soviet leader retired to his country *dacha* for three days and refused to answer the telephone. He was eventually lured out of hiding by members of the Politburo and addressed the Soviet nation on 3 July, eleven days after the invasion had begun, by which time Minsk had already fallen to the advancing Germans.

On 12 June code-breakers at Bletchley Park had deciphered a telegram sent from the Japanese Embassy in Berlin, which revealed the date of the invasion. Eden ensured the information reached the Russian ambassador, Ivan Maisky, but his tip-off, along with evidence provided by Russian spies who sent back to Moscow first-hand reports of the German troop build-up, was ignored. The general view in Britain was that Russia would be obliterated if it ever had to confront the German war machine. The Russian army had performed embarrassingly in the Finnish war of 1939-40, and the Chief of the General Staff was of the opinion that Russia would not last six weeks. Churchill held a rather different view, saying he would bet 500-1 'that the Russians are still fighting, and fighting victoriously, two years from now.'[2]

Communism had for decades been seen as the greatest enemy of peace in Europe. Churchill had even welcomed the rise of National Socialism in Germany, as it was a counter to what he once called 'the foul baboonery of Bolshevism'. The Communist revolution in Russia had led to the country exiting the First World War and ceasing to be Britain's ally only twenty-four years previously. In line with the Communist manifesto, the property of the bourgeois had been confiscated and among those denuded of all their possessions and summarily sent packing were a number of British subjects. One British woman, whose family lost their entire fortune when a cotton mill they owned was confiscated following the 1917 revolution, wrote to Churchill in 1920 asking for his assistance. She lamented, 'I know there are hundreds of British subjects living now in this country in poverty, who were turned out of Russia with nothing more than they could carry, and only enough money to pay their fares home, the rest of their possessions being appropriated by the Bolsheviks.'[3]

The British government did not just accept the dethroning of the tsar, and as Russia descended into civil war, British money, men and arms were sent to support Russian nationalists. The Russian civil war ended in victory for the Communists, who made no secret of their plans to expand their ideology into parts of the British Empire. Communist Russia was, in ideological terms, Britain's most natural enemy on the European continent, a problem Churchill had to navigate carefully when he addressed the British public on the evening of the German invasion. In his address, Churchill openly admitted the rather unique position Hitler's action had now placed him and his government in. 'No one has been a more consistent opponent of Communism for the last twenty-five years [than I have] … But all this fades away before the spectacle which is now unfolding.' He added that 'the cause of any Russian fighting for his hearth and home is the cause of free men and free people in every quarter of the globe.'[4] In short, the practicalities of war meant that any enemy of Hitler was Britain's friend.

On 20 July Stalin dispatched his first personal message to Churchill. Maisky decoded it, translated it and typed it up in person, before driving to Chequers to deliver the note to Churchill. The Soviet ambassador was impressed by his surrounds: 'Dark halls, old paintings, strange staircases … how it should be in a respectful, solid English house several centuries old.'[5] Churchill met him in relaxed attire; a pair of grey-blue overalls which Maisky thought looked like 'a cross between a brick-layer's work clothes and an outfit suitable for a bomb shelter'. The two went into a drawing room and sat by the fire, where Churchill read Stalin's communiqué. The Soviet leader called for Britain to launch a second front in France, but Churchill was adamant that it was risky and would end in disaster. It was a demand Stalin would make again and again over the following years.

One of Eden's first tasks was to patch up relations between Britain's new ally and the exiled Polish government, which had taken up residence in London. The Poles showed a remarkable amount of grace in supporting Eden's efforts, despite the fact that Stalin and Hitler had jointly invaded Poland in 1939. They demanded the release of the Polish deportees and prisoners of war still being held in Russia and sought to reconfirm the borders that had been negotiated between both countries at the end of the Polish-Soviet war in 1921.[6] Ambassador Maisky acquiesced to the release of the prisoners of war, but was insistent that any discussion of the frontiers of Poland should be left aside. Over multiple meetings and lunches of sandwiches and caviar, Eden managed to hammer out an agreement, which was signed on 30 July. Eden immediately informed the House of Commons, announcing that it was an historic event, which he stated would 'lay a firm foundation for future collaboration between the two countries in the war against the common enemy.'[7] Privately, Eden was very conscious that the Soviets were still refusing to commit to where Poland's border would be drawn when hostilities ended.

Eden was not the only one concerned with what would happen when the fighting ceased, even though the war in the East had only just begun. In the midst of his negotiations with the Poles and the Soviets, Eden was paid a visit by Harry Hopkins, Roosevelt's unofficial envoy. Hopkins was officially in charge of the Lend Lease programme, through which the United States supplied aid and military assistance to Britain, but in practice he was the American president's emissary in London. Hopkins informed Eden that Roosevelt did not want any commitments made on any frontiers prior to a peace treaty, asserting, '[the] U.S. would come into the war and did not want to find after the event that we had all kinds of engagements of which they had never been told.'[8] Eden was diplomatic, but was privately irked by Roosevelt involving himself when America was not even fighting, noting, 'the spectacle of an American President talking at large on European frontiers chilled me with Wilsonian memories.' But Hopkins' intervention on the president's behalf was just the beginning.

A few weeks later the British prime minister quietly boarded the HMS *Prince of Wales*, which sailed at high speed taking an erratic course across the Atlantic. Churchill was going to meet Roosevelt. They held discussions in Newfoundland aboard the US Navy cruiser *Augusta*. At Roosevelt's suggestion, they drew up what Churchill later described as 'broad principles which should guide our policies'.[9] In Churchill's eyes, they were a handy set of post-conflict ideals that might help swing American public opinion in favour of US intervention to aid Britain's plight, by outlining the rights of nations; rights that were being trampled on by the German and Japanese armies across Europe and the Far East. For Roosevelt, the Atlantic Charter's eight principles were nothing less than the founding document of a new world order. Roosevelt would go on to use the charter's third principle – that all peoples had the right to 'choose the form of government under which they will live' – as a way of criticising Britain's empire. Even during his discussions with Churchill, Roosevelt pushed him on Britain's colonies, angering Churchill by suggesting future trade should bring wealth to all and pointing the finger: 'those Empire trade agreements are a case in point. It's because of them that the people of India and Africa, of all the colonial Near East and Far East, are still as backward as they are.' Churchill brushed the criticisms aside and returned to discussion of the war, but the moment was not quickly forgotten. Late that night, after the fractious meeting, while he sat smoking a cigarette in bed, Roosevelt confided in an aid, 'Winnie has one supreme mission in life, but only one. He's a perfect wartime prime minister. His one big job is to ensure that Britain survives this war … He changes the subject away from anything post war.' The president added, 'His mind is perfect for that of a war leader. But Winston Churchill lead Britain after the war? It'd never work.'[10]

At the start of September Eden tried to take a few days' holiday in the country, but was dragged back to London by the news that Maisky was delivering to Churchill another personal message from Stalin. In it, the Soviet leader admitted, 'we have lost more than one half of the Ukraine and in addition the enemy is at the gates of Leningrad.'[11] The Germans were also less than 200 miles from Moscow. Russia was on the brink. Stalin stated that without Britain launching a second front to draw away at least thirty German divisions and supplying their new ally with tanks, aircraft and aluminium, Russia would be defeated. Churchill was spurred into action and shortly afterwards he did discuss with Eden a potential invasion of France, but there were more German divisions in France than the British would be able to land, even if they could find the boats to do so, and the Luftwaffe had complete local air superiority. They agreed to Stalin's plea for tanks and aircraft, and Churchill cabled Stalin in reply, promising to deliver what had been asked. He also added that it was his own 'personal opinion' that the 'violence of the German invasion is already over and that winter will give your heroic armies breathing space.'[12] Churchill was deliberately misleading Stalin. Far from being his 'personal opinion', it was the code-breakers at Bletchley Park who had found out that the Luftwaffe was struggling with supplying and maintaining aircraft, and that German commanders were increasingly of the view that the Russians would not be defeated before winter set in. On 12 October the first Arctic supply convoy from Britain to Russia reached Archangel carrying 193 fighters and twenty tanks. German troops were only sixty-five miles from Moscow. Stalin continued to demand more material and British action to draw away German forces attacking Russia. British representatives in Moscow were getting short shrift from the Soviet leader, who wanted a 'clear statement' of Britain's war aims and also sought to discuss, rather prematurely, a post-war settlement. On 20 November, after extended discussion, Churchill messaged Stalin to tell him that they would shortly be sending the foreign secretary to Moscow. Eden began preparations for the long journey east.

Churchill dined with friends at Chequers on the evening of 7 December. At nine o'clock he turned on the wireless to listen to the news. The announcer began with a bulletin on Russia, after which followed a few lines on 'an attack by Japanese on American shipping at Hawaii.' The Japanese had bombed Pearl Harbor. Churchill made an immediate telephone call to Roosevelt and was put through. In response to Churchill's question, 'What's this about Japan?', the President responded, 'It's quite true. They have attacked us at Pearl Harbor. We are all in the same boat now.'[13] Eden had just arrived in Scotland by train in preparation to sail to Russia. He was coming down with gastric flu and had spent most of the journey from Euston feeling chilled and sick, and was hoping to proceed straight to his ship and go to bed. Instead, he was driven to a naval headquarters to take a call on a secure line. On hearing the news of attack, he later admitted, 'I could not conceal my relief ... I felt that whatever happened [in the war] now, it was merely a question of time.'[14]

Chapter 10

Uncle Joe and FDR

A thick fog shrouded Murmansk harbour when Eden's boat docked. He disembarked in the early afternoon of 13 December 1941 in a swirling snow storm, as the premature winter darkness was already closing in. The original plan to fly to Moscow was shelved in view of the weather and the delegation traipsed to the station, to begin the sixty-hour train ride to the Russian capital. As he boarded his carriage, Eden remarked to Maisky, who was accompanying him, on the placement of a Union Jack next to the Soviet Union flag on the platform. The Soviet ambassador replied, 'That is a symbol … the hope of final victory over Hitler.'[1]

Eden's train reached Moscow at 11.30pm on 15 December, and after an official welcome the delegation went to bed. Eden met Stalin the next day. It was not the first time the two had encountered one another. Eden had visited Moscow in 1935 during his first stint as foreign secretary, but felt like he was starting from scratch. Initially, meetings went well, and Eden messaged Churchill after the first day, 'I believe I have established friendly relations with Stalin. I am sure that he is entirely with us against Hitler. Our first day has definitely been good.'[2] Stalin had presented Eden with two draft treaties, one for a military alliance and another agreeing common goals for a post-war settlement, which would not be for publication. Stalin was seemingly emboldened by the success of Russia's first counter-attacks against German troops, which had seen the Soviets push back the Germans from the gates of Moscow and Leningrad. In his conversations with Eden, Stalin was already suggesting dividing up Germany after the war, but Eden had to insist that he could agree nothing concrete as such ideas had not even been discussed in Cabinet. Stalin seemed, Eden wrote in his diary, 'a quiet dictator in his manner. No shouting, no gesticulation, so that it is impossible to guess his meaning, or even the subject of which he is speaking until the translation is given.'

It was a very successful negotiation approach, as Eden later admitted: 'if I had to pick a team for going into a conference room, Stalin would be my first choice ... He never wasted a word. He never stormed, he was seldom even irritated. Hooded, calm, never raising his voice ... he got what he wanted without having seemed obdurate.'[3]

The following day, the mood changed. Stalin opened discussions by asking for recognition of Russia's 1941 frontiers to be included in any treaty. Eden replied that such a request was impossible, as Churchill had already publicly stated that Britain did not recognise any of the territorial changes which had taken place in Poland since 1939, although he neglected to mention that he himself had given the same personal assurance to the exiled Polish government. Eden tried to explain that his hands were tied, in part blaming the need to consult the Dominions: 'if they were to hear tomorrow that I had agreed upon the Polish-Russian frontier, without any consultation with them, they would have every right to the strongest complaint.' Stalin was restrained, but critical in his reply, hinting that Eden was weak, while slamming Churchill and Roosevelt's Atlantic Charter. 'I certainly do not want to demand the impossible from you and I fully realise the limitation of your powers, but I am addressing myself to the British Government and I am genuinely surprised. I thought that the Atlantic Charter was directed against those people who were trying to establish world dominion. It now looks as if the Charter was directed against the U.S.S.R.'[4] The debate dragged on all day and into the next, leaving Eden considerably irritated. Eventually Eden and Stalin agreed the wording of a joint communiqué, which was light on detail, but strong on symbolism, although the sticking point of the frontiers remained.

On his final night in Moscow, Eden attended an 'awful' banquet for Stalin's birthday, which lasted until 5am and included thirty-six toasts. However, as he left the Russian capital, his last message to Churchill from Moscow was upbeat, 'Final discussions with Stalin were the best and I am sure that the visit has been worthwhile. We have allayed some at least of the past suspicions. Stalin, I believe, sincerely wants military agreements but he will not sign until we recognise his frontiers, and we must expect continued badgering on this issue.' He closed with mention of the banquet: 'We drank your health and some others. Stalin spoke very warmly of you.'[5] Eden spent Christmas at sea, finally reaching London on 30 December, more than three weeks after his departure.

On 11 December Germany declared war against the United States, finally bringing about the event Churchill had been eagerly hoping for since 1939. Having begun 1941 alone against Hitler, Britain now had two allies. An immensely relieved prime minister telegraphed Eden, then en-route to Murmansk, 'The accession of the United States makes amends for all, and with time and patience will give certain victory.'[6] Churchill decided at the last minute to visit Washington to discuss strategy in person with Roosevelt, a decision which appalled Eden, as he considered it deeply foolish for them both to be undertaking risky overseas visits at the same time. But Churchill would not be dissuaded and crossed the Atlantic aboard a battleship in stormy weather (and was one of the few among the eighty-strong political entourage not to get seasick). He arrived on American soil on 22 December and Roosevelt invited him to spend Christmas at the White House, much to the dismay of Roosevelt's wife, who had been away in California and only found out hours before the prime minister's arrival.

In meetings, Roosevelt and Churchill agreed to a strategy of 'Germany first' and discussed the potential of a joint Anglo-American landing in North Africa, while deciding that American bombers would be based in Britain. Churchill's stay in the White House also led to one of the most oft-repeated anecdotes of the war. After emerging from the bath, Churchill began dictating a memo, still naked and dripping wet. When there was a knock at the door, Churchill responded 'Come in!' and in came the president of the United States. Roosevelt made a swift retreat, but Churchill stopped him and said, 'You see, Mr. President, I have nothing to hide from you.' The two men enjoyed their time together. On Christmas Day Roosevelt telegrammed Clementine, wishing her a Merry Christmas, adding, 'It is a joy to have Winston ... I want you to know how grateful I am [to you] for letting him come.'

Distance did not appear to make the heart grow fonder for Churchill or Eden. A number of their most vicious spats during the war took place while one or other of them was overseas, often exacerbated by Churchill's penchant for sending extremely forthright telegrams. On 5 January 1942 Churchill flew to Florida for five days' rest. That day, Eden messaged him, encouraging him to consider Stalin's request for some form of recognition of the 1941 border with Poland in the name of 'stark realism'. In what would transpire to be a prophetic statement, Eden candidly told Churchill, 'nothing we and the US can do or say will affect the situation at the end of the war.' He received an angry reply four days later, in which Churchill stated, 'Your telegram surprised me … We have never recognised the 1941 frontiers of Russia … They were acquired by acts of aggression in shameful collusion with Hitler.'[7] He also dismissed Eden's prophecy, claiming no one could foresee where the balance of power would lie. But Eden had correctly divined that Europe's future course would be set in Moscow, once Russian forces turned the tide against Germany.

Eden's efforts to envision future policy met with stony opposition from Churchill, who seemed to regard himself as a realist when it came to post-war policy. In practice it meant that when anyone discussed it, he reverted the conversation back to the immediate conflict. When Eden submitted a draft document outlining what he called a 'Four Power Plan' in which Britain, the US, Russia and China would attempt to maintain world peace, Churchill was scathing: 'I hope that these speculative studies will be entrusted mainly to those on whose hands time hangs heavy, and that we shall not overlook Mrs Glass' Cookery Book recipe for Jugged Hare – "First, catch your hare."'[8] Eden's perspective was not just that of an internationalist, but also that of a man determined to maintain Britain's place in the world. Tellingly, he replied to Churchill that the vision of the Four Power Plan was so that policy was not made 'hand to mouth', adding, 'the only consequence of doing so is that the U.S. makes a policy and we follow, which I do not regard as a satisfactory role for the British Empire.' It was a battle for forward thinking that Eden fought and lost throughout the entire war. Churchill revelled in last-minute, late-night decision-making and never seemed to comprehend the perspective of anyone for whom such seat-of-the-pants government was anathema.

On the issue of Russia's border with Poland, Eden now pushed Cabinet, again advocating 'stark realism' so that a treaty could be agreed with Russia. Although the debate also split the Cabinet, the difference of opinion between Eden and Churchill was one of the occasions in which Eden's view prevailed. After weeks of discussions, on 7 March Churchill cabled Roosevelt, stating, 'the principles of the Atlantic Charter ought not to be construed so as to deny Russia the frontiers she occupied when Germany attacked her … I hope therefore you will be able to give us a free hand to sign the treaty which Stalin desires as soon as possible.' Reluctantly, Roosevelt agreed.

In May 1942 Vyacheslev Molotov arrived in London. The balding, bespectacled Russian foreign minister was the acceptable, external face of Communist Russia. He wore a suit, in contrast to Stalin who always wore a uniform, but in person could be both dull and brusque in equal measure. One senior Foreign Office civil servant recorded that Molotov had 'all the grace and conciliation of a totem pole'. While Churchill had poured oil on the waters of discontent over Britain's acceptance of Russia as a war ally, there were still several members of parliament who strongly opposed a formal treaty. Eden received violent letters from several senior MPs, including the Chief Whip, none of whom knew the details, but who knew enough to know they did not like it. The Russians were also being obdurate. Eden found discussions painful, recording, 'It was despairing to try to negotiate with the Soviet Government when they invariably raised their price at every meeting.' The Soviet insistence on the Polish frontier was forcing Churchill and Eden into a bind. Without it, they could not seemingly get Russia to agree a treaty, but if it were included they would upset not just the exiled Polish government, but a number of their own Cabinet. As a workaround, Eden came up with a completely new draft treaty that made no mention of frontiers at all. Churchill regarded it as a masterstroke, which avoided the problem of Poland, telling his friend that if it came off 'it would be the biggest thing I [Eden] had done'. The treaty agreed a twenty-year alliance, a commitment to ongoing military assistance and a commitment to principles of post-war collaboration, but made no mention of specific borders. To Churchill and Eden's surprise, it was almost immediately accepted. The change of heart was entirely Stalin's, who had decided he was happy to accept Eden's revised version, as it gave Russia 'free hands' in the future. His focus was on securing a commitment to a second front, not from Churchill, but from Roosevelt. The Soviet leader's instruction to Molotov simply stated, 'It is desirable to hastily conclude the treaty, after which fly to America.'[9] Eden had secured his treaty, but it was a largely pointless document.

A fortnight later a triumphant Molotov returned from Washington and dined with Churchill and Eden. He had with him a formal communiqué from Roosevelt, stating that 'full understanding' had been reached 'with regard to the urgent tasks of creating a second front in Europe in 1942.' Roosevelt had initially prevaricated, but he was assured by General Marshall that he could encourage Molotov, although it would depend on the British who would have to supply the majority of the troops. By giving Molotov what he wanted, Roosevelt was making Churchill be the bearer of bad news. Over dinner, Churchill attempted to explain to the Russian foreign minister the difficulties of mounting a European invasion. While not rejecting Roosevelt's communiqué, he stressed he could not promise anything.

On the first anniversary of Hitler's invasion of Russia, Maisky wrote in his diary, 'Much has changed ... A year ago the Germans were convinced they would win – the only question was when? Now they have lost that belief. They don't yet perceive their defeat is inevitable, but its terrible spectre already troubles their minds.'[10] It no longer seemed to be tempting fate to talk of the potential end of the war and victory for the Allies. But Churchill and Eden were starting to discover that around them a new world was being forged, a world in which Britain played second fiddle to the United States.

Chapter 11

Avoiding losses

History has painted Churchill's wartime premiership as an almost unalloyed success and the man himself as a hero war leader. While few would criticise the second judgement, politically, Churchill's time as prime minister was not all plain sailing. In the summer of 1942 there was serious criticism of Churchill's leadership. An early indication of what was to come took place at a lunch with members of the Chief of Staff in early April, at which Eden was present, when someone suggested Churchill should give up his dual role as Minister of Defence to safeguard his health. He angrily shot down the suggestion and Eden recorded afterwards, 'He sees himself … as sole director of war', adding, 'the Chiefs of Staff are only too ready to compromise where issues should be decided and Winston's unchecked judgement is by no means infallible.'[1]

The crisis was precipitated by the fall of Tobruk at the end of June. In 1941 Allied troops had held the Libyan city under siege for 241 days, before it was relieved in one of the periodic swings of fortune of the North African campaign. In 1942 it fell within twenty-four hours to Rommel's renewed advance. Nearly 33,000 soldiers were taken prisoner. Churchill was again on a trip to America and was staying in the White House when Roosevelt brought him the news. At first, he refused to believe it. A few hours later, at 5am, Eden was awoken by a telephone call from Churchill. Churchill was distressed by articles in American newspapers which he said 'were full of the impending fall of the government' and wanted to know from Eden how the military catastrophe had been received at home. Eden assured him that nothing had yet happened that would shake them, but that had changed by the time Churchill returned.

While Stalin had been pressing for debate on post-war frontiers and Roosevelt had been assuring the Soviet leader of the United States' and Britain's commitment to opening a second front, the reality remained that Britain was not at that moment winning the war, even though the politicians were talking about it. The Atlantic convoys were still under grave threat, a situation worsened by the fact that the British had lost the ability to read U-boat cipher signals in February, when the *Kriegsmarine* altered their Enigma code settings. Singapore had fallen to the Japanese and the initially successful campaign in North Africa was again in reverse, greeted by the headline in the *New York Times* that read 'Nazis near Egypt'. Churchill was frequently on trips overseas, but held tight control of decision-making and maintained his unique working habits, which stressed and exasperated his political colleagues and civil servants. Eden was well aware of the situation. Three months before, he had admitted in a letter to a friend that he was 'troubled' by Churchill's management of the military campaign, noting, 'One would not boggle at that, if the results were good, but they're not! Brilliant improvisation is not substitute for carefully planned dispositions ... What troubles me is that I, and I suppose other members of [the] War Cabinet, are regarded by [the] public as those running the war, and we don't one little bit.'[2] That summer, he confided in one of his close aides that Churchill was being 'more and more obstinate and at the same time losing his grip.'[3]

On 2 July the Conservative MP Sir John Wardlaw-Milne put forward a motion of no confidence in Parliament. The wording was damning: 'That this House, while paying tribute to the heroism and endurance of the Armed Forces of the Crown in circumstances of exceptional difficulty, has no confidence in the central direction of the war.'[4] As the 'central direction of the war' was the responsibility of one man, it was a barbed attack on Churchill. The motion was seconded by Labour MP Aneurin Bevan, who told the House, 'The Prime Minister wins debate after debate and loses battle after battle. The country is beginning to say that he fights debates like a war and war like a debate.' Churchill faced criticism from his current and former party, with one Liberal MP questioning his lack of delegation in the face of the unrelenting burden of wartime leadership.

Churchill responded with what Eden described in his memoirs as 'one of his most effective speeches, beautifully adjusted to the temper of the House'. The prime minister criticised the open negativity, pointing out, 'Only the hostile speeches are reported abroad, and much play is made with them by our enemy.' In closing, Churchill dramatically flung himself at the mercy of his parliamentary colleagues: 'I ask no favours either for myself or for His Majesty's Government. I undertook the office as Prime Minister and Minister of Defence, after defending my predecessor to the best of my ability, in times when the life of the Empire hung upon a thread. I am your servant, and you have the right to dismiss me when you please.' In the event, he won the vote of confidence by resounding 476 votes to twenty-five, with thirty abstentions, but he was personally shaken. That evening, over dinner, Churchill admitted to Eden he was 'ashamed' because they 'had not done as well as we should [have]'.[5]

The focus of the debate had been on Churchill's monopoly on wartime strategy, from his position as Minister of Defence. In responding to his critics, Churchill defended his holding of both posts by stating that if a military man were appointed in his place, they would have remarkable powers, but not be democratically accountable to Parliament. But there were also members of Parliament who questioned whether he should remain as prime minister. Eden was regarded as the most viable alternative and immediately before his visit to the US in June, Churchill had written to the king, advising the monarch that in the event of his death Eden should replace him, as he was 'the most outstanding minister in the largest political party ... who I am sure will be found capable of conducting Yr. [*sic*] Majesty's Affairs with the resolution, experience and capacity which these grievous times require.'[6] Churchill was not alone, but there were a number of backbenchers who were actively considering whether Eden should take over from Churchill, regardless of whether or not death intervened. For all Eden's misgivings over Churchill's management of war strategy, he rebuffed suggestions that he should consider himself as an alternative or conspire to stab Churchill in the back. When visited by a backbencher in August who suggested that Churchill should go and Eden should take his place, Eden replied that he 'would do no plotting against Winston, now, or ever'.[7] It was a principled stand, but Eden's loyalty to Churchill would not be fully reciprocated.

The opposition to Churchill did lead to significant change in Eden's responsibilities. As the Leader of the House of Commons, Sir Stafford Cripps, had been strongly critical of Churchill's war management, he was moved on to be Minister of Air Production and lost his seat at the War Cabinet. Churchill gave the post to Eden, which left him responsible for managing the day-to-day government business in Parliament. He wrote in his diary, 'If I had had time, I should have enjoyed my new job, but meetings of the Defence Committee, the War Cabinet and work of the Foreign Office were sufficiently onerous. I had to be almost continually at hand in the House of Commons during the day, while the Defence Committee often sat late into the night.' He was good at the role, as his charm and diplomacy helped smooth over difficulties with MPs, although privately he wrote that most were 'prima donnas' who 'like attention, which is a time-consuming form of flattery'. It was an additional work commitment that would eventually harm his health.

The summer of 1942 brought one more disaster. Sailing on the edge of the Arctic circle, where the sun never set throughout the summer, the Russian convoys were constantly vulnerable to air and submarine attack. In April the Admiralty had demanded that sailing be halted during the months of continuous daylight, but the decision was made at War Cabinet to carry on.

Convoy PQ 17 formed up off Iceland on 27 June. It comprised thirty-five merchant ships and a close escort of destroyers and corvettes, while two British and two American cruisers provided a screen forty miles to the north. It was the largest convoy to have set sail for Russia. Early attacks by Luftwaffe aircraft were beaten off and a brief fog provided a short respite, but the Admiralty then received intelligence that the battleship *Tirpitz*, sister ship of the sunk *Bismarck*, had sailed from its base in Norway. Admiral Dudley Pound ignored his senior officers and ordered the cruiser escort to retreat and the convoy to scatter. It was a disastrous decision, made worse by the fact that the intelligence on the *Tirpitz* was wrong. The merchant ships were left to the mercy to the Luftwaffe and prowling U-boats.

On 14 July the Russian ambassador went to see Eden, who informed him that out of thirty-five merchant ships, nineteen were known to be sunk and only four had made it to Archangel. The following day Maisky and his wife were invited for dinner at 10 Downing Street. Churchill admitted that three quarters of the convoy had been lost, telling Maisky, 'Four hundred tanks and three hundred planes lie on the sea bed!' He banged his fist on the table, adding, 'There's no sense in sending tanks and planes to certain ruin. We might just as well sink them in the Thames.'[8] Maisky strongly objected, pointing out that the supply convoys were essential to the Soviet war effort and that stopping them would also affect 'psychology'. Once again, he pressed the proposed second front. 'So, you are ceasing delivery of military supplies at the most critical moment for us. In that case, the question of a second front becomes all the more urgent. What are the prospects here?' Churchill was adamant, however, replying, 'In 1942 we are simply in no condition to undertake serious operations in order to open a second front. There is no sense getting involved in an absurd adventure which is bound to end in disaster. This will help neither you nor us. Only the Germans will profit from it.' After dinner, Churchill and Maisky retired to a neighbouring room to smoke cigars, shortly after which Eden arrived. Clearly under the impression that conversations were planned to take place after dinner, he opened with, 'So, shall we discuss the convoys?', to which Churchill gloomily replied, 'We already have.'

Five days later Maisky was again at Number 10, this time delivering an angry message from Stalin in response to the decision that the Arctic convoys were to be suspended. In it, Stalin accused Churchill of failing to fulfil his obligations. Maisky recorded that Churchill was in a bad mood and 'must have had a drop too much whisky. I could tell from his face, eyes and gestures.'[9] The Russian ambassador noted, 'At times his head shook in a strange way, betraying the fact that in essence he is already an old man and that it won't be long before he starts sliding downhill fast.' The two men argued into the night. Eden summoned Maisky the following morning and confided that Churchill was 'hurt and in some distress' as a result of Stalin's message. Ever the diplomat, he suggested that Stalin's message should be left unanswered until a calmer atmosphere prevailed. Smiling, he explained, 'Two great men have clashed … They've had a tiff … You and I need to reconcile them.' It was a rare admission of Eden's unheralded, but crucial role as peacemaker, which he played for the duration of the war. As they parted, Eden said to Maisky, apparently on a whim, 'Too bad they've never met face to face.'

Chapter 12

To Moscow

On 12 August 1942 Churchill arrived in Moscow. In the words of his wife, Clementine, he was going to 'visit the Ogre in his Den.'[1] Churchill flew via Cairo and then Tehran in a US-made Liberator bomber, which had to climb to 15,000ft to cross the Zagros Mountains, an altitude that required all the passengers to wear oxygen masks, although Churchill had his modified so that he could still smoke his cigars. Ahead of his visit he had personally cabled Stalin, proposing that the two leaders could 'survey the war together and take decisions hand-in-hand,' adding that he 'could then tell you plans we have made with President Roosevelt for offensive action in 1942.'[2]

After inspecting the guard of honour at the airport and being driven to a specially prepared villa, the first thing Churchill did was to have a bath. He was much impressed by the plumbing system, which had a single spout for both hot and cold water 'mingled to exactly the temperature one desired'. At 7pm, accompanied by Molotov, Churchill went to meet Stalin. Churchill recorded that the first two hours were 'bleak and sombre' during which he admitted to Stalin that it would not be feasible to mount a cross-Channel invasion in September, the last month calm weather could be relied upon. On hearing the news, Stalin's face 'crumpled to a frown' and he tersely enquired why the British 'were so afraid of the Germans'. Churchill cheered his gloom by unfurling a map of Southern Europe, the Mediterranean and North Africa. Like a magician pulling a rabbit from a hat, he dramatically announced that he had come to Moscow to discuss a second front in 1942, but France was not the only place such an operation could be undertaken. Churchill said that he had been authorised by Roosevelt to impart to Stalin the 'secret' plan that had been decided upon. It was Operation Torch: the Anglo-American invasion of North Africa. To explain the plan, Churchill drew Stalin a sketch of a crocodile, outlining how Torch was an attack on the 'soft belly' of the enemy, and if successful would enable a deadly attack to be mounted on Hitler the following year. It was, Churchill later wrote, a 'turning point' in the conversation. The two men spent the rest of their four-hour meeting examining maps and standing over a globe, before parting. Churchill went to bed 'feeling that at least the ice was broken and human contact established.'[3]

Churchill thoroughly enjoyed staying at the villa, which was surrounded by gardens and a twenty-acre fir wood. The goldfish in the pond were so tame that they would eat out of a person's hand and Churchill made a point of going to feed them every day of his stay. The weather was pleasantly warm, 'just like what we love most in England – when we get it', Churchill wrote.

His second meeting with Stalin the following day was less congenial. Churchill was handed a document which was deeply critical of Britain's actions and Stalin then proceeded to accuse his allies of breaking their pledge to invade mainland Europe and failing to deliver the promised supplies to Russia. Among other things, the document asserted, 'the refusal of the Government of Great Britain to create a Second Front in 1942 in Europe inflicts a mortal blow to the whole of Soviet public opinion … [and] it complicates the situation of the Red Army at the front and prejudices the plan of the Soviet command.'[4] It was exactly the same approach Stalin had adopted with Eden during his visit nine months before in the depths of the Russian winter: allowing the visitor to leave the first meeting with a sense of a developing relationship, before hitting them the following day with a pre-prepared written document to which they could never agree. Churchill flatly rebuffed every single accusation, telling Stalin that he pardoned his effrontery 'on account of the bravery of the Russian army'. Eventually, Stalin stated that he must accept the situation and tersely invited his guest for dinner the following night. Churchill accepted and described in an animated fashion how Britain had been left alone to fight Germany and Italy, but now that the three great nations of Russia, the United States and Britain were linked victory was certain 'provided we did not fall apart'. Churchill's passion thawed the mood, with Stalin admitting that 'there was no mistrust [between them], but only a difference of view.'[5]

The real success of Churchill's trip was achieved during a private dinner in Stalin's quarters on Churchill's final night. The Permanent Under-Secretary at the Foreign Office, who accompanied Churchill on the trip, was summoned to Stalin's private rooms at 1am and found the two wartime leaders, and Molotov, 'with a heavily-laden board between them: food of all kinds crowned by a suckling pig, and innumerable bottles.' He recounted, 'What Stalin made me drink seemed pretty savage: Winston, who by that time was complaining of a slight headache, seemed wisely to be confining himself to a comparatively innocuous effervescent Caucasian red wine. Everyone seemed to be as merry as a marriage bell.'[6] The meeting broke up at 3am after Stalin and Churchill had agreed a warmly worded joint communiqué, which spoke of the 'close friendship and understanding' between Great Britain and the Soviet Union. The delegation then grabbed a few hours' sleep before boarding the plane home the following morning. Churchill reversed his previous route and on the ground at Tehran dispatched a telegram to Stalin: 'Thank you for your comradeship and hospitality. I am very glad I came.' In Churchill's view, by personally being the bearer of the bad news of the postponed European invasion and also of the good news of Torch, he had stopped the two nations drifting apart. In truth he had achieved little more than Eden did with his visit to Moscow, leaving after having consumed a significant amount of hard liquor, clutching a letter of friendship. But Eden did acknowledge that Churchill's trip served an important purpose, because from then on Stalin 'ceased to insist that a second front [in Europe] should be opened in 1942.'[7]

In the autumn and winter of 1942 the tide of the war began to turn in the Allies' favour. Over a few short months the British scored a major victory against Rommel, which was followed by the Anglo-Allied landings in North Africa. The same period also witnessed the Soviet defence of Stalingrad, which led to the defeat of the German 6th Army, and the first major offensive against the Japanese, which took place around the Pacific island of Guadalcanal.

Bernard Montgomery was never meant to be in command of British forces in North Africa. Churchill had originally decided to appoint General Gott as head of the Eighth Army, a decision that had delighted Eden as he had a warm affection for Gott, whom he had met before the war and who had commanded Eden's former regiment. But a plane Gott was travelling in was shot down and he was killed before he reached his new post. Montgomery was appointed in his stead. Eden recorded that he was 'not only grieved but shaken' by Gott's death and it brought home again the fact that senior commanders and political leaders faced significant risks when flying. Eden's wife, Beatrice, was very apprehensive about Eden's air travel, not without good reason given his near-miss during his Sunderland flight to Gibraltar in October 1940. She was even more concerned when their eldest son joined the RAF and began his training in October 1942. Eden wrote in his diary, 'Simon had breakfast with us and left during the day … It is sad to see him go, and he is so very young. Not yet eighteen.'

Montgomery began his offensive on the night of 23 October and Churchill received a telegram with the prearranged code word 'zip' to inform him the attack was underway. The initial phase more closely resembled a battle from a previous war; a monstrous artillery barrage was followed by a slow infantry advance as sappers worked to clear dense minefields. Montgomery had bided his time and built up a significant superiority in men and tanks. He also had the advantage of complete air superiority. Three days into the fighting there was another stroke of luck, as British aircraft sunk several tankers that had been transporting fuel for Rommel's forces off the North African coast. The Germans were short of ammunition and fuel, and Rommel himself was serious ill; he had been receiving treatment at a hospital in Germany when the attack was launched and was rushed back to the battlefield without time to convalesce. A few days later it was clear that the Eighth Army was in the ascendency. On 2 November Montgomery began his decisive breakthrough. Two days later Rommel was in full retreat and Montgomery's tanks were advancing across open desert. Churchill telegrammed General Alexander, the Commander-in-Chief, 'I send you heartfelt congratulations on the splendid feat of arms achieved by the Eighth Army under the command of your brilliant lieutenant, Montgomery … it is evident that an event of the first magnitude has occurred which will play its part in the whole future course of the World War.'[8] Churchill added, 'I propose to ring the bells all over Britain for the first time this war.' In the end Churchill had second thoughts and held off from permitting bells to be rung until Operation Torch had been completed successfully. Following the victory at El Alamein he famously stated in a speech, 'Now this is not the end. It is not even the beginning of the end. but it is, perhaps, the end of the beginning.'

The Torch landings were a three-pronged simultaneous amphibious operation that put Allied troops ashore around Casablanca in Morocco and at Oran and Algiers in Algeria. The straight-talking, Texan-born General Dwight D. Eisenhower was in overall command of the invasion force, in which American troops outnumbered British by more than three to one. Both Morocco and Algeria were still under the control of the Vichy French government, although the expectation was that there would not be significant opposition from Vichy French forces. The Allies had also secretly communicated with a number of sympathetic French commanders and although the surprise of the landings caused confusion, Allied casualties were low. Two days after the invasion the French authorities in Algiers ordered their men to cease fighting.

The most problematic element of the invasion for Churchill and Eden was political. To start with, no one had told Charles De Gaulle. Even though the British had formally recognised him as the leader of the Free French in 1940, it was thought that he would be unable to keep his mouth shut and so he knew nothing of the planned invasion of French North Africa. Roosevelt and Churchill conspired to keep him out of the loop, with Churchill messaging the president three days before the landings, 'It will be necessary for me to explain "Torch" to de Gaulle some time during D minus 1'; i.e. an hour before the troops planned to go ashore. Roosevelt replied, 'I am very apprehensive in regard to the adverse effect that any introduction of de Gaulle into the "Torch" situation would have on our promising efforts to attach a large part of French African forces to our expedition … I consider it inadvisable for you to give de Gaulle any information … until subsequent to a successful landing.'

The Americans had settled on General Henri Giraud to be leader of the French in North Africa. The sixty-three-year-old had been captured by the Germans in 1940, but escaped from captivity and was smuggled out of the south of France on a British submarine just days ahead of the Torch landings. On his arrival in Algiers, Giraud found an icy reception. No one of any importance was willing to accept him as being in charge. Keen to ensure the Vichy French forces came over to the Allied side, Eisenhower struck a deal with Francois Darlan, the senior Vichy French commander. On 15 November Eisenhower passed on the news of his deal to Churchill. Darlan was to be the political head of the French in North Africa, while Giraud would be in charge of the military. Eden recorded that he 'Didn't like it one bit, and said so.' The following morning, Churchill and Eden met with De Gaulle. His position on Darlan was clear-cut and he stated he 'could not justify having dealings with a traitor.'[9] Eden sympathised with De Gaulle's position, the Free French leader claiming that at their meeting Eden was 'moved to the point of tears' by the situation, which he viewed as a travesty.[10] When Roosevelt officially announced American acceptance of Eisenhower's deal, Eden and Churchill ended up in a shouting match on the telephone. Eden could not get Churchill 'to see the damage Darlan may do to the Allied cause', while Churchill still harboured strong suspicions about the Free French leader, at one point telling Eden that Darlan was 'not as a bad as De Gaulle anyway'.[11] Churchill presented a far more united front to Roosevelt, however, writing to him, 'The more I reflect upon it the more convinced I become that it [the arrangement with Darlan] can only be a temporary expedient, justifiable solely by the stress of battle. We must not overlook the serious political injury which may be done to our cause, not only in France but throughout Europe, by the feeling that we are ready to make terms with the local Quislings.'[12] The Darlan debate was settled in December 1942, when he was assassinated by an opponent of the Vichy regime, but it would not be the last time Churchill and Eden rowed over De Gaulle. Eden confided in his diary that Christmas Eve after he heard of Darlan's death, 'I have not felt so relieved by any event for years.'

Chapter 13

Churchill, Eden and the Holocaust

On Boxing Day 1942 Eden wrote in his diary, 'Tired. There is always a reaction after these long periods of work and strain, and the spring seems to uncoil more and more. A cold day.' It was in fact not unusually cold that December, the first few weeks being mild, but Christmas brought a cold snap and a sharp drop in temperature that seemed to coincide with Eden's mood. His work as Leader of the House of Commons ended on 17 December when Parliament went into the Christmas recess. But it had closed on a sombre note.

Reports of the mass execution of Jews in Poland had made the newspapers in Britain as early as July 1942, when the *Daily Telegraph* published a story headlined 'Germans murder 700,000 Jews in Poland'. The information had come from a member of the exiled Polish government. The newspaper reported the use of poison gas chambers and the starvation of Jews in ghettos, but the government did not respond until months later. On 2 December Eden met with Maisky, who suggested a joint statement by all three Allies against what he described as a 'systematic attempt' to eliminate the Jewish population.[1] At a Cabinet meeting two weeks later Eden told his stunned colleagues that, while he could not confirm the methods used, there were indications that large-scale massacres were taking place. He also stated that it was known that Jews were being transported from German-occupied territories, adding that it might well be that they were being undertaken 'with a view to the wholesale extermination of Jews.'[2] The Cabinet agreed to Eden's proposed wording of a joint official statement, which the foreign secretary told his colleagues 'committed us to punishing those responsible'.[3] Eden read the joint statement to the House of Commons on 17 December, confirming that 'the German authorities, not content with denying to persons of Jewish race in all the territories over which their barbarous rule has been extended the most elementary human rights, are now carrying into effect Hitler's oft repeated intention to exterminate the Jewish people in Europe.'[4] After the statement, the members stood for a minute's silence. Lloyd George told Eden afterwards, 'You were very impressive this morning. I cannot recall a scene like that in all my years in Parliament.'[5]

Eden and Churchill have faced criticism for not doing more to prevent the Holocaust, but when the full barbarity of the programme of extermination began to be revealed, they had few options at their disposal. By Christmas 1942 the invasion of the European mainland had been postponed until spring 1943 and was eventually delayed until D-Day in 1944. The only weapon that could be brought to bear against the Nazis' extermination of the Jews was air power, but other than agreeing that the perpetrators should be punished, Eden and Churchill (and their government) did nothing for two years. In 1944 Eden met with the Zionist Jewish campaigner, Chaim Weizmann. As Eden recounted in a note to Churchill, Weizmann proposed that 'we should do something to mitigate the appalling slaughter of Jews in Hungary [who were being transported en masse to Auschwitz].'[6] In response, Eden stated he was in favour of bombing the railway lines to the death camps, to which Churchill agreed. Eden claimed in his meeting with Weizmann that it was an idea which had 'already been considered', although there is no clear evidence of this. However, both he and Churchill pushed for action. Eden wrote to the Secretary of State for Air, Liberal leader Archibald Sinclair, asking him to study the feasibility of the proposals, adding 'I very much hope that it will be possible to do something. I have the authority of the Prime Minister to say that he agrees.'[7] Sinclair replied just over a week later, stating that there was nothing that could be done, as the camps were out of the range of the RAF's heavy bombers. He proposed passing the request on to the Americans, who ran the daylight bombing raids over Europe. But in the event, no action was taken. Even though the Americans were under pressure from other quarters, all calls for military action were denied.

It is difficult, particularly now that the scale of the mass murder of Europe's Jewish populations is known, to excuse Eden and Churchill. There is no doubt that air action against the death camps was a problematic proposal, but why was it seemingly not properly explored until 1944, when Chaim Weizmann personally pressured Eden? Eden placed significant faith in international institutions. He had previously played a key role in the League of Nations and would go on to be a champion of the UN, and from the outset he envisioned post-war prosecutions, but even though he spoke about it in Parliament, it seems he did not fully grasp Hitler's genuine intention to completely exterminate the Jewish race. In some quarters he was seen as having less sympathy for the Zionist cause, with one civil servant noting that the Foreign Office's pro-Arab stance affected him, recording, 'The Arab myth clouds his mind.'[8] Eden himself admitted to his private secretary, 'If we must have preferences, let me murmur in your ear that I prefer Arabs to Jews.'[9] In July 1944 Eden's predecessor in the Foreign Office, Lord Halifax, passed on to Eden an American plan to repatriate German citizens from Uruguay to Germany, in exchange for Jewish detainees in concentration camps. The plan, far-fetched thought it was, was quashed by Eden, who feared those released would eventually end up entering Palestine, where they would 'cause trouble' for Britain. He wrote that facilitating the exchange was 'doubtful', but that there was 'ground for hope' that the Germans 'will abstain from exterminating these unfortunate people and will keep them in camps open to outside inspection'.[10] His hope was profoundly naïve.

The year before Eden stood up in Parliament and spoke of the 'extermination' of the Jews by Hitler, Churchill had recognised the threat. In a radio broadcast in August 1941, Churchill stated that 'whole [Jewish] districts are being exterminated', adding, 'We are in the presence of a crime without a name.'[11] Churchill, in the words of his most eminent biographer, saw Zionism as part of the 'great tide of history' and consistently supported the establishment of a Jewish state in Palestine. He saw himself as a friend of the Jews. In October 1942 Churchill wrote to the then Archbishop of Canterbury, 'The systematic cruelties to which the Jewish people – men, women, and children – have been exposed under the Nazi regime are amongst the most terrible events in history.'[12] But he was as guilty as Eden of letting the 1944 proposal to bomb Auschwitz slip by.

Although the Air Ministry told Eden that the camps were out of range, they then requested details of the topography and the layout of the camps. The details were not forthcoming, which Churchill discovered in late September. He wrote to his private secretary, 'We are therefore technically guilty of allowing the Air Ministry to get away with it without having given them (though we had it) the information they asked for as a prerequisite.'[13] He ended his note, 'In all the circumstances I think perhaps (though I feel a little uneasy about it) we had better let this go by.' By the time Churchill discussed it with his private secretary, Chaim Weizmann had already been officially informed by the Foreign Office that the proposal had been rejected. Multiple accounts have claimed that the decision not to bomb Auschwitz was taken because the British had received intelligence that the transportation of Hungarian Jews to the camp had been stopped. At best this may have provided a convenient excuse, but it is not the reasoning stated by Churchill, or by the Foreign Office, who informed Weizmann it was because of the 'technical difficulties involved' that the plan had been rejected.

Churchill and Eden were both aware that from early in the war Hitler had begun a campaign of extermination against the Jews. They also knew to a significant extent the methods used and the sophistication of the logistical operation that transported Jews to the death camps. Even in the face of this evidence, and despite making public declarations of support, they did nothing to try and stop it. There is no doubt that there were sceptical elements within the Foreign Office whose stance bordered on the anti-Semitic. In January 1945, the same month that Russian troops liberated Auschwitz, one Foreign Office official criticised the reports of mass murder, writing, '[The] Sources of information are nearly always Jewish whose accounts are only sometimes reliable and not seldom highly coloured … One notable tendency in Jewish reports on this problem is to exaggerate the numbers of deportations and deaths.'[14] There is no evidence that Eden shared this view. However, he was certainly naïve in thinking that publicity would stay Hitler's hand and seemed to regard the problem as a criminal one, which would be correctly dealt with through post-war prosecutions of those responsible. Churchill was stridently pro-Jewish, but the Jews were not his priority: winning the war was. As he candidly admitted in another letter to the Archbishop of Canterbury in 1944, 'There is no doubt in my mind that we are in the presence of one of the greatest and most horrible crimes ever committed … [but] the principle hope of terminating it must remain the speedy victory of the Allied Nations.'[15]

Chapter 14

Casablanca

Churchill had hoped that the year 1943 would open with the first tripartite conference between the Allied leaders. At the start of December 1942 Roosevelt had accepted his proposal for a three-way meeting, replying to Churchill's suggestion, 'I agree with you that the only satisfactory way of coming to the vital strategic conclusions the military situation requires is for you and me to meet personally with Stalin.' Roosevelt suggested a place south of Algiers, but added, 'I don't like mosquitos.'[1] Churchill immediately sent a message inviting Stalin, but he replied that he would 'not be in a position to leave the Soviet Union.' Roosevelt also tried to convince him to attend, but to no avail. Despite Stalin's refusal, Roosevelt still decided he wanted to meet Churchill and sent him a cheery note. 'I've not had an answer to my second invitation to Uncle Joe, but, on the assumption that he will again decline, I think that in spite of it you and I should get together'. At Roosevelt's insistence, neither Eden nor his opposite number, US Secretary of State, Cordell Hull, were invited.

The two settled on Casablanca in Morocco as the eventual venue, although the composition of the replacement for the Vichy government in North Africa was still causing difficulties following Darlan's assassination. Churchill penned a telegram suggesting the inclusion of Darlan's predecessor, M. Pierre-Etienne Flandin, in the administration. Churchill had known Flandin before the war and he and Clementine had lunched with the former French air force pilot in Paris in 1935. Flandin had been appointed by Pétain as Vichy Foreign Minister in 1940 and Churchill later stated that at the time he thought, 'here is a friend of England in a high position in the Vichy Government.'[2] Eden did not share Churchill's view that the promotion of another former Vichy man into the government was a good idea. Before its dispatch, the message was flagged to Eden and he ordered it to be held back. Eden caught Churchill as he was heading into Parliament the following day, and opened the conversation with, 'By the way, about that telegram you thought of sending last night to Algiers…'

'Thought of sending? What do you mean? I sent it,' Churchill replied.

Eden admitted that he had held it up, as he wanted to talk it though. Churchill was livid and gripped his jacket with both hands, demanding Eden explain by what right he was 'interfering' with his private correspondence. He was not placated by Eden's reply that, as foreign secretary, he saw all important messages. Churchill told Eden that 'he was not dead yet and would send any telegrams he chose.'[3] Eden left it be, but was called to see Churchill following the prime minister's afternoon nap. Churchill was in a better mood, and tore up the telegram in front of Eden with the words, 'Oh, by the way, you remember that message I intended to send? Perhaps we had better not send it.' It was another example of Eden's careful manoeuvring around Churchill's reactions, which succeeded in securing the outcome the foreign secretary preferred.

Eden was left in London when Churchill departed for Casablanca in the second week of January. Roosevelt did not arrive for two days and Churchill spent much of the time walking on the rocky beach with the Chiefs of Staff for company. The British and American generals, Eisenhower among them, discussed the next move in the Mediterranean theatre, debating whether they should invade the island of Sardinia, or attack the preferred option, Sicily. Once Roosevelt arrived, conversations began in earnest, although Churchill and Roosevelt also found time to attend a small formal dinner with the Sultan of Morocco. Out of respect to the Sultan's Islamic beliefs, no alcoholic beverages were served before, during, or after the meal. One of Roosevelt's aides recorded that Churchill 'started to glower' on discovering the fact. Just after the party was seated, Churchill was summoned to read an urgent message and returned twenty minutes later having 'taken time out to have a quick drink or two while handling his urgent dispatch.'[4]

One aim of the Casablanca conference was the attempt to get De Gaulle, the official leader of the Free French, and Giraud, the head of the French government in North Africa, in the same room. At first, De Gaulle refused to attend. It did not help his cause with the Americans. De Gaulle's position was that France needed unanimity of leadership, which in the eyes of Roosevelt seemed arrogant and self-serving. In Roosevelt's own words, De Gaulle was 'well-nigh intolerable' and at one point during the war Roosevelt suggested to Churchill, 'Possibly you could make him [De Gaulle] governor of Madagascar.' As Eden admitted in a message to the British ambassador in Washington, 'He is of autocratic and uncompromising temper (indeed, his personality is a grave impediment to his cause) ... He has small use for the normal processes of international discourse and has more than once brought our relations near to breaking-point. For all that, we have in the end always had patience with him, for the sake of France whose resistance he worthily represents.'[5] But Churchill's patience was wearing thin and there was an empty villa at Casablanca intended for De Gaulle. Churchill wrote to Eden, stating that, if he thought it was a good idea, he should pass on a forthright message that Churchill had drafted. In it, Churchill informed the Frenchman that if he refused to attend, 'The position of His Majesty's Government towards your [Free French] Movement while you remain at its head will also require to be reviewed.'[6] He was threatening to withdraw British support for De Gaulle as Free French leader if he did not play ball. Churchill told Eden he could amend the message if he wished, closing with the line 'For his own sake, you ought to knock him about pretty hard.' Eden spoke with De Gaulle and the Frenchman grudgingly agreed to fly out to North Africa. An impatient Roosevelt telegrammed Eden ahead of the Frenchman's arrival, 'I have got the bridegroom, where is the bride?'[7] A carefully choreographed press conference was held on the lawn outside one of the villas. Four chairs were set out and then De Gaulle and Giraud, accompanied by Churchill and Roosevelt, were seated. After they had spoken to the assembled journalists, a photographer called out, asking for the two men to shake hands. They hesitated. The president encouraged them into it with the words, 'You two Frenchmen are loyal to your country, and that warrants a cordial handshake anytime.'[8] It made for a great photo, but it did not herald the start of a new friendship, although Eden later wrote that it was 'as good a result as could be expected from a shotgun wedding.' Churchill's harsh line and Eden's encouragement had headed off another De Gaulle disaster.

The Casablanca Conference is most noted for the agreement that the Allies should push for the 'unconditional surrender' of both Germany and Japan. Churchill communicated with the War Cabinet throughout and they agreed to the proposal, with the caveat that Italy should be excluded from the demand.

The demand for unconditional surrender that sprang from the Casablanca Conference subsequently triggered great debate amongst historians. It is suggested that by obstinately sticking to the requirement for 'unconditional surrender' (instead of a negotiated end to the fighting), Churchill and Roosevelt prolonged the war. By refusing to compromise they played into the hands of Hitler, who made the German people his last line of defence, and made it more likely that the Japanese would refuse surrender terms, encouraging America's unleashing of the atom bomb. Churchill, while denouncing the view that it prolonged the war, claimed in his memoirs not to have discussed the proposal at length, writing that it was 'with some feeling of surprise' that he heard Roosevelt inform journalists at the press conference of the plan to enforce unconditional surrender. Roosevelt himself later admitted to his Secretary of State that the announcement was unplanned, blaming the lapse on being distracted by the furore surrounding De Gaulle and Giraud: 'We had so much trouble getting those two French generals together that I thought to myself that this was as difficult as arranging the meeting of [Civil War generals] Grant and Lee – and then suddenly the Press Conference was on, and Winston and I had had no time to prepare for it, and the thought popped into my mind that they had called Grant "Old Unconditional Surrender", and the next thing I knew I had said it.'[9]

A policy of unconditional surrender was certainly discussed between Churchill and Roosevelt at Casablanca, but it was never intended to be announced. It placed both statesmen in a bind for the remainder of the war. Even though it might well have been adopted as Allied policy anyway, it was a lapse in judgement by Roosevelt. In interviews conducted for the iconic 1970s television series *The World at War*, Eden also stated that the announcement itself came as a surprise: 'we were told about it in advance actually, though I think Winston was taken aback by the actual moment of the announcement. I'm sceptical whether it had much effect either on Germany or Japan, but we were troubled in the Foreign Office.'[10] Publicly, Churchill supported the policy, but a few months later he admitted to Eden that 'continually uttering the slogan "Unconditional Surrender" would lead to the German people becoming 'fused together in a solid desperate block for whom there is no hope.'[11]

For all their carefully worded later criticism of the policy, in the immediate context of Casablanca, Churchill and Eden were in fact united. When Maisky met with Eden at the end of January, the Russian ambassador mused with the foreign secretary about the possibility of Hitler being forced from power by his own generals. He told Eden, 'The generals know what is going on at the front and they do not share Hitler's mysticism. It must already be clear to them by now that Germany cannot win the war on the battlefield ... if military victory is impossible, what is left for the generals?' Maisky said he would not be surprised to wake up one morning and read in the papers that Hitler had committed suicide or died in a 'car accident' and that the generals might then offer a peace deal. Maisky had correctly guessed the minds of a number of Hitler's generals, but there would not be an assassination attempt until 1944. It was unsuccessful and the plotters paid dearly. Even though it was a tempting proposition, Eden quashed the notion of making peace, rising from the armchair in which he was sitting and telling Maisky with 'uncharacteristic energy', 'As long as Churchill is Prime Minister and I am Foreign Secretary, there will be no compromise with Germany!'[12]

Before Roosevelt departed North Africa, Churchill insisted they go together to visit Marrakesh and see the Atlas Mountains. Churchill had been captivated by the region ever since he spent the winter of 1935 on a painting holiday in Morocco, a vacation which he used to distract himself from the bleakness of being out of government. Arriving after a five-hour drive from Casablanca, Churchill was adamant they should witness the sunset that night and cajoled two of Roosevelt's aides into making a chair out of their arms to carry the disabled president to the top of a nearby tower. Roosevelt was delighted with the view, remarking 'I feel like a sultan'.[13] After the president left for home, Churchill stayed another day and completed his only canvas of the entire war. Painted in oils, it depicts the tower of Marrakesh's Katoubia mosque and, in the background, the white-topped shadows of the Atlas mountains rising into a blue sky. Churchill later gave it as a gift to Roosevelt, who hung it in his New York home.

Chapter 15

East to west

Nearly 3,000 miles east of Casablanca, the tide had turned at Stalingrad. It was arguably the single most decisive moment of the entire war: from then on, Hitler's armies would never truly go on the offensive again. In November 1942 a surprise Soviet counter-offensive had encircled the entire German Sixth and Fourth armies. Instead of allowing his generals to break out from the trap, Hitler personally ordered them to 'stand and fight'. After enduring a freezing winter with dwindling supplies, they finally surrendered on 31 January 1943. The Russians took 91,000 prisoners. Ambassador Maisky recorded in his diary, 'The moral and psychological significance of Stalingrad is colossal. Never before in military history has a powerful army, besieging a city, itself become a besieged stronghold that was then annihilated – down to the very last general, the very last solider.'[1] On 2 February Churchill sent Stalin a personal message of congratulation on the 'wonderful achievement'.

The heroic defence of Stalingrad had captured the imagination of the British public, some of whom drew a parallel with the brave defence of the island of Malta against German and Italian air attacks. Churchill received a letter from three young female typists from the Roads and Bridges Department of Salop County Council in Shropshire. They wrote, 'We most humbly beg to suggest that as in the case of Malta, some recognition of the valour of our allies the Russian soldiers, airmen and civilians be made to that city.'[2] In April 1942 the population of the island of Malta had been awarded the George Cross in recognition of their bravery in the face of the hardship and unrelenting air assault they had endured. Eden was in favour of the idea of similar recognition of Stalingrad, but there was a snag, as he explained to Churchill: 'I would myself like to see the George Cross bestowed on Stalingrad. I understand, however, that the Honours Committee see [a] difficulty in that foreigners are not eligible for the George Cross ... The only alternative to the George

Cross would be the Victoria Cross, which has never been bestowed on a foreign town, or some lesser decoration such as the Military Cross ... I think, however, that it would be difficult to explain to the Russians why such lesser decorations were chosen in view of the precedent of Malta.' In the end, a compromise was reached and Churchill instead presented Stalin with a bejewelled sword from King George VI engraved with an inscription to 'the steel-hearted citizens of Stalingrad'.

Churchill, Eden and Maisky met frequently in the early part of 1943 as the Russian ambassador delivered messages from Stalin to Churchill. Maisky's entries in his diary from the time are revealing. He wrote of Churchill's 'boyishness', the entertaining telegrams the prime minister often dispatched and the joy he took in explaining the subterfuge and security arrangements around his foreign travel. But the Russian ambassador also saw what he viewed as a deterioration in Churchill's abilities. In February he noted, 'Churchill is definitely growing old. Yesterday he lost the thread of our conversation several times and, turning to Eden, asked with impatience: "Remind me – what were we saying?"' Churchill, who hated being ill, was bed-ridden with a severe cold for a few days in late February. Eden took a message from Maisky into Churchill's bedroom and on returning, poured the ambassador and himself a whisky and soda, and suggested they sit down for a chat. Stalin was now once again pressing for a second front and Maisky told Eden that his own preference would be to postpone the planned invasion of Italy and instead focus on a cross-Channel operation. Eden agreed, admitting to Maisky that he thought the Mediterranean plans were 'inexpedient' and that a direct attack on Germany through France was 'undeniably preferable to indirect blows via Italy'.[3] It was a rare moment of candour from Eden, in which he let slip his quiet dissatisfaction with Churchill's direction of the war effort.

The following month, Eden travelled to Washington for an eighteen-day trip to the United States. The visit was Eden at his diplomatic best. He visited US troops, delivered a well-received speech and made a good impression with Roosevelt; unlike Churchill, he also managed to keep his clothes on during his stay at the White House. The British ambassador afterwards informed London, 'he clicked with everyone from the President downwards ... He has never put a foot wrong.'[4] In the words of Eden's private secretary, he 'put himself across everywhere ... as the successor to the P.M.'[5]

At the start of his tour Eden dined alone with President Roosevelt and his aide, Harry Hopkins. Among the topics they discussed were Soviet ambitions to 'Communise' Europe. Eden later recalled in his memoirs that he told Roosevelt, 'Even if those fears were to prove correct, we should make the position no worse by trying to work with Russia and by assuming that Stalin meant what he said in the Anglo-Soviet Treaty.' Eden found Roosevelt more receptive than Churchill was to discussing the post-war settlement and vice versa. Every time Eden pushed Churchill he received the same response. Once, Churchill did admit to Eden in conversation that 'It would be a measureless disaster if Russian barbarism overlaid the culture and independence of the ancient States of Europe,' but then he cut the discussion short with the words, 'the war has prior claims on your attention and mine.'[6]

If Roosevelt was receptive to Eden's concerns about the future with Russia, he completely failed to grasp Eden's perspective on Poland. The president suggested to Eden that if the Poles were given parts of East Prussia there should be 'no issue' over frontiers, and that Britain, the US and Russia should decide the future border and 'Poland would have to accept'. Eden was completely unimpressed with Roosevelt's line of thinking, later writing in his memoirs, 'Roosevelt was familiar with the history and geography of Europe. Perhaps his hobby of stamp-collecting had helped him to this knowledge, but the academic yet sweeping opinions which he built upon it were alarming in their cheerful fecklessness.' When conversation moved to the Far East, the president waxed lyrical about China and its leader, Chiang Kai-shek, saying that it would be neither an aggressive nor imperialist nation and would act as a 'counterpoise' to the Soviet Union. Eden was sceptical, telling Roosevelt that he feared the country might go through a revolution after the war, a prophesy that proved correct as China became a Communist People's Republic under the leadership of Mao Zedong in 1949. During their meal Roosevelt also suggested that, at the end of the war, Korea and Indochina would, instead of being colonies, be transferred into international trusteeship, details of which could be finalised in the 'ironing out of things after the war'. Eden's response was that the idea of unilaterally internationalising their former colonies was 'being very hard on the French'.[7] Eden recalled that Roosevelt 'seemed to see himself disposing of the fate of many lands, allied no less than enemy. He did all this with so much grace that it was not easy to dissent. Yet it was too like a conjuror, skilfully juggling with balls of dynamite, whose nature he failed to understand.'[8]

Eden spent three days watching US Army training. General Marshall took him to Montgomery, Alabama, where great pains were made to fly the Union Jack alongside the Stars and Stripes. Some of the American soldiers were not even familiar with the British national anthem and on one occasion when *God Save the King* was played, Eden heard a whisper from one soldier, 'Why the heck do we salute at *My Country, 'tis of Thee*?' (the hymn shares the same melody). Eden witnessed the 82nd Airborne conduct a mass parachute drop at Fort Bragg, a demonstration which most impressed him, and then visited naval shipyards in Norfolk, Virginia, which were repairing a number of damaged Royal Navy warships.

Before Eden departed, Roosevelt suggested he should make a speech. Eden proposed San Francisco as a venue, so he could use the opportunity to 'remind the West Coast that we are with them in the Japanese war until the end', to which Roosevelt warmly assented, but in the end he decided Eden should speak 'closer to home'. On 26 March Eden delivered a speech at Annapolis State House in Maryland. He talked of the post-war world, telling the gathered listeners, 'We cannot have prosperity in one country and misery in its neighbour, peace in one hemisphere and war in another.' A month before, he had written a paper for the British Cabinet on the idea of a new international organisation, for which he proposed the title of 'the United Nations'. Eden's speech at Annapolis was one of the first times the idea of collective international interest under the title of the 'United Nations' was mentioned publicly. Warming to his theme, Eden stated, 'We shall never find security or progress within heavily defended national fortresses. The United Nations, and in particular the United States, the British Commonwealth, China and the Soviet Union, must act together in war and peace.'[9] It was a high ideal and one that would be quickly dashed. Just before he returned to London, Eden sent a long and detailed telegram to Churchill outlining the proposed structure of the organisation that would bear the name. He suggested it should have a 'general assembly' where representatives of the smaller powers 'could blow off steam' at once-yearly meetings and a committee of the 'Four Powers' – Eden proposed Britain, the US, Russia and China – '[who] would take all the more important decisions and wield [the] police powers of the United Nations.'[10] At the heart of Eden's proposal was his gentlemanly sense of diplomacy that had been so mauled by the actions of Hitler and Mussolini in 1939. One line in his Annapolis speech asserted, 'Never again must the civilised world be ready to tolerate unilateral infraction of treaties.'

Spring 1943 witnessed an event that strained relations between the Allies. In April the German press gleefully reported the discovery of the bodies of 10,000 Polish officers in a mass grave in Katyn Forest near Smolensk. They had been murdered by the Soviets in 1940. Russia quickly denounced the findings as German propaganda, even though the exiled Polish government insisted they were accurate and explained the disappearance of thousands of Polish officers whom the Polish government had been unable to track down in camps in Russia. Stalin's response was to immediately break off relations with the Polish government. His message to that effect reached Maisky on 23 April: Good Friday. Maisky telephoned Number 10 and was informed that Churchill had gone to Chartwell for the Easter weekend, but that he was welcome to go to Churchill's family house in Kent for dinner. The Russian ambassador arrived by 8pm and waited around for Churchill to appear. He emerged in his siren suit and after they shook hands, Maisky gave Churchill Stalin's message. He read it impassively, but told Maisky, 'Publicity would be most unfortunate. Only the Germans would stand to gain by it.' Churchill ordered his secretary to telephone Eden and he returned to report that Eden was 'very upset' by the news, which shattered his earlier efforts in 1941 to bring the Poles and the Russians together when Russia became Britain's ally. After a sparse meal of milk soup, fried salmon, and asparagus picked from the Chartwell gardens, Churchill and Maisky sat and smoked until midnight. Maisky recorded that Churchill 'stressed he of course does not believe the German lies about the murder of 10,000 Polish officers,' but even Maisky thought Churchill was saying what he thought the Russian wanted to hear, writing in his diary, 'But is this so?' Churchill did, however, tell the ambassador, 'Even if the German statements were to prove true, my attitude towards you would not change. You are a brave people, Stalin is a great warrior, and at the moment I approach everything primarily as a soldier who is interested in defeating the common enemy as quickly as possible.'[11]

Privately, Churchill had little doubt the Russians were guilty and that the German film reels showing piles of excavated bodies were not faked, admitting to an aide, 'Alas, the German revelations are probably true.

The Bolsheviks can be very cruel.'[12] Eden shared Churchill's opinion, but was desperate not to jeopardise relations with Russia. He makes no mention of Katyn in his memoir of the war, and with good reason. The Polish government had called for the International Red Cross to investigate the massacre, which was the catalyst for Stalin to break off relations, but when the leader of the Polish government confronted Eden he found him unresponsive. Eden stated that if the Poles wished to have diplomatic relations with Russia, they would have to call off the Red Cross investigation and agree to blame the Germans for the massacre. When asked point blank what the government's position was, Eden replied, 'First of all, the British government did not believe the Germans, and secondly, it could not estrange such a powerful ally [Russia].'[13] The Poles withdrew their request to the Red Cross, but refused to state the Germans were responsible for Katyn and Stalin broke off relations anyway. It was a dark chapter in British-Polish relations, in which the perceived need to keep Soviet Russia onside to win the war overruled action being taken against the perpetrators of mass murder. Churchill and Eden were equally guilty.

Chapter 16

Second-in-command

In spring 1943 Eden was faced with one of the biggest decisions of his entire political career. The prestigious and important position of viceroy of India had become vacant. The role was anything but ceremonial. The viceroy was head of the British administration in India, which in 1943 also included the countries of Pakistan and Bangladesh, and historically had wielded near-unquestioned power over millions of subjects. The position had always been a key appointment, but as support for the independence movement in India had gathered momentum following the First World War, Britain's new viceroy would need to be a politician of clout and tact. Eden quite liked the thought of taking on the challenge.

Eden and Churchill had long discussions about the idea. At first Churchill was opposed and then gradually warmed to it. The two chatted late into the evening of 21 April. Churchill told Eden that he would hate to lose 'his chief lieutenant and only really intimate friend among his colleagues,' but also added 'what a calamity it would be to win the war and lose India'.[1] Churchill had always had strong feelings about India. He had found himself in the wilderness prior to the war because he had resigned over proposed Conservative support for the idea that India be granted dominion status. As he wrote in 1934, 'The loss of India would mark and consummate the downfall of the British Empire.'[2] Given Churchill's view of India as central to the future of the British Empire, it is not illogical for him to have come around to the idea of tasking Eden, whom he trusted, with the role of holding on to what was once described as the 'jewel in the Empire's crown'.

Eden had in fact been quietly contemplating his personal life and career for several months. His relationship with his wife, Beatrice, was increasingly becoming one of professional convenience, although they remained fond of each other and connected to their children. In autumn 1942 he had discussed with her his political future and written of his own doubts about his abilities to hold high office after the war: 'Beatrice saw the force of all this but argued I had gone too far [in politics] to turn back now. 'Tho she admitted India was only [a] possibility. Truth is I feel too tired to tackle these post-war problems. I am desperately in need of a change and I do not know enough of economics.' The viceroyship would offer a change, remove him from the vexations of working closely with Churchill, but in all likelihood also mean it would be highly unlikely he would ever become prime minister. Leo Amery, the Secretary of State for India, was one of a number of ministers in favour of Eden's appointment, writing that Eden realised 'the greatness of the task and [is] prepared to take his chance over his future political position ... I am not sure that he is not by nature a much better viceroy than a leader of the Conservative Party.'[3] For others, including Eden's private secretary, it was a disastrous idea: 'to go would be to lose all he had now gained – to miss the P.M.ship, to miss the vital peace-making years, to confound his friends and confirm his critics.'[4]

Unlikely as it seemed, the trajectory of travel was moving towards Eden's appointment as viceroy and his departure from London to Delhi, until the king intervened. On 28 April George VI wrote to Churchill that there were several strong arguments against dispatching Eden to India, 'From the point of view of the general conduct of the war he is, I know, very much in your confidence. He is, so to speak, your second-in-command ... As regards Foreign Affairs ... He enjoys, in an exceptional degree, the confidence of both the United States and of our Soviet Allies. If he were to go away to India now, the benefit which the country derives from his very special position would be, to a large extent, lost.'[5] George VI also personally contacted Eden, who began to change his mind. In his own words, Eden stated he 'pondered the decision and grew increasingly to feel that I ought not to leave London, despite the appeal of a job of this magnitude and of work so much one's own.'[6] One of Eden's biographers claims it was a 'watershed moment' in Eden's career, writing, 'In 1943, being in Churchill's shadow was less attractive than New Delhi [taking up the viceroy position], but Eden chose the shadow, not because he wanted to guarantee his future premiership, but because he genuinely believed – and was encouraged to do so by the King – that it was in Cabinet as a counter-balance to Churchill's wilder excesses, that he could make the most valuable contribution to the war effort.'[7] Once the decision was made, Eden concluded he had made the correct choice. He noted in his diary that as he and Beatrice arrived back at the family home in Surrey after driving from London, 'It looked and smelt as lovely as usual. We are glad not to be giving it up for a splendid palace at Delhi.'

As spring turned to summer Eden again found himself at loggerheads with Churchill over De Gaulle. In May, De Gaulle was in negotiations with Giraud over the formation of a joint French committee but discussions had stalled. Churchill was again in Washington and his own misgivings about De Gaulle were stoked by Roosevelt, who informed him of a number of 'allegations' about De Gaulle's conduct. Churchill messaged the entire War Cabinet calling for 'urgent consideration whether De Gaulle should not now be eliminated as a political force, the [London-based] French National Committee being told that we would have no further relations with them, nor give them any money, so long as De Gaulle was connected to them.'[8] The War Cabinet almost entirely disagreed with Churchill, and Eden, with the support of Deputy Prime Minister Clement Attlee, replied, stating that De Gaulle was an important figurehead of the Free French military forces, who, following their absorption into the Allied armies after the invasion of North Africa, now constituted more than 80,000 men. The message to Churchill ended, 'we are convinced that the Americans are wrong … We do hope that a decision on this question can await your return.'[9]

De Gaulle and Giraud put aside their differences sufficiently to officially form the Algiers-based French Committee for National Liberation at the beginning of June, but in Roosevelt's view, it was only a matter of time before things turned sour. He informed Churchill, 'you and I will be sitting on top of a probable volcanic explosion.' Reusing his metaphor from Casablanca, he added, 'the bride [De Gaulle] evidently forgets that there is still a war in progress … Best of luck in getting rid of our mutual headache.' Having earlier accepted De Gaulle as a necessary difficulty, but one which would eventually be advantageous for Britain once France was liberated, Churchill now moved entirely over to Roosevelt's side. When Giraud and De Gaulle had yet another, well-publicised quarrel over the composition of the Algiers committee only a fortnight after its creation, the US president personally messaged Churchill, 'I am fed up with De Gaulle, and the secret, personal and political machines of that committee in the last few days indicate that there is no possibility of us working with De Gaulle … he would doublecross us both at the first opportunity. I agree with you that the time has arrived when we must break with him.'[10]

Two nights after Allied forces landed in Sicily, finally taking the land war onto European soil for the first time since the evacuation of Dunkirk, Churchill and Eden had another spectacular disagreement. After the other dinner guests had left Downing Street on 12 July, Eden stayed on to talk with Churchill. They argued until 2.15am over De Gaulle. Churchill was at his bellicose worst and in 'a crazy state of exultation', having consumed considerable amounts of champagne, brandy and whisky over the course of the evening. Rather than making peace the following day, he drafted a fiery memo for circulation to the War Cabinet, saying of De Gaulle, 'Wherever he went he left behind him a trail of Anglophobia ... I have therefore for some time regarded him as a personage whose arrival at the summit of French affairs would be contrary to the interests of Great Britain ... He is animated by dictatorial instincts and consumed by personal ambition ... he shows many of the symptoms of a budding Führer.'[11] Eden also wrote his own memo for that Cabinet meeting and then discovered that he and Churchill would effectively be presenting to Cabinet two completely different policies.

The evening before the Cabinet meeting, the foreign secretary went to see his prime minister. Churchill threatened to place both memos before the War Cabinet the following day, effectively presenting the possibility of a repeat of the circumstances that had led to Eden's resignation in 1939 and thus leaving him as the voice in Cabinet opposing the prime minister's view. During their argument, Churchill told Eden that he did not like his paper and 'thought we might be coming to a break'. In the face of Churchill's violent opposition, Eden backed down. Churchill in the end held back from presenting his memo to Cabinet and the following week came around to Eden's position. He told Eden he had 'swallowed his thesis whole' and Eden noted 'Winston was in very good form and could not have been more friendly.' The episode again showed Churchill eventually moderating his position for Eden, but he only did so after treating him viciously and effectively threatening to place Eden in an extremely difficult position in front of Cabinet. Eden was one of only a handful of people in Churchill's life who demonstrated the stamina and eloquence to occasionally manage to change his mind.

The invasion of Sicily had precipitated a crisis in the Italian government and led to an occasion which enabled Churchill to be the bearer of good news. On 25 July Mussolini was forced from power and arrested by Italian police. Churchill telephoned Eden in person at 11.30pm that evening to tell him. Eden had never changed his mind about the Italian dictator, recording in his diary that night, 'It is terrific news for me. Eight years since all my troubles with Musso[lini] began.' The following day the king of Italy dismissed the Fascist government. The man he appointed was not entirely a surprise: Marshal Pietro Badoglio had earlier made contact with the British through an intermediary in the Special Operations Executive. Churchill and Roosevelt were united in the desire to swiftly take Italy out of the war, ideally with as little fighting as possible. The hope was that dealing with Badoglio could bring about an early armistice. Ten days before, Allied aircraft had carpet-bombed Rome with leaflets bearing 'a message to the Italian people from the President of the United States of America and the Prime Minister of Great Britain.' It read, 'Your Fascist leaders sent your sons, your ships, your air forces, to distant battlefields to aid Germany in her attempt to conquer England, Russia and the world … The sole hope for Italy's survival lies in honourable capitulation.'[12] It was a logical move, but a strategy that had the potential to alienate elements of the British public, who had a strong desire to see Italy crushed in the war. As Churchill later admitted to Roosevelt and Stalin, 'The British people would not easily forget that Italy declared war on the Commonwealth in the hour of her greatest peril, when French resistance was on the point of collapse, nor could they overlook the long struggle against them in North Africa before America came into the war.'[13]

Secret negotiations began in Lisbon in the second week of August, with much subterfuge. Eden recounted there was 'toing and froing of envoys, crossing and double-crossing in Lisbon, Tangier and Sicily, but all ending up on September 3rd on terms which were sensible rather than drastic.'[14] The final outcome was a simple one: the day the Allies invaded the mainland, the Italian government agreed an armistice. Churchill and Eden were in Canada by the time it happened, but the hoped-for outcome did not materialise. Hitler quickly mobilised the German forces in Italy and instead of proving to be the 'soft underbelly' of Europe, fighting there continued until 1945.

Chapter 17

Visiting friends

One of the remarkable and less reported facts of Churchill's tenure as wartime prime minister is how much time he spent abroad. It has been calculated that he made twenty-five foreign trips, totalling 369 days overseas. Churchill spent one whole year of the five that Britain was at war not in the country. His trips were hazardous, arduous, and in a number of cases, completely unnecessary. In August 1943 Churchill and Eden went to Quebec in Canada to meet up with Roosevelt and senior US military and diplomatic staff. For Churchill, it was another opportunity to see his friend.

Roosevelt and Churchill had a strong personal friendship, stretched occasionally by the travails of war, but certainly one of the closest in history between a British prime minister and a US president. Roosevelt had a nickname for Churchill and the two exchanged regular gifts, delighted in the whimsy of using codenames on correspondence while overseas, and met and got on well with their respective wives. Churchill once wrote to Roosevelt, 'I cannot tell you how much I value your friendship or how much I hope upon for the future of the world, should we both be spared.'[1] A few historians have suggested that Churchill's chumminess, while genuine, was also a studied tactic to ensure that Britain's most important ally was always onside. While this view may contain an element of truth, and Churchill's war memoirs certainly gloss over a number of difficult periods in their relationship, Churchill certainly was not a man to completely fake friendship.

Eden was never as starry-eyed about Roosevelt, although he conceded that the American president was 'a charming country gentleman'. In truth, there seems to have been an element of insecurity to Eden's view of Roosevelt. Eden correctly dismissed Roosevelt's views of what to do in Europe after the war as naïve, but the well-dressed, well-spoken foreign secretary could occasionally come across as arrogant when he knew his own mind and did not wish to hide the fact. While Eden often had to work extremely hard to change Churchill's mind, Churchill on occasion seemed to move at the whim of Roosevelt. Eden did not view this positively. Shortly after returning from Canada he noted, 'I am most anxious for good relations with the U.S. but I don't like subservience to them and I am sure that this only lays up trouble for us in the future,' adding that Churchill's lengthy stays in Washington strengthened that impression. It is problematic to speculate on Eden's private view, but he at times doubted his own abilities. This insecurity, and the contrast of his own relationship with Churchill and that of Churchill and Roosevelt, perhaps provoked in him an element of jealousy. Four days into the Quebec conference, Eden was annoyed with the pair, noting in his diary that night, 'W.[inston] and F.D.R. did not get back from [a] fishing expedition until 8.30, so that our dinner was unpleasantly late.' Eden had arrived on time and been waiting around for Churchill, as he had done five-and-a-half years previously ahead of a lunch on the French Riviera. Dinner that night at Quebec was 'not a very agreeable meal'.

The Quebec Conference produced an agreement on a new plan for the invasion of France, codenamed 'Overlord'. The provisional invasion date was set as 1 May 1944, nine months away. Churchill, in view of the vastly superior number of US troops who would be landing in France, suggested to Roosevelt that the overall military commander should be an American. Churchill had previously told General Alan Brooke that he would be leading the future invasion and later had to break the news to him that he would not; Brooke, Churchill later claimed, 'bore the great disappointment with soldierly dignity.'

The conference also led to an agreement of sorts over De Gaulle, in which the British would formally recognise the French Algiers Committee, but the Americans would not. Eden personally undertook the negotiations with Cordell Hull, although they both got very heated when Eden remarked that he had to live twenty miles from France and 'wanted to rebuild her so far as I could.' Hull retorted with the accurate riposte that the British were 'financing De Gaulle,' but, as Eden noted, 'he has an obsession with the Free French which nothing can cure.'[2] Churchill explained the outcome in a reporting telegram to the Cabinet in London, stating that they had reached a 'settlement' over recognition of the French Committee, but adding 'we all had an awful time with Hull, who has at last gone off in a pretty sulky mood, especially with the Foreign Secretary [Eden], who bore the brunt.'[3] The agreement to disagree solved the problem of US animosity towards De Gaulle in the short term, but it was to flare up again as soon as Allies landed in France, and the previously theoretical question of who should be in charge of the freed French became a very practical one.

Plans were also agreed for a foreign secretary's conference, which would put Eden, Hull and Molotov in the same room. Eden had hoped for it to be held in London, but his hopes were dashed by the Americans. Roosevelt agreed 'with alacrity' to make Moscow the venue. Eden disappointedly wrote, 'His [Roosevelt's] determination not to agree to a London meeting for any purpose … is almost insulting considering the number of times we have been to Washington.' Once Eden got back to London from Canada, he would only have a brief window before he again trekked abroad.

Following the conference, Churchill and Eden both took a few days off, initially in different locations outside Quebec, which put a mountain range between them. However, Eden's attempts to fish were interrupted by communications from Churchill. One 'urgent' message, which Eden's private secretary had to drive thirty miles each way to pick up, enquired whether Eden would like to join him at some point for lunch or dinner. Eden eventually caved to Churchill's hassling and went to stay with him at the Lake of Snows, as 'evidently the beauties of the scenery and the teeming trout were not absorbing him sufficiently.' There was perhaps another element to Churchill's call for company. After Eden arrived, Churchill's doctor confided in him that he was worried about his patient, as Churchill seemed to be 'unduly depressed by troubles which are not immediate and to be unable to shake them off.'[4] Churchill himself admitted to Eden that he needed a 'longer change' and Eden, who thought he looked in 'bad colour', encouraged him. The upshot was that Churchill stayed on in Canada for an extended rest, later travelling down to Washington, while Eden and the remainder of the delegation returned to London. Eden's departure worried Churchill. On the foreign secretary's final night, the two were discussing politics while Churchill splashed about in the bath and Churchill remarked that he was concerned that Eden, along with the Generals Brooke, Portal and Admiral Mountbatten, planned to fly back on the same plane. 'I don't know what I should do if I lost you all,' he said. 'I'd have to cut my throat. It isn't just love, though there is much of that in it, but you are my war machine.' Back in London, Churchill's absence again caused problems for Eden. On 10 September he wrote in his diary, 'Felt depressed and not very well all day, partly, I think, because of [the] exasperating difficulty of trying to do business with Winston over the Atlantic.' A few weeks later he left for Moscow.

The scenery out of the plane window on Eden's flight to the Russian capital was largely uninspiring: 'Fine view of tops of Caucasus [mountains] above the clouds and of the Volga [river], a few miles east of Stalingrad. But the country generally appears flat, treeless and monotonous from the air.'

The meeting of the three foreign ministers began the following day, although US Secretary of State Cordell Hull proved rather high maintenance. The Tennessee senator had a dislike of travel, perhaps understandably given he was seventy-three years of age. Unlike Churchill, he was not wearing the advance of the years well and at Quebec had risen from dinner to go to bed at midnight, remarking it was late, to which a dismayed Churchill had pointedly told him, 'Why, man, we are at war!' On the first day of meetings in Moscow, Hull was cold and demanded his overcoat be fetched. Eden thought the meeting room was 'reasonably warm', remarking that Hull liked to work in a temperature of about ninety degrees. The next day, the Russians turned up the heat in the room so much that Eden thought he would faint. The first major agreement between the British, Americans and Russians was upon a suitable room temperature.

Top of the agenda, Molotov had put 'Measures to shorten the war'. Once more, Eden found himself in Moscow being asked about the plans for a second front. The Russians wheeled in two generals to probe the Allies' invasion plans, seemingly intent on proving they were deliberately delaying, but General Ismay for the British and Major-General John Deane, who had accompanied Hull, explained with 'exemplary patience' the complexities of mounting a cross-Channel invasion to the Russian military men, whose only experience was of fighting on land. As well as the second front, the talks planned to cover a number of other points, including the treatment of Germany and other nations after the war, the future of Poland and the organising of a meeting between the leaders of the three Allied nations. Eden reported to Churchill, 'We are making fair progress though we have yet to tackle the most contentious issues, e.g. Poland ... But the work is heavy and not very rapid, [the] language difficulty causing inevitable delay.'[5]

Eden was annoyed that he could not get out much, even though the Moscow weather was fine and sunny. He was permitted to walk around the 'ill-kept' garden where he stayed, but only allowed in the streets of Moscow in a bullet-proof car. As guests they were well fed, but Eden noticed that the general Russia populace were not, recording, 'There never was a country where two standards of living were more plainly marked, the official and the rest.'

Before Eden's departure from London, he had not expected to meet with Stalin while in Moscow, but after he had arrived he asked Molotov to arrange it, so he could personally explain to Stalin why the Russian convoys had been suspended. He found Stalin in a dejected mood. Eden recorded, 'He spoke glumly, as if we did not want to fight the war as Allies.' But Eden managed to relax the atmosphere and detailed to the Soviet leader the major naval operation that every convoy entailed and the ongoing struggle of the war against the U-boats. Stalin accepted Eden's explanation and went on to talk about the Russian front, admitting that the invasion of Italy did seem to be helping as the Germans were no longer moving fresh reserves to the Eastern Front. Eden found Stalin personally friendly, but problematic to talk with: 'he still has that disconcerting habit of not looking at one as he speaks or shakes hands,' Eden wrote in his diary that night. 'A meeting with him would be in all respects creepy, even a sinister experience, if it weren't for his readiness to laugh, when his whole face creases and his little eyes open.'

Eden returned to talks with Molotov and Hull, but they seemed to be achieving little. After a week of fruitless discussions on a number of subjects, Hull cornered Eden and complained that they were getting nowhere. With Hull's consent, Eden agreed to raise the issue with Stalin if he met him again. He shortly had another opportunity, as Churchill cabled him with orders to inform Stalin that the promised cross-channel invasion planned for May 1944 might again have to be postponed. Churchill stressed that Operation Overlord was not being abandoned, but that the need for landing craft in Italy 'may cause a slight delay, perhaps till July.'[6] Fortunately for Eden, Stalin took the news of another postponement with little complaint. Eden also told the Soviet leader of his conversation with the US Secretary of State. Stalin asked, 'What do you want?', to which Eden replied, 'Decisions on the subjects we have been discussing for more than a week.' After days of delays, Molotov's attitude completely changed and in an hour they reached conclusions on almost everything they had been discussing. Eden noted the Russian foreign minister 'was always a superb workman, as skilful at disentangling as at stalling.'

There was no dramatic agreement following the meeting of the foreign ministers, but the Allies did set up a joint European Advisory Committee in London, which looked at the practicalities of governance once Hitler's regime collapsed. It was this committee that later proposed 'zones of occupation' within Germany, a plan which would lead to the division of the country between East and West at the start of the Cold War. Molotov refused to discuss Poland, however, and Hull would not give Eden significant support. Eden described the absence of diplomatic relations between Russia and Poland as an embarrassment and stressed the hard work that had gone into the agreement between the two nations in 1941, but Molotov was insistent. He stated the question of Polish-Soviet relations was one to be decided between the two nations. Eden's attempts to place himself as mediator were ignored.

After weeks away, Eden cabled Churchill on 2 November, 'So far as I can judge the mood of these incalculable people, they are now in the current to move with us ... provided that they can be made to feel that they are in all things our equals.'[7] That was perhaps the greatest achievement of Eden's second trip to Moscow: that by the time he and Hull left, the Russians seemed to feel that they really were allies. Churchill summed it up with the words, 'the mounting deadlock in our working with the Soviet Union had in part been removed. Those who took part in the conference sensed a far more friendly atmosphere, both on and off duty, than had ever existed before.'[8]

Chapter 18

A very small country

In late autumn of 1943 the outlook of the war had changed beyond recognition from a few years previously. London's streets were still gloomy and rain-washed, but the city was no longer under nightly siege from the air. British bombers were now pounding Germany and it was the citizens of Berlin, Cologne, Dortmund and Dusseldorf who now cowered under their stairs at night. Hamburg had been reduced to a splintered shell of a town in ten nights of bombing over the summer of 1943, which flattened historic landmarks and then whipped up a firestorm so hot it melted the asphalt on the roads. Ten square miles of city simply no longer existed; 900,000 inhabitants had fled, while more than 40,000 had lost their lives. The series of raids had been codenamed Operation Gomorrah, a reference to the Biblical destruction of the eponymous town with fire and brimstone. Churchill was an ardent supporter and proponent of the Allied strategic bombing campaign, but his private secretary later recorded that he was troubled by its effects. Air Marshall Arthur 'Bomber' Harris proudly showed Churchill a film reel of the results of the raids on Hamburg in the Cabinet room cinema and when the projector had rattled to a stop and the lights went up, tears were streaming down the prime minister's face. He is said to have asked Harris, 'Are we beasts that we should be doing these things?'[1]

Allied soldiers were now fighting Germans on the ground, not just in North Africa, but also in Italy and across a Russian Front that stretched thousands of miles. Hitler, like Napoleon before him, had discovered to his cost that the glittering prize of Moscow was one that he would never grasp. Of far greater strategic relevance was the reversal at Stalingrad, which put paid to Hitler's hopes of using the Caucasus oil fields to fuel his armies. In time, shortages would come to cripple the fabled ability of German armour to counter-attack or even to mount any meaningful offensive. In the Atlantic, merchant shipping losses to U-boats had fallen dramatically in 1943, partly as a result of an increase in the number of escorts, but primarily due to improvements in technology and tactics; losses would continue to decline until the end of the war. The U-boats were still a threat, but their chokehold on Britain's critical sea supply line had been broken.

The seemingly unstoppable advance of Japanese forces across the Pacific had also been halted in 1943. Following victory against the Japanese at Guadalcanal in the Solomon Islands, the vicious island fight towards Japan itself was beginning. From east to west, the tide of war was decisively turning. Against this backdrop, Churchill, Roosevelt and Stalin met together for the first time.

After arriving back in London from Moscow, Eden had less than a fortnight at home before flying to Cairo and then on to Tehran for the grand meeting. The easing of relations following his Moscow visit was a welcome outcome for Eden, who for months had been pushing to involve the Russians more, joining in Churchill's calls for a meeting of the 'big three'. In July he had written to Churchill, 'You have often met President Roosevelt, and we have both met Stalin, but there have as yet been no triangular meetings … There has been a tendency for us to agree matters with the Americans first and to present results to the Russians, and there are signs the Russians resent this procedure.'[2] Now, it seemed there would be a moment of shared progress between the Allies. Before Eden left for Tehran, the Polish prime minister, M. Stanislaw Mikolajczyk, came to see the foreign secretary. He understood that Poland was on the agenda for Tehran and sought reassurance from Eden that there would be no decisions made on Poland's future without consultation. Eden told him he would do his best, but warned them not to be hopeful.

At Cairo, Churchill and Roosevelt held discussions with the Chinese leader, Chiang Kai-shek, ahead of flying on to Persia. Eden was 'very much impressed' by him in the short time they had together, recording in his diary, 'He has a constant smile, but his eyes don't smile so readily and they fix you with a penetrating, unswerving look, in marked contrast to Uncle Joe's [Stalin's] habit of looking at one's naval. His strength is that of a steel blade.' There was a late dinner the night before Eden and Churchill travelled from Cairo to Tehran. Churchill was on fine form throughout the evening, but the following morning had lost his voice. Eden noted he '[felt] sorry for himself until he had a stiff whisky and soda, at 8.45 a.m.'[3]

On arrival Eden was whisked off the plane and separated from Churchill. He was driven to the British Embassy in the city, although his car was held up by a 'characteristic Persian donkey and its owner' who were blocking the gates. It 'took much shouting, gesticulation and police activity' to dislodge them. He was annoyed to later find out that Churchill had been brought in the back door, effectively making him Churchill's decoy. His use as a decoy was a rather pointless exercise. The route from the airport was lined with spectators and Persian cavalry, who Churchill noted would have been 'no kind of defence at all against two or three determined men with pistols or a bomb.' At one point, Churchill's car was held up and remained stationary for nearly five minutes 'amid the crowded throng of gaping Persians'.[4] Stalin stayed at the grand Soviet Embassy, which was just across the road from the British legation, but Roosevelt was at the American Embassy, more than a mile away through the narrow Tehran streets. The British Embassy was well-guarded by British-Indian troops, and the Soviet Embassy by Russian soldiers, so in the interests of removing Roosevelt from potential harm's way, he was eventually prevailed upon by Churchill to transfer his staff and retinue over to the Soviet Embassy. Churchill could now safely walk the hundred yards or so for meetings.

The Tehran conference was the moment of the war when Stalin began to move from being an awkward ally to a dominant dictator. It was not by accident. The Americans, on their part, had already realised who held sway over the future of Europe. At Quebec four months before, the American delegation had discussed internally a secret paper entitled 'Russia's position', which openly stated, 'Russia's post-war position in Europe will be a dominant one. With Germany crushed, there is no power in Europe to oppose her tremendous military forces.' The paper added that it was 'essential to develop and maintain the most friendly relations with Russia.'[5] The president now set about doing just that. Before the first joint meeting at Tehran, Roosevelt met face to face with Stalin. Personally, Roosevelt still clung to a hopelessly optimistic notion that Stalin's bark was worse than his bite and that Soviet statements of a desire for world domination were mostly posturing. The president had previously cabled the US ambassador in Moscow, 'I have just a hunch that Stalin doesn't want anything but security for his country, and I think that if I give him everything I possibly can and ask nothing from him in return, *noblesse oblige*, he won't try to annex anything and will work for a world of democracy and peace.'[6]

For Eden, the rushed meeting at Cairo with the Chinese had resulted in a serious misstep. He later admitted, 'The Americans and ourselves had to go to Tehran without having had an opportunity of reaching a decision upon our combined plans for Europe in 1944.'[7] Poland was the casualty. In Stalin's presence, Churchill was more dismissive of the issue of Russia's future border with Poland. When the three discussed Russia's post-war frontiers, Churchill was content to hold the Polish-Russian frontier at the border drawn after the end of hostilities in 1920, adding, 'We should never get the Poles to say they were satisfied [anyway].' In Eden's version of events, Roosevelt was 'unhelpful' about Poland. He later discovered that Roosevelt had told Stalin in person that he did not want to be publicly associated with any agreement on Poland and that it could wait another year. Eden noted that after Tehran, 'Above all, I began to fear greatly for the Poles.'[8] Around six weeks later, Russian soldiers advanced across Poland's eastern border.

In three-way discussions, Roosevelt morphed from Churchill's confidant to a man opposed to one of the things Churchill held most dear: the British Empire. The president made no secret of his distaste for imperial Britain, openly talking with Stalin about the future independence of India during the conference, as well as freeing Indochina from French control post-war. Roosevelt had always been deeply suspicious of Britain's imperial legacy, once remarking to Churchill, seemingly only partly in jest, 'The British would take land anywhere in the world even if it were only a rock or a sand bar.'[9]

Singlehandedly, Roosevelt made Tehran a very difficult conference. A senior British civil servant recorded, 'Without any previous Anglo-American consultation, [the] President, in his amateurish way, had said a lot of indiscreet and awkward things.'[10] Over lunch on 30 November he informed Stalin of the planned date for Operation Overlord, which Eden had been careful not to let slip during his visit to Moscow a few months previously. Roosevelt opened the conversation by saying he wanted to tell Stalin 'a good piece of news' and went on to state that the invasion of France was planned for May 1944. Churchill interjected that the precise date would depend on the phases of the moon, to which Stalin replied that he was 'not asking to be told the exact date'.[11] Roosevelt, ignoring Stalin's statement, informed him that it would be between 15 and 20 May. It may have been a deliberate ploy on Roosevelt's part to make Stalin feel in his confidence, or simply that the affable American found it hard to keep his mouth shut.

Either way, it exposed the true balance of power. Churchill later confided in a friend, 'When I was at Teheran [sic], I realised for the first time what a very small country this [Britain] is. On the one hand the big Russian bear with its paws outstretched – on the other the great American elephant.'[12]

Although in formal discussions the British felt side-lined, there were lighter moments. One evening, the leaders and foreign ministers sat in a circle with coffee and cigars. At one point Churchill remarked, 'I believe that God is on our side. At least I have done my best to make him a faithful ally.' Stalin grinned when Churchill's words were translated and replied, 'And the devil is on my side. Because, of course, everyone knows that the devil is a Communist and God, no doubt, is a good Conservative.'[13] Churchill also celebrated his sixty-ninth birthday while at Tehran. Most of the dinners were held at the Soviet Embassy, but Churchill insisted on hosting his birthday evening meal on 30 November at the British Embassy. The paranoid Soviet security searched the building from top to bottom before Stalin was allowed across the road. Churchill sat with Roosevelt, who was in his wheelchair, on his right and Stalin on his left, surrounded by tens of other guests. The president gave Churchill a delicate Persian porcelain vase as a gift, which was smashed to pieces on the homeward flight, although Churchill had it reconstructed and kept it for posterity. Toasts flowed freely. Harry Hopkins, Roosevelt's official head of Lend Lease and trusted envoy, proposed one to Churchill. The American said he had made 'a very long and careful study of the British Constitution, which is unwritten, and of the War Cabinet, whose authority and composition are not specifically defined.' He told the assembled company that his study had enlightened him to the fact that 'the provisions of the British Constitution and the powers of the War Cabinet are whatever Winston Churchill wants them to be at any given moment.'[14] The gathering descended into laughter and Churchill took the jest in good spirit, but he later felt the need to include and refute it in his memoirs. The party broke up around 2am.

Officially, Tehran was a great success. The *New York Times*, once the meeting was made public on 4 December having been leaked by Russian radio, ran the headline 'Roosevelt, Stalin, Churchill agree on plans for war on Germany in talks at Tehran', although at the time the newspaper had no details of what had actually been discussed.[15] It was not the only news being kept hidden. At the end of the Tehran conference Churchill had flown to Cairo and then on to Tunisia, with the intention of going on to visit the Italian front, but on the plane he became seriously ill.

Chapter 19

Maladies

Air traffic control in El Aouina, Tunis, mistakenly diverted Churchill's aircraft to an alternative airfield on his arrival and the Avro York in which he was flying spent an hour on the ground. By then, Churchill was already unwell. General Brooke, who was on the flight, later wrote, 'They took him out of the plane and he sat on his suitcase in the cold morning wind … he was chilled through.'[1] Churchill's doctor also saw that the prime minister's face was glistening with perspiration. On finally arriving at El Aouina, Eisenhower greeted Churchill, who told the American general, 'I am afraid I shall have to stay with you longer than I had planned. I am completely at the end of my tether.' Churchill was taken to a villa and slept the whole afternoon. The following day, Sunday 12 December, he pottered into his doctor's bedroom in a dressing gown complaining of a headache and pain in his throat. He was running a temperature of 101°F. Churchill thought he had just caught a chill from the draughty plane, but his doctor was gravely concerned, stating, 'We have nothing here in this God-forsaken spot – no nurses, no milk, not even a chemist.'[2] He was also worried about Churchill's heart as his pulse was 'shabby'. Another doctor and nurses arrived the following day and an x-ray machine and electro-cardiograph were secured on loan from an American hospital in Tunis. Churchill was weak and drowsy, but still working from his bed. He messaged Eden, 'I am caught amid these ancient ruins with a temperature and must wait until I am normal. Future movements uncertain.'[3] X-rays showed he had pneumonia and over the next few days his pulse and breathing sped up. On 15 December Churchill reached his lowest point. He told his doctor, 'My heart is doing something funny – it feels to be bumping all over the place.' He was prescribed digitalis, which slowed his heart rate, and antibiotics to try and fight back against the infection. Churchill telegrammed Roosevelt that he was 'stranded … with a fever which has ripened into pneumonia', but the cheery tone of his message belied his own and his doctors' concerns. As one of the doctors left the room, Churchill asked him, 'I am dying am I not?' The reply was blunt, but positive. 'No sir, you are not. I thought you were, but you are on the way up.'[4]

The following day, Attlee made a statement in the House of Commons that the prime minister had been in bed with a cold and had developed 'a patch of pneumonia'. Further proof of the seriousness of the situation came when Clementine was bundled onto a plane to Tunis, so she could be by her husband's bedside.[5] By the time Clementine arrived, Churchill was over the worst. He had had no idea she was flying out. Churchill forever made light of it, but without the concerted effort that was made to get the necessary drugs and medical equipment, he might well have not survived the combination of pneumonia and repeated attacks of atrial fibrillation. On Christmas Day he was out of bed and holding a conference with Eisenhower on the planned landings at Anzio in western Italy, which would put the Allies within striking distance of Rome, although he was still in a dressing gown. Churchill's private secretary rather exasperatedly admitted, 'The doctors are quite unable to control him, and cigars etc have now returned.'[6]

While Churchill was in North Africa he had lunch with De Gaulle. Out of respect to his host, De Gaulle started by speaking English, while Churchill, 'to make things equal', tried to speak French. It was probably the worst of both worlds. The Frenchman continued to exasperate him. Both men were already of the opinion that the liberation of France was a matter of when, not if, but Churchill stressed to De Gaulle that he should be wary of acting against former Vichy supporters in a manner that would cause a rift in French society. It was a warning De Gaulle would entirely ignore. At one point, when irked by his guest, Churchill blurted out, 'Look here! I am the leader of a strong, unbeaten nation. Yet every morning when I wake my first thought is how I can please President Roosevelt, and my second thought is how I can conciliate Marshall Stalin. Your situation is very different. Why then should your first waking thought be how you can snap your fingers at the British and Americans?'[7] Two days later, on 14 January 1944, Churchill returned to London, having spent nearly eight straight weeks out of the country.

Eden meanwhile had travelled back after the Tehran Conference and spent the next few months preoccupied with the continuing saga of

Poland and preparations for Overlord. The outcome of Tehran was that the Poles were being offered the option Roosevelt had suggested to Eden during his trip to Washington: that they should give up eastern Poland to Russia in exchange for territory taken from Germany. It was exactly the kind of scenario that the Polish prime minister had hoped to avoid when he visited Eden just before he left for Persia. Churchill had misgivings, admitting that if Poland was 'overrun by the advancing Soviet armies, the result might hold great dangers in the future for the English-speaking peoples,' but still pushed the exiled Polish government to accept Stalin's assurance that he would allow Poland to be 'free and independent'.[8] The Polish government, insulted by the suggestion, flatly refused the proposal. Eden still had strong sympathy with the Poles, but admitted to Churchill, 'The truth is that in the present atmosphere of overwhelming Russian victories there is public impatience with the Poles. This may not be just, but it is true.'[9] At heart, Eden was an ally of the Polish government, but the Foreign Office still publicly painted the Russians in as positive a light as possible. Privately, Eden remarked that while he understood the value of the Anglo-Soviet understanding, 'I confess to growing apprehension that Russia has vast aims and that these may include the domination of Eastern Europe.'[10] Instead, the British tried to encourage the Poles to enter into direct negotiations with the Russians. When the Poles finally agreed to accept the proposal of negotiations, the Russians refused, unless the Poles agreed beforehand to the 1941 frontier. Eden recognised the element of futility in the entire exercise, admitting, in perhaps his most telling comment on the Polish situation in the entire war, 'I do not want to throw the poor Poles to the Russian wolves. That was never in my thought, even though my power to help them may be limited.'[11]

Eden also continued to support French interests. In February he wrote a memo for Cabinet on the future of Indochina. It began by stating openly that 'President Roosevelt has recently made it clear that, in his opinion, Indochina should not revert to France [after the war].'[12] He added that it was not simply a long-term issue, but 'one affecting our day-to-day relations with the French and our political warfare policy towards Indochina.' The Japanese had taken control of Indochina in 1941, although they nominally left in charge a French administration. De Gaulle's London-based French Committee of National Liberation had asked the Foreign Office if they could be involved in the Special

Operations Executive's clandestine work in the region, but were roundly told they could not be, primarily because Indochina might not end up being French, although the Foreign Office could not tell them this. The result, it was noted, was 'suspicion and ill-feeling'. Indochina was strategically important because, as a War Cabinet sub-committee had secretly admitted in January, Indochina's loss to Japan was a potential threat to India, Australia and New Zealand. The difficult reality was that only the United States was in the position to win the battle for Indochina, and Roosevelt had no intention of handing it back to the French again afterwards. Eden informed his colleagues in his own memo, 'If the Cabinet favour the continuance of French sovereignty it will be desirable to take the matter up with the United States Government with a view to avoiding a conflict of policy.' The Cabinet discussion and Eden's paper proved irrelevant, as Churchill was in no hurry to press the British view of what should happen in Indochina with the Americans. He wrote to Eden a few weeks later, 'Nothing is going to happen about this for quite a long time.'[13]

Preparations for Overlord were occupying both Eden and Churchill's time, and from early 1944 until the invasion itself Churchill had a weekly meeting dedicated to the planning of the operation. After the landings at Anzio in Italy had been completed, landing craft were rushed as quickly as possible across the Mediterranean to Britain in preparation for the invasion of France, which was still expected to take place in May.

The stress that Eden had been feeling for some time finally caught up with him in April. He was shattered as a result of trying to manage his dual duties as Leader of the House of Commons and foreign secretary, and was being plagued by stomach ulcers. Churchill insisted he take several weeks entirely off work, telling Eden, 'You are my right arm; we must take care of you.'[14] There is no doubt that Eden was concerned about his health, something that a number of his contemporaries, including his private secretary, viewed as 'fussing'. He regularly drank milk to try and stave off flare-ups of his ulcers, but the ever-present possibility that work could leave him confined to bed troubled him. As one Conservative MP recorded in their diary at the time, Eden's problem was that his natural diplomacy made him an excellent Leader of the House: 'Anthony is obliged to retain the leadership (which he does admirably) and may have to give up the F.[oreign]O.[ffice] … I am afraid his last illness has really pulled him down.'[15] However, the position of Leader of the House was one that, personally, Eden felt he was ill-suited to. He once noted in his diary, 'I am not much use as a party man ... I seem forever to be seeing the other feller's point of view. In other words, I am not a political warrior like Winston but only [a] civil servant.'[16] Eden never relinquished his post as foreign secretary, but there is no doubt that the dual stresses affected his health. While Eden rested, Churchill took over leadership of the Foreign Office in his absence, with one senior civil servant remarking that he seemed 'to be enjoying his new toy'.[17] It was the first time that Eden's ill-health had compelled him to give up his duties and leave them in the hands of a man who was much older. The moment was a harbinger of what would take place over the coming decades: Churchill would continue to defy age and the medical odds, while Eden would grow old and ill before his time.

Chapter 20

D-Day, De Gaulle and Doodlebugs

The English Channel is a stretch of sea that narrows to only twenty miles between Dover and Calais. But the often-choppy waters were sufficient to halt Hitler's seemingly unstoppable advance across Europe. Having failed to achieve air superiority over the RAF, the planned invasion was cancelled in September 1940. Four years later the Allies prepared for the invasion of France, putting together the largest amphibious operation in history. To try and gauge what they would face, detailed aerial reconnaissance was undertaken across the entire French coastline, the French Resistance supplied maps and information and the BBC put out a request for the public to send in postcards of the coast of Europe, to which millions responded. Normandy was chosen as the landing site in the hope that the Germans would least expect the Allies to come ashore on the beaches furthest from the south coast. The initial selected invasion date, of which Stalin had been informed, was 17 May, but the planned alternative, based on the tides and predicted weather, was 5 June. Rough weather forced the move to June and on 28 May the personnel of the invasion force were sealed aboard their ships or at their shore bases in preparation.

Churchill had wanted to watch the invasion from a cruiser off the Normandy beaches, but was eventually prevailed upon to stand down. Even the king appealed to him not to go to sea, writing to Churchill on 2 June, 'You will see very little, you will run a considerable risk, you will be inaccessible at a critical time, when vital decisions have to be taken.'[1] Instead, Churchill was forced to content himself with visiting troops as they prepared to embark at the south coast. He took the prime ministerial train, which was rather limited in its accommodation space, having only one bath and one telephone. The inconvenience of it all annoyed Eden, who remarked, 'Mr Churchill seemed always to be in the bath and General Ismay always on the telephone,' making it 'almost impossible to conduct any business.'[2] The weather forecast worsened and a steadily increasing westerly wind built up a moderate sea. The decision was taken to postpone by twenty-four hours. Churchill later recorded, 'We were haunted by the knowledge that if the bad weather continued and the postponement had to be prolonged beyond June 7 we could not again get the necessary combination of moon and tide for at least another fortnight.' The men stayed on their ships and D-Day was set for 6 June. Now in London, Eden anxiously waited for news.

While the military operation was foremost in Churchill's mind, there were still wranglings with the Americans over the future political situation in France. After much cajoling, Roosevelt had invited De Gaulle to Washington to try and make peace, but made a point of doing so unofficially. Churchill described it as a 'friendly message to come over', but Roosevelt pointedly told him, 'Please for the love of Heaven do not tell de Gaulle that I am sending him a "friendly message to come over to see me". The whole point of it is that I decline absolutely as head of State to [formally] invite him to come over here.'[3] As D-Day loomed, there was still no agreed arrangement between the Americans, the British or the French on how liberated French territories were to be administered. De Gaulle's committee was carrying on anyway and in mid-May underwent a rebrand. Instead of the French Committee for National Liberation (FCNL), it announced that the organisation was now to be called the 'Provisional Government of the French Republic.' Roosevelt clung to his great personal dislike of De Gaulle and dressed up his distaste in the noble guise of peoples being allowed to freely determine their own leaders. On 20 May he replied to a message from Churchill stating, 'I really cannot go back on my oft-repeated statement that the Committee and de Gaulle have aimed to be recognised as the Provisional Government of France without any expression or choice by the people themselves.'[4] Churchill insisted that Britain should side with the Americans, but once again found himself at loggerheads with Eden. This time Eden had the backing of several members of the Cabinet, who also wrote to Churchill in support of a formal agreement recognising the authority of De Gaulle's organisation on the ground. Public perception also mattered. The British public had only ever had De Gaulle portrayed to them in a positive light as Britain's ally. He had been recognised by Churchill at the start of the war and it was De Gaulle who, when permitted, spoke on British radio on behalf of the French nation. To the public, and certainly to the French leader himself, France was De Gaulle and De Gaulle was France. As

Eden phrased it in a message to Churchill, 'I am deeply concerned at the situation which is developing in respect of Anglo-French-American relations ... Failure to reach an agreement will not be understood in this country ... Parliament and public wish to see an agreement.'[5]

On 4 June De Gaulle accompanied Eden to the south coast where they rendezvoused with Churchill. They met at Droxford, near Portsmouth – where Churchill's train had terminated – the prime minister walking down the tracks, arms outstretched, to embrace De Gaulle. Churchill's affectionate greeting, Eden later wrote, was a product of him being 'moved by his sense of history', but it left De Gaulle nonplussed, as he had no idea why he had been driven down from London to meet Churchill at a railway siding. He quickly became aware, when Churchill informed him of the invasion plans. It was the second time the Allies had kept him in the dark. Churchill recorded that De Gaulle was 'bristling' and demanded to be allowed to telegram Algiers to inform them. Churchill refused. He did, however, ask De Gaulle if he would prepare a public message to France, to be broadcast once the invasion was underway. Eden then attempted to broach the subject of the administration of France, encouraging De Gaulle to accept Roosevelt's offer to go to Washington. In reply, De Gaulle asserted that the administration of France should have been sorted long ago. At this, Churchill lost his temper and told the Frenchman that the US and Britain were willing 'to risk the lives of scores of thousands of men to liberate France'. If De Gaulle wanted the British to ask Roosevelt 'to give him the title-deeds of France', then the answer was no, but if he wanted them 'to ask the President to make the Committee the principal body with whom he should deal in France', the answer was yes.[6] An offended De Gaulle visited Eisenhower's camouflaged headquarters in nearby woods and then declined Churchill's invitation to dine on the train, instead driving back to London.

The De Gaulle situation came to a head on D-Day itself. As Allied soldiers fought their way off the beaches around midnight on 6 June, Churchill telephoned Eden. They argued for at least forty-five minutes. Churchill was annoyed because he had received letters from two Labour MPs in the Cabinet – Deputy Prime Minister Attlee and Minister for Labour, Ernest Bevin – who both took Eden's side. Churchill insisted De Gaulle should go. Eden recorded in his diary, 'I was accused of trying to break up the Government ... He [Churchill] said that nothing would induce him to give way ... F[ranklin].D.R[oosevelt]. and he would fight the world.' Over the following days, Eden held multiple meetings with De Gaulle, who was a far better host than he was a visitor, talking easily and enjoying meals with his guests. He told Eden at one meeting that he was aware of the price the Americans and the British were paying to liberate France: 'I understand … and we feel with you for the losses which your army will suffer.'[7] Eden was still entertained by the pomp and circumstance with which the French General surrounded himself. For his trip to De Gaulle's headquarters at Carlton Gardens, an elegant three-storey white-stone building overlooking St James's Park, he was received with considerable ceremony. Eden wrote in his diary that it was 'rather like a visit to the Führer. Guard of honour drawn up outside, officers at intervals up the stairs and eventually shown in to the great man's salon.'

In practice the supposed great debate about the administration of France, over which Eden, Churchill and Roosevelt had so long argued, was resolved fairly quickly. As one senior civil servant noted, 'Roosevelt, P.M. [Churchill] and … de Gaulle all behave like girls approaching the age of puberty,' but whatever plans the Americans might have had for De Gaulle not to run France after the liberation were rendered irrelevant by what unfolded on the ground.[8] The outcome also solved Eden's long-standing problems with Churchill over De Gaulle: 'As France was liberated,' he wrote, 'its administration fell without question into the hands of the Resistance which acknowledged General de Gaulle as its chief and this chapter of our difficulties, the cause of so many hard feelings, naturally resolved itself.' Eden, ever more sympathetic to the Frenchman than Churchill had ever been, later concluded, 'Whatever de Gaulle's gifts or failings, he was a godsend to his country at this hour, when France must otherwise have been distracted by controversy or bathed in blood.'[9]

Stalin responded warmly to the positive news from the beaches, telegramming Churchill on the evening of 6 June, 'I have received your communication about the success of the beginning of the "Overlord" operations. It gives joy to us all and hope of further success. The summer offensive of the Soviet forces, organised in accordance with the agreement at the Teheran [*sic*] Conference, will begin towards the middle of June.'[10] There was other good news as well. Rome had been liberated by Allied forces on 5 June. Churchill was in a buoyant mood and on 10 June finally crossed the Channel to France aboard a British destroyer. He arrived on the beach by landing craft and strolled on the sand before visiting Montgomery's headquarters five miles inland. Over lunch at the château,

Churchill discovered that Montgomery did not have a continuous forward line set up at the front, which was only three miles distant, and he asked the general, 'What is there then to prevent an incursion of German armour breaking up our luncheon?', to which Montgomery replied that he 'did not think they would come'.[11] Churchill departed a few hours later on the destroyer *Kelvin*, which sailed a few miles out of its way so Churchill could watch some battleships and cruisers bombarding German positions on the Allies' left flank. As the destroyer was about to turn for home, Churchill asked, 'Since we are so near, why shouldn't we have a plug at them ourselves before we go home?' The ship's commander agreed and loosed off a few rounds from the main guns before the destroyer steered for Portsmouth. Churchill was delighted. It was the only time he had ever been on a naval vessel that had fired its guns 'in anger' and recorded that it was altogether 'a most interesting and enjoyable day'.

Eden did not accompany Churchill on his jaunt to Normandy, although he conducted his own brief trip to the beachhead in France a month later. He visited a field hospital at Arromanches and was profoundly impressed by the improvement in medical care for the wounded from what he had experienced in the previous war. 'Ever since the first world war and the memories of casualty clearing stations, I have not been good at military hospitals,' he wrote, 'but this one was a revelation. Its swift, aseptic handling of the wounded and the injection of pain-killing drugs were far removed from the mud and stretcher bearers of Flanders, though the initial wounds were as savage and searing.'[12]

Within less than a week of the D-Day landings, V1 flying bombs started dropping on London. Effectively the first cruise missile, each winged bomb was powered by jet engine, the distinctive insect-like sound of which earned the weapons the name 'doodlebugs'. On 18 June one landed in the garden of Eden's house, blowing out many of the windows. 'I had plenty of time to think,' he wrote in his diary afterwards, 'I thought it was the end but was not particularly perturbed. Surprised and impressed that the house stood up. Yet an approaching shell always terrified me in [the] last war.' It was the second time Eden had narrowly avoided becoming a wartime casualty. The same day, fifty civilians and sixty-three soldiers were killed when a flying bomb landed on the Guards Chapel in London during a service. The newspapers adhered to government requests and initially kept details of the new threat secret, but on 6 July Churchill publicly acknowledged the danger they posed. He announced in Parliament that the government had been aware of Hitler's attempts to develop a 'flying bomb' and 'long range rocket' since 1943, and that Bomber Command had located and bombed the German's development site at Peenemunde and had targeted launch sites in France. Churchill effectively admitted there were almost no counter-measures to the new threat, but called upon the stoic British public to once more display a stiff upper lip: 'This form of attack is, no doubt, of a trying character, a worrisome character, because of its being spread out throughout the whole of the twenty-four hours, but people have just got to get used to that. Everyone must go about his duty and his business, whatever it may be – every man or woman – and then, when the long day is done, they should seek the safest shelter that they can find and forget their cares in well-earned sleep. We must neither under-rate nor exaggerate.'[13]

Privately, Churchill seemed to be strained by being powerless in the face of bombs once more raining down on the capital. That evening, the Defence Committee gathered to hold a meeting on strategy in the Far East. General Brooke wrote in his diary that it was a 'frightful meeting' that lasted until 2am. 'It was quite the worst we have had with him [Churchill]. He was very tired as a result of his speech in the House concerning flying bombs, he had tried to recuperate with drink. As a result he was in a maudlin, bad-tempered, drunken mood, ready to take offence at anything, suspicious of everybody and in a highly vindictive mood against the Americans.'[14] Churchill criticised Montgomery's command of the troops in France as overcautious, argued with Attlee about the future of India and accused most of those present of trying to push him into a corner. Eden remembered it as 'a deplorable evening', with Brooke noting that he left 'having accomplished nothing beyond losing our tempers and valuable sleep!'

It was the second time in just over a month that Churchill had clashed with Attlee, one of the non-Conservative members of his government. The adroit move of assembling a wartime cabinet of politicians from all sides seemed to be starting to unravel and Churchill began contemplating a future without the coalition. A few days later, Churchill and Eden lunched together alone. Churchill was in good spirits, but he told Eden that when the coalition broke up 'we should have two or three years of opposition and then come back together to clear up the mess!' At this suggestion, Eden noted in his diary, 'My face fell'.

Chapter 21

'A deathless memory'

The Soviet armies had achieved a remarkable reversal of fortunes. Having fought to the death to defend Moscow, by late July 1944 they had pushed the German armies back more than 700 miles and reached the Vistula river in Poland. Russian soldiers were only six miles from Warsaw and the sound of Russian artillery could be heard in the Polish capital. For months, a Polish 'underground army' had been preparing for that very moment and on 31 July messaged the Polish government in London, 'We have started fighting at 1700 hours … Send urgently ammunition and anti-tank weapons.'[1] Eden wrote to Churchill, calling for a 'maximum effort' to support the Poles.

The German response to the Warsaw Rising was swift. Heinrich Himmler personally informed Hitler of the news. It was, he said, 'difficult' timing, but he told the Führer, 'From a historical point of view, the action of the Poles is a blessing … Warsaw will be liquidated … [the] Poles themselves will cease to be a problem for our children and for all who follow us.'[2] Four armoured divisions were given the task of crushing Warsaw and another armoured division and two SS divisions were dispatched to Poland from Italy. The city was to be razed to the ground. Churchill telegrammed Stalin that the Poles were asking for Russian aid, stating that 'a Polish revolt against the Germans [in Warsaw] is in fierce struggle.' Stalin responded on 5 August, 'I have received your message about Warsaw. I think the information which has been communicated to you by the Poles is greatly exaggerated.'[3] The same day, the head of the Nazi military administration in Poland informed the Reich Chancellery, 'Warsaw is in flames. Burning down the houses is the most reliable method of liquidating the insurgents' hideouts … Indescribable poverty reigns among the million inhabitants. Warsaw will be punished with complete destruction.'[4] RAF planes were able to drop small amounts of arms and aid flying from bases out of Italy, but the run involved a hazardous round trip of 700 miles and what could be supplied was nowhere near sufficient. Ten days into the Rising, German armoured columns had scythed the city into three parts and artillery and planes were bombarding indiscriminately. 'We are conducting a bloody fight,' began the message from the Polish commander in Warsaw to London. 'The [Polish] soldiers and the population of the capital look hopelessly at the skies, expecting help from the Allies. On the background of smoke they see only German aircraft.'[5]

The inaction of the Russians, who could see for themselves the smoke rising from the Polish capital, roused Churchill's suspicion. He wrote to Eden that it was 'very curious' that the Russian offensive against Warsaw halted the moment the uprising began, adding, 'For them to send all the quantities of machine-guns and ammunition required by the Poles for their heroic fight would involve only a flight of 100 miles.'[6] The only solution was for US Air Force long-range bombers to undertake the supply-drop flying from airfields in England, but to do so they would need to refuel on Russian territory. The Russians refused permission, with the US Ambassador to Moscow being informed 'the Soviet Government do not wish to associate themselves either directly or indirectly with the adventure in Warsaw.' Roosevelt himself also proved unresponsive. In a continuation of the attitude he had displayed at Tehran, he resisted a direct appeal from Churchill that he apply pressure to Stalin to allow the US to supply Warsaw and consented only to a joint telegram to the Soviet leader, expressing 'hope' that he would agree to the plan.

On 22 August Eden sent Churchill a top secret document containing messages from an escaped British prisoner of war who had found himself in Warsaw and was the Foreign Office's only direct source of information; everything else came from the exiled Polish government. The officer's early messages spoke of thousands of civilians being made homeless each day, along with hundreds killed, adding, 'About 40 per cent. of the city centre is already completely destroyed.' His report on the day Eden passed the note to Churchill read, 'The Soviet Army is … standing again inactive at the gates of Warsaw … breaking of the deadlock … is not possible without serious droppings of arms and ammunition. The prolongation of the present phase leads to the total destruction of Warsaw.'[7] Churchill forwarded a number of the officer's reports directly to Roosevelt, who expressed sympathy but concluded, 'I do not see what steps we can take at this present time.'

In Warsaw the situation was becoming increasingly desperate. Stalin always claimed that the Russian delay was the result of Soviet forces being unable to capture the city because of German counter-attacks, but while the Rising was in progress the Red Army managed to occupy most of Romania, cross into Bulgaria and reach the Yugoslav border. The real suspicion was that Stalin simply wanted armed supporters of the exiled Polish government in London eliminated. Public opinion in Britain was also swinging in the Poles' favour, leading the War Cabinet, on a day when Eden was chairing, to take the unprecedented step of directly messaging Stalin. They stated, 'public opinion in this country is deeply moved [by events in Warsaw[... Your government's action in preventing ... help being sent seems to us at variance with the spirit of Allied co-operation.'[8] Churchill and Eden both faced awkward questions in Parliament. In response to an accusation that acting in aid of the Poles was a matter of principle, Eden responded with the unconvincing assertion 'our responsibility has been fully, and I might add gallantly, discharged.'

The repeated hassling of Stalin did eventually bear fruit and in mid-September the Soviet leader acquiesced to allowing American aircraft to drop supplies for the Poles and to refuel at Russian bases on their way home. Eden was delighted and messaged Churchill, who was by now at Quebec for another conference with Roosevelt, 'This is really a great triumph for our persistence in hammering at the Russians ... Your judgement was correct when you said that Stalin had not understood the significance of his refusal on world opinion.' A triumph it was not. A high-ranking Russian officer close to the front made a careful analysis of the 1,000 containers that descended from the bellies of the 110 Flying Fortress bombers and floated down to the city. He calculated that twenty-one reached the insurgents, nineteen landed on the Soviet lines, while 960 were picked up by the Germans. His message to Moscow was blunt: 'The English and American airforce is not aiding the insurgents, it is supplying the Germans.'[9]

On 5 October, with the Russian forces still only on the outskirts of the city, the leaders of the Warsaw Rising surrendered. Emerging from the shattered, torched ruins, they gave up their weapons. Thousands of ragged civilians then followed, to be herded into German transit camps. The devastation wreaked upon Warsaw during the sixty-six days of the Rising was not like that in Stalingrad, where months of constant fighting had gradually reduced the city to ruins. While large areas were destroyed by the fighting, there was a systematic effort to raze the city which went on for months, even in places where the fighting had ended. A nineteen-year-old lieutenant from Berlin was wounded and given a new job of furnishing German officers' flats from the ruins. He wrote to his parents, 'From half-ruined houses we take the best stuff: sculptures, sofas, rugs, etc. – soon it will all go up in flames ... That's the propagators of European culture for you.'[10] The day of the Poles' surrender, Churchill addressed Parliament: 'When the final Allied victory is achieved, the epic of Warsaw will not be forgotten. It will remain a deathless memory for the Poles, and for the friends of freedom all over the world.'[11]

Chapter 22

The post-war world

September 1944 again saw Eden and Churchill journeying to Quebec to meet with Roosevelt. Churchill left on 5 September at the height of the Warsaw Rising and sailed to Canada on the *Queen Mary*, and after arriving decided Eden should be there as well. Eden received a summons via telegram. The night before he departed, he refused to accept a midnight call from Quebec, instead getting 'a good night's sleep' before beginning a tortuous plane journey via Iceland, which was interrupted by bad weather. 'Left 10.a.m local time,' he wrote, 'and began our interminable flight to Canada, nearly thirteen hours which seemed as many days … Finished my book and felt very bored. Not expected at Quebec which was a relief as I was desperately unshaven.' Eden bathed and shaved and arrived at the conference in time for dinner. He sat next to Roosevelt, who he thought 'looked very drawn'.

One of the primary objectives of the second series of meetings at Quebec was to discuss the plans for what would happen to post-war Germany. The Americans had their own ideas which were presented by the Secretary of State for the Treasury, Henry Morgenthau Jr. The premise of the 'Morgenthau Plan' was that Germany's military strength rested on the country's industrial strength. Instead of demanding vast reparations of the kind that had crippled Weimar Germany after the First World War, it was proposed that large areas of Germany's industrial regions in the Ruhr and Saar basins would be stripped of their manufacturing industries and turned into pastoral land. Eden described it 'as if one were to take the Black Country and turn it in to Devonshire.'[1] Arriving late to the conference, Eden discovered that Churchill had already agreed to the scheme. Churchill later claimed in his memoirs that he did not have time to examine the plan in detail and that, had it ever been implemented, it would not have been right to depress Germany's standard of living. But the fact remains that at Quebec he acquiesced with no opposition. All the objections came from Eden. For months, the Foreign Office had been working on their own plan for post-war Germany and there was a clear expectation that whatever plan was adopted would be decided upon after discussion and consideration. When Churchill told Eden he had agreed to the Morgenthau Plan, Eden 'flew into a rage', at one point shouting at Churchill, 'You can't do this.'[2] Churchill refused to move and openly showed his displeasure at Eden in front of Roosevelt, the only time in the war, Eden later admitted, that he did so. Eden found an unlikely ally in the form of Secretary of State Cordell Hull, who was annoyed at seeing the Treasury Committee putting its oar into foreign policy. Eden noted that Hull 'was as much against it as I was, with an added spice of indignation towards Morgenthau for prowling on his preserves.'[3] The staunch objection of both foreign secretaries was strengthened by a supporting message from the Cabinet in London. It was noted by the Treasury that if Germany were unable to manufacture she would also be unable to pay for imports, which would have a catastrophic impact on world trade. Morgenthau's plan was later dropped nearly as quickly as it had been taken up. Being so clearly opposed appeared to irk Churchill, who was 'troublesome' for most of the rest of the trip, refusing to be pushed into making decisions and quibbling over minor points of wording on documents. Quebec did produce the creation of a Royal Navy task force to fight in the Pacific, but little else. The joint communiqué which Roosevelt and Churchill sent to Stalin talked of agreement to 'press on with all speed to destroy Germany' and to 'intensify the offensive against Japan in all theatres': hardly tough collective decisions of the kind that needed Churchill and Eden to cross the Atlantic.[4] The debate over what to do with Germany was postponed.

The actual, concrete achievement of Quebec was kept secret. It is only hinted at in Churchill's memoirs, where he comments that he was glad to see Morgenthau 'as we were anxious to discuss financial arrangements between our two countries for the period between the conquest of Germany and the defeat of the Japanese.'[5] In short, Britain needed another loan from Uncle Sam. It has been speculated that Churchill's ready agreement to the abortive Morgenthau Plan was in fact an exchange: Morgenthau got to decide the fate of foreign lands and Churchill got six and a half billion dollars. Hull thought as much, writing it was 'the quid pro quo with which the Secretary of the Treasury [Morgenthau] was able to get Mr. Churchill's adherence to his cataclysmic plan for Germany.'[6]

Privately, Eden was also well aware of what had taken place, confiding in his diary the day before he flew home that he had finally 'got through [a] draft on this wretched pay business which is really about all I have achieved by this journey.'

Exactly as it had in 1943, Eden's trip to Quebec was almost immediately followed by one to Moscow. But this time Churchill was to accompany him. They travelled on separate planes for the first leg of the journey and were on the same plane from Cairo to Moscow. Churchill was the only passenger who needed to be roused by the steward for breakfast before they landed 'triumphantly' at the wrong airfield on 9 October. They met with Stalin for the first time that evening, with only interpreters present. Churchill suggested they should 'settle about our affairs in the Balkans', and while the translators spoke, he wrote down on a half-sheet of paper suggestions for what he called 'predominance' in different countries. For Romania he wrote that Russia would have ninety percent, with Britain getting ninety percent in Greece. Yugoslavia and Hungary were fifty-fifty, with Bulgaria seventy-five percent Russian. He slid the paper across the table to Stalin who paused, before writing a big tick in blue pencil. Churchill said to Stalin, 'Might it not be thought rather cynical if it seemed we had disposed of these issues, so fateful to millions of people, in such an off-hand manner? Let us burn the paper.' To which Stalin replied, 'No, you keep it.'[7] Churchill and Stalin's infamous 'percentages agreement' would forever become the ultimate example of imperial arrogance: the futures of entire nations decided on a whim with the stroke of a pencil. Eden was deeply unimpressed as he was the one who 'had to follow it up with Molotov', his opposite number. The following evening Eden and Molotov convened. Molotov wanted to 'haggle over the percentages'. Eden was clearly exasperated by the entire exercise and later wrote, 'Finally I told him that I was not interested in figures. All I wanted was to be sure that we had more voice in Bulgaria and Hungary than we had accepted in Roumania [sic], and that there should be a joint policy in Yugoslavia.'[8] Churchill had already sensed that Eden might not be happy with the blasé method of dividing up Eastern Europe and the night he proposed the percentages agreement admitted in private to his doctor, 'the Foreign Secretary could be obstinate, he must be told that there is only one course open to us – to make friends with Stalin.'[9]

The prospect of 'making friends with Stalin' was even less palatable after the Warsaw Rising, which demonstrated anew the Soviets' callousness. Churchill, however, remained very pragmatic about it. He expressed a response similar to Eden's during the foreign secretary's first visit to meet Stalin in Moscow, writing to Clementine during the trip, 'I like him [Stalin] the more I see him. Now they respect us here and I am sure they wish to work with us.'[10] On one night Churchill and Stalin went to the Bolshoi theatre, arriving late as the first act of the ballet *Giselle* was already underway. At the interval, when the house lights were turned up, the audience broke out into spontaneous applause at the sight of Churchill. The ballet was followed by a two-hour performance by the Red Army Choir, which Churchill clapped along to. It did not auger well for the representatives of the Polish government who arrived in Moscow on 12 October.

Thanks to Stalin's manoeuvring, they found they were no longer the only 'Polish government'. Taking a leaf out of De Gaulle's book, in July 1944 Polish Communists created an organisation named the Polish Committee of National Liberation. Establishing a base in Lublin, which had been liberated by the Russians, they set themselves up as an alternative administration to the exiled Polish government in London. Unsurprisingly, Stalin flung his full weight behind them. It has been repeatedly alleged that the Red Army's defiant halting outside of Warsaw, which left the city to be obliterated, was a deliberate action, aimed to result in the eradication of the significant number of armed supporters of the London Polish government.

The first meeting between the Polish prime minister, Mikolajczyk, and the Russians ended in a stalemate, with the Poles refusing for the umpteenth time to recognise any Polish 'border' that was not the one immediately prior to the Soviet invasion. After the London Poles were sent on their way, two representatives from the Lublin Poles were ushered in and they were only too keen to accept the Russian request that the frontier of Poland be set as a 'compromise' at the place where the border had been drawn following the war between Russia and Poland in 1920. It also happened to fairly closely align with the area the Soviets had partitioned when they had invaded Poland in 1939. The Lublin representatives were fulsome and servile toward the Russians and Eden whispered in Churchill's ear that they were 'the rat and the weasel'.[11] Despite the recent events in Warsaw, Churchill retained the unsympathetic attitude he had demonstrated toward the Poles at Tehran and insisted that they should accept the offer of the 1920 frontier. Eden sat down with Mikolajczyk, and in another demonstration of his adroit negotiation skills managed to persuade the Polish premier to agree that the Poles would treat the 1920 border as a 'demarcation line' and not as a frontier. It was a nuanced proposal, but one which allowed the Polish government to save face while at the same time giving the Russians the territory they wanted, allowing a future negotiation to take place. Churchill moderated his stance and accepted Eden's compromise, which he put to Stalin. Eden glumly messaged Cabinet, 'The Prime Minister used all possible arguments, but was unable to move him [Stalin].'

On 18 October, the final night of the visit, the toasting session of the six-hour banquet at the Kremlin was interrupted with the news that Russian forces had entered Czechoslovakia. Stalin's armies were slowly but surely making whatever agreements the Allies came to over the post-war world a practical irrelevance. Less than three months after Churchill and Eden departed from Moscow, the Russians liberated the burnt-out shell of Warsaw from Nazi tyranny. The Polish government would be in exile until the end of the Cold War.

Chapter 23

Vive la France

In the midst of Churchill's and Eden's angst with Roosevelt and Stalin over the Warsaw Rising, there was a moment of joyous victory. In late August Paris was liberated.

As with Warsaw, the news of the approaching Allied armies and the obvious departure preparations of the German occupiers, which included significant amounts of looting, inspired the general populace. French citizens hung tricolours from buildings and the Communist resistance elements began an uprising. Barricades blocked the roads of the French capital and the fashionable street cafés that had been crammed with smoking, drinking Germans just days before were deserted. Eisenhower meanwhile insisted that any advance on Paris should be delayed. A furious De Gaulle pleaded with him to change his mind, but for two days he stood firm. While the Allies waited, Hitler sent a direct order to the commander of German forces in Paris that he was to fight to the last man and leave the French capital 'a pile of ruins'.[1] Finally, on 23 August Eisenhower relented and ordered the French Second Armoured Division to press for Paris.

The French soldiers riding on American-made half-tracks and Sherman tanks crawled through muddy roads to the town of Rambouillet, thirty miles from Paris itself. On arrival, the French discovered that Ernest Hemingway had expanded his wartime correspondent's brief to round up a band of local armed Frenchmen, with whom he had already scouted out different approach routes to Paris. That night the small town was the base for De Gaulle, Hemingway and the French commander of the Second Armoured, General Leclerc, all of whom harboured grand notions of personally liberating Paris. In the end, it was Leclerc's men who achieved it, De Gaulle who took the plaudits and Hemingway who wrote about it. German resistance delayed the advance another day, but on 25 August French troops entered Paris. After sporadic fighting at a few key strongholds, the German commander of the city surrendered. He ignored Hitler's orders to fight to the last man and raze the city. De Gaulle arrived in Paris shortly afterwards and was greeted by marching bands. As late as a week before the liberation, Churchill had still questioned De Gaulle's leadership, writing to Eden that they should still not recognise the French Committee and wait 'till we can see more clearly what emerges from the smoke of battle.'[2] Divisions remained within the French, the greatest being between De Gaulle and Communist factions, but the French General's overwhelming public popularity quickly made him the de facto leader of liberated France, a fact which Churchill finally acknowledged in Parliament on 27 October.

Once again seized with a sense of history, Churchill determined to visit Paris. Only the strenuous efforts of the newly appointed French ambassador, Duff Cooper, persuaded Churchill to wait for a formal invitation from De Gaulle, which was eventually grudgingly extended. Churchill, accompanied by Eden, landed at Orly airfield on 10 November and they were conveyed to the Quai d'Orsay palace, which had only recently been vacated by the Germans. Churchill and Eden stayed in the same lavish rooms which the king and queen had occupied during their final pre-war visit to Paris. Much to Churchill's delight, he had the finer suite. On the second morning of their visit, Eden went into Churchill's bedroom to show him a telegram, only to discover he was in the bath. Churchill yelled, 'Come in; that is, if you can bear to see me in a gold bath when you only have a silver one.'[3] Churchill accompanied De Gaulle at a parade down the Champs Élysées to mark the 11 November First World War armistice, laying a wreath at the grave to the unknown soldier, while crowds of overjoyed Parisians lined the route watching in the bright sunshine. Churchill revelled in the reception he and De Gaulle received, flashing the V-for-victory sign. One journalist wrote that they were a curious couple, 'the one so round and merry, the other so tall and grave; like Mr Pickwick and Don Quixote.'[4] The visit ended with a long meeting with De Gaulle, during which the new French ambassador recalled, 'There was not an unpleasant word said'. The visit marked a temporary rapprochement for Churchill and De Gaulle. Afterwards he wrote to Roosevelt, 'I certainly had a wonderful reception from about half a million French in the Champs-Elysees ... I re-established friendly private relations with de Gaulle, who is better since he has lost a large part of his inferiority complex.'[5] However, De Gaulle's preoccupation with shoring up his own position in Paris was about to result in him offending one of his staunchest allies: Anthony Eden.

Within France itself, De Gaulle had to contend with powerful internal opposition from Communist elements. He was also acutely conscious that the new centres of world power were Washington and Moscow, and that a revived France would need allies if it were to regain its former status as a world power. Eden sympathised with De Gaulle's aims and indeed it was Eden who had, on multiple occasions, stressed to the Americans his desire to see France as an ally. What he had not seemingly intuited was that if De Gaulle could not make an ally in Washington, his next port of call was Moscow. On 20 November Churchill received a message from Stalin which stated openly in its second paragraph, 'General De Gaulle expressed his wish to come to Moscow … The French are expected to arrive in Moscow towards the end of this month … after our conversations with De Gaulle I will let you know about it.'[6] It was the first Churchill or Eden had heard of it. A few days later came a message from Moscow that De Gaulle was likely to ask for a Franco-Soviet pact. In principle, as Churchill admitted in reply to Stalin, the British were hardly in a position to object; Eden himself had negotiated the Anglo-Soviet Pact in 1942.

Eden was annoyed because, in the first instance, he felt France should have consulted Britain in advance and in the second, he was busy concocting his own ideas for the defence of Europe, and he did not have in mind including the Russians. 'It has always seemed to me', Eden wrote, 'that the lesson of the disasters of 1940 is precisely the need to build up a common defence association in Western Europe, which would prevent another Hitler … The best way of creating such an association would obviously be to build up France.' He added, 'There seems every reason to start thinking about it now, since if our Western European allies and more especially the French have the impression that we are not going in future to accept any commitments on the Continent … they will come to the conclusion that their only hope lies in making defence arrangements, not with us, but with the Russians.'[7]

While Eden was penning his note, De Gaulle was in Moscow chatting up Stalin. Once the news of De Gaulle's trip was out, a message arrived from the British ambassador in Washington, suggesting that opinion across the Atlantic would view such a pact 'as a move by France away from Great Britain.'[8] For Eden, De Gaulle was ignoring all the efforts he had made for him and climbing into bed with an ally Eden increasingly viewed as a likely future enemy. In reality, De Gaulle was far more concerned with domestic issues and a Franco-Soviet pact was a guaranteed way of neutering the threat he faced from Communists within France itself: if De Gaulle was Stalin's ally, French Communists could hardly call for Soviet support to overthrow his government. In the midst of his annoyance, Eden seems to have entirely missed De Gaulle's motive, instead getting caught up in the apparent slight and all the while forgetting that Roosevelt's violent hatred of De Gaulle had given the Frenchman no real alternative. On 22 December 1944 De Gaulle agreed the Franco-Soviet Treaty.

The solution arrived at was that Britain would negotiate its own pact with France, which Eden immediately supported. Churchill could not grasp the need for any hurry however, writing to Eden, 'Surely we should wait until we are asked by the French?'[9] Eden wanted to secure a French pact as swiftly as possible in order to make clear that France remained a close ally and was not drifting towards Moscow, but Churchill's view was that what mattered was whether or not it benefitted Britain: 'we are losing nothing from the point of view of security, because the French have practically no army and all the other nations concerned [in Eden's plans for a European Defence organisation] are prostrate or still enslaved ... I do not know what our financial position will be after the war, but I am sure we shall not be able to maintain armed forces sufficient to maintain all these helpless nations even if they make some show of recreating their armies.'[10]

Churchill and Eden were managing to disagree when in fact their perspectives were beginning to align. To some degree, each had realised that the balance of power had already diverged west and east, to Washington and Moscow. Eden, more than Churchill, recognised that Britain's place in the new world order was as yet undefined, but saw the future as one in which Western Europe, with France at its heart, allied together in defence. He wrote to Churchill, 'I find it difficult to contemplate a future in which France will not be a factor of considerable importance. She must be interested in almost every European question.'[11] Churchill was unmoved and for all the euphoria of his trip to Paris had not been able to shake his dislike of France's new leader. He replied to Eden with a personal letter, 'I cannot think of anything more unpleasant and impossible than having this menacing and hostile man [De Gaulle] in our midst, always trying to make himself a reputation in France by claiming a position far above what France occupies, and making faces at the Allies who are doing the work.'

Chapter 24

Hands off the British Empire

In December 1944 Churchill sent Eden his now famous note on his view of what their priority should be in post-war negotiations: 'There must be no question of being hustled or seduced into declarations affecting British sovereignty in any of the Dominions or colonies. "Hands off the British Empire is our maxim" and it must not be weakened or smirched to please sob-stuff merchants at home or foreigners of any hue.'[1] It was not a conclusion Churchill had suddenly arrived at. In 1942, following the invasion of North Africa, he had grandly told Parliament, 'I have not become the King's First Minister in order to preside over the liquidation of the British Empire,' a statement greeted by loud cheers in the chamber.[2] Eden was also in firm agreement with the principal and sent a note to Churchill which read, 'The aim of British policy [post-war] must be, first, that we continue to exercise the functions and responsibilities of a world power.'[3]

The areas of the Empire that most exercised Churchill and Eden were the Far East and India. Eden had come within a whisker of giving up his duties at the Foreign Office to become viceroy of India in the spring of the previous year, narrowly avoiding being viceroy during the disastrous Bengal famine of 1943. Although it has become fashionable in some circles to lay the blame for the Bengal famine at Churchill's door, he was not personally responsible and neither was his decision-making as callous as has been alleged. The primary cause of the famine was the war itself: the Japanese invasion of Burma cut off the country from its main reserve supplier of rice imports, leaving it more vulnerable to falls in domestic production. The famine was an unspeakable tragedy that cost the lives of at least one and a half million civilians who, at the time, were British subjects. There is no doubt that elements of British wartime policy and the ineptitude of local authorities on the ground exacerbated the situation, but it is deeply naïve to singularly lay the blame for a complex food shortage at the feet of one man.

Some of Churchill's comments at the time have also led to the now much-repeated allegation that he was 'racist'. At a Cabinet meeting in September 1943 he stressed that 'Indians are not the only people who are starving in this war,' adding in an excessively jocular turn of phrase, '[the] starvation of anyhow underfed Bengalis is less serious than that of sturdy Greeks.'[4] In hindsight his remark can be viewed as that of a callous racist, but at the time the full extent of the famine was not known. Even then, a fortnight later, Churchill directly instructed authorities in India to take action, writing, 'The hard pressures of world-war have for the first time for many years brought conditions of scarcity, verging in some localities into actual famine, upon India. Every effort must be made, even by the diversion of shipping urgently needed for war purposes, to deal with local shortages.'[5] Churchill also displayed a genuine concern for the situation of the general populace in India, and the impact of poverty and the notorious cultural caste system: 'The contrast between wealth and poverty in India ... require searching re-examination ... No form of democratic Government can flourish in India while so many millions are by their birth excluded from those fundamental rights of equality between man and man, upon which all healthy human societies must stand.'[6] Another aspect seemingly deliberately ignored by Churchill's critics is the fact that there were political aspects to the difficulties encountered in aiding the situation in Bengal. As was later noted, '[the] shortage in Bengal was partly political in character, caused by Marawi supporters of Congress [Gandhi's party which sought Indian independence] in an effort to embarrass the existing Muslim Government of Bengal, the [British] Government of India and His Majesty's Government.'[7] Churchill was critical of plans for the mass repurposing of vessels carrying war material to Britain as grain shipments to India, but in the context of a conflict throughout which he emphasised at every turn the primacy of defeating the enemy above all other concerns. Reading through the memoranda for Cabinet from the time conveys the extent to which other pressing matters of war crowded out news of food shortages in India. The failure of the British government to mount an immediate, large-scale, sustained effort to alleviate the suffering in Bengal is a stain on Churchill's leadership. However, he did not wish to see British subjects starve. Whether more would have been done if Eden had been viceroy is a matter of conjecture.

Churchill and Eden in 1935. (Wikimedia Commons)

Churchill, Eden and Lloyd George discussed the 'threats of the two dictators' when they met for lunch on the Riviera in January 1938; pictured are Hitler and Mussolini together in Munich eight months later. (Bundesarchiv, Bild 183-H12940 / CC-BY-SA 3.0)

Anthony Eden chatting with U.S. Secretary of State Sumner Wells during his December 1938 trip to Washington. (Library of Congress, Prints & Photographs Division, photograph by Harris & Ewing, LC-DIG-hec-25569)

The formal portrait of Winston Churchill's coalition government in May 1940. Clement Attlee is pictured sitting between Eden and Churchill. (Wikimedia Commons)

Eden greets a lady officer in charge of nurses during a trip to Palestine in February 1940. Eden genuinely enjoyed the opportunities he had to meet service personnel. (Library of Congress, Prints & Photographs Division, LC-DIG-matpc-20130)

A gathering in the garden of 10 Downing Street following the signing of the Anglo-Soviet Treaty in May 1942. Russian Ambassador Maisky stands next to Churchill with Molotov on Maisky's right. (Department of Foreign Affairs and Trade, Australia, www.dfat.gov.au, CC BY 3.0 AU)

De Gaulle (centre) and Giraud (left) shake hands at Casablanca, 24 January 1943. Eden remarked that the slightly forced rapprochement was 'as good a result as could be expected from a shotgun wedding.' (FDR Presidential Library & Museum, https://www.flickr.com/photos/fdrlibrary/6311839881, CC BY 2.0)

Eden greets a smiling Roosevelt at the Quebec conference in August 1943. (Wikimedia Commons)

Churchill and Eden in summer suits at Quebec, 1943. (Wikimedia Commons)

Eisenhower with Churchill pictured on Christmas day in Tunis 1943, while Churchill was still recovering from his 'fever which has ripened into pneumonia' following the Tehran Conference. (Wikimedia Commons)

Churchill and Eden sit either side of De Gaulle at the Armistice Day parade in Paris, November 1944. (Wikimedia Commons)

Churchill preparing to disembark from HMS Ajax to go ashore in Athens for his and Eden's 'Greek Christmas', December 1944. (Wikimedia Commons)

The Yalta Conference, February 1945. The 'Big Three' sit in front of the foreign secretaries (left to right), Eden, Stettinius and Molotov. (Wikimedia Commons)

Churchill leaves Truman's residence at Potsdam following talks, with Eden behind. Following the election, Churchill and Eden's places at the conference were taken by Attlee and Bevin. (U.S. National Archives Records Administration, NAID 198765)

Clarissa and Anthony Eden, pictured together in 1952. (Wikimedia Commons)

President Truman gifts Churchill a signed photograph from the Potsdam conference during Churchill's 1952 visit. Churchill and Eden (pictured looking on) are on board the presidential yacht *Williamsburg*. (U.S. National Archives Records Administration, NAID 199024)

Churchill, Truman, Acheson and Eden in the salon of the presidential yacht.
(U.S. National Archives and Records Administration, NAID 199025)

Churchill shakes hands with Eisenhower during their trip to Washington in 1954. Eden and Dulles stand behind; to the right is Vice President Richard Nixon. (Library of Congress, Prints & Photographs Division, LC-DIG-ppmsca-51668)

Churchill and Eden after landing at Ottawa airport during a brief visit to Canada in June 1954. (Library and Archives Canada)

Eden, fists clenched, addresses the final plenary session of the Geneva Conference on Indochina, July 1954. (Wikimedia Commons)

Egyptian President Gamal Abdel Nasser announces the nationalisation of the Suez Canal on 26 July 1956. Churchill's response was, 'I think France and Britain ought to act together with vigour, and if necessary with arms.' (Wikimedia Commons)

The official monthly report provided for Cabinet in December 1944 on the Dominions and the colonies showed how the effects of war were being felt in Britain's far-flung territories. In Australia there was widespread industrial unrest and in November 1944 the government released more than 20,000 men from the army to bolster the number of industrial workers. Data compiled in October showed the average cost of living in the Union of South Africa increased by thirty percent in one month alone. It was not the only place struggling. In Ceylon (Sri Lanka), Crown ministers reported that since rice supplies had been 'cut off from Japanese occupied territories [Burma] and also from India this ration has stayed at the very level of 1lb per head per week.'[8] In response, ministers sanctioned the import of an additional 9,000 tonnes of rice per month.

The loss of Burma to the Japanese had been keenly felt, but the general picture in the wider Far East region demonstrated the increasing dominance of the United States. Britain's lack of involvement in the Far East battle particularly troubled Eden, who wrote to Churchill, 'If we are merely dragged along at the tail of the Americans in the Pacific, we shall get no credit whatever for our share in the joint operations ... the Americans are not anxious that we should play any notable part in the Pacific war. We want to make it plain to the world that we have played our part in regaining our Far-Eastern Empire.'[9] Above all, it was the recapture of Singapore that represented the restoration of British pride and prestige in the Far East. When Singapore fell in January 1942, accompanied by the surrender of tens of thousands of British, Australian and Indian troops, an angry and appalled Churchill described it as 'the worst disaster and the largest capitulation in British history.'[10] It affected him even months later; one night the prime minister was sat in the bathroom enveloped in a towel when he stopped drying himself and stared at the floor. He sadly told his doctor, 'I cannot get over Singapore.'[11]

By the end of 1944 the Americans had advanced as far as Leyte in the Philippines, while, further west, the British had secured a decisive victory against the Japanese at Imphal in the Indian state of Manipur, which ended the Japanese effort to invade India from Burma. The war in Burma, a campaign that has largely been forgotten in the annals of history, was to take on great personal significance for Eden. In December 1944 Eden's eldest son, Simon, was posted out to Burma with the RAF, having completed his flying training. The campaign was typified by extended jungle warfare, difficulties with supply and the multi-ethnic nature of the soldiers fighting under British colours. A significant level of prejudice against non-white soldiers still existed, even though British-Indian soldiers had fought bravely in the First World War and Ghurkha units in particular were legendary fighters. Supply by aircraft was a crucial part of the campaign's eventual success, but it meant that pilots had to navigate through monsoon weather and jungle-covered mountains at great risk. Eden, having come so close to an air disaster earlier in the war, was well aware of the perils his son was going to face. The fight for Burma was first and foremost a fight to secure India, but it became Britain's single largest contribution to the Far Eastern campaign. Singapore itself was not retaken until after the Japanese surrender in 1945.

The desire to cling on to empire also exercised the French. Churchill had initially vehemently opposed De Gaulle's request for the French to take part in clandestine operations in Indochina, telling Eden, 'The more the French can get their finger into the pie, the more trouble they will make in order to show they are not humiliated ... by the events through which they have passed. You will have de Gaullist intrigues there ... [Roosevelt] has been more outspoken to me on the subject than any other colonial matter, and I imagine it is one of his principal war aims to liberate Indochina from France.'[12] But following D-Day and the fall of Paris, Churchill's attitude softened and he permitted De Gaulle to send French soldiers, who went on to form the *Corps Expéditionnaire Français en Extrême-Orient* (French Far East Expeditionary Corps). The Americans were kept mostly informed of what was going on, but seemingly were not fully seized of the fact that the aim of the French mission was to guarantee Indochina was returned to France. In early 1945 Eden received a top secret communication from the political advisor to the South-East Asia Command which reported that the French operations were going 'satisfactorily', adding, 'In view of the President's [Roosevelt's] attitude, I feel it would be [prudent] to stop pressing for his decision [on the future of Indochina] at the risk of it being unfavourable.'[13] The hope was that, like Paris, when the liberating soldiers finally arrived they would be French and events on the ground would lead to the establishment of a French administration, regardless of the wishes of the American president. Eden was working not just to secure the future of the British Empire, but also to help the French retain what was left of theirs.

Chapter 25

A Greek Christmas

Not every country liberated from under the heel of the German jackboot was taking to its new-found freedom as comparatively easily as France. Greece had its De Gaulle figure in the form of the nationalist Georgios Papandreou, a silver-haired, fifty-six-year-old former minister, who headed a Greek government in exile in Egypt. It also had strongly Communist resistance movements operating within the country, along with the added complication of a monarch in exile in London. The future of the nation was an open one. Depending on how events played out following the departure of the German occupiers, Greece could have become a monarchy, a republican democracy, or a Communist state. The British supported a government headed by Papandreou, who they helped return to Athens after the Germans marched out in October 1944. The largest resistance group had meanwhile established its own administration in the areas it controlled. On 1 December Eden noted the situation in Greece was 'extremely precarious' because 'The Greek Government's authority extends at present only to Athens and Piraeus and the immediate neighbourhood. Of the rest of Greece the greater part is under E.A.M. [National Liberation Front] control.'[1] Churchill had a very clear idea of where Britain should stand, informing Eden, 'Having paid a heavy price to Russia for freedom of action in Greece [a reference to the 'percentages agreement' that gave Britain a ninety percent], we should not hesitate to use British troops to support the Royal Hellenic Government under M.Papandreou.'[2] The situation swiftly came to a head when Communist supporters clashed with police in Athens. Communist fighters ignored government orders to disarm and leave the capital and instead joined the fight. Papandreou wrote to Eden, 'Everything is degenerating … we must make up our minds whether we will assert our will by armed force, or clear out altogether.'[3] Churchill's response was swift and decisive. He ordered British troops to enter Athens and open fire on the Communists. In the following outbreak of fighting the British lost 169 men, with nearly 700 wounded.

Parliament and the country was, in Eden's words, 'confused and disturbed by events in Athens.' Parts of the British and American press were deeply critical. On 8 December a Labour member told the House, 'Today, on the sacred soil of Athens, in the shadow of the Acropolis, British soldiers and Greek patriots lie dead side by side, each with an Allied bullet in his heart, and I ask the Government to put an end immediately to this fratricidal strife.'[4] In reply, Eden stressed that Papandreou's government was 'the only constitutional Government there is,' but added that Britain really only wanted peaceful elections: 'We do not say this Government has to endure forever … it is our hope that at the earliest possible moment elections may be held.' Rumours circulated that Britain wanted to reinstall the king of Greece, a position King George VI was known to be in favour of, which made it impossible to properly deny, even when Eden secured an agreement from the Greek king that he would only return following a plebiscite in favour of him taking up the throne again. Eden proposed a regency as a temporary alternative, suggesting as the frontrunner a Greek Orthodox Archbishop. As Christmas approached, the Greek situation remained on a knife-edge.

Churchill's solution was action. He telephoned Eden at 5.30pm on Christmas Eve to tell him that the weather was good and they should leave for Greece that night. Eden had to miss his last Christmas with his son, Simon, before he deployed to Burma, writing bitterly in his diary, 'Hell. I was looking forward to [a] quiet family Christmas.'

Churchill and Eden landed at Kalamaki airfield on the afternoon of Christmas Day. The flight at least had been comfortable, as the prime ministerial plane was now a luxuriously fitted-out American-built C-54 Skymaster, which had bunks for many of the passengers and a dining salon. The additional comforts extended to the aircraft's facilities, although Churchill demanded during the flight that the electronically heated toilet seat in the bathroom be disconnected. On arrival, Eden and Churchill travelled to the port in armoured cars and transferred to a British cruiser that was anchored safely offshore. The following morning, Boxing Day, Churchill messaged Roosevelt, 'Anthony and I are going to see what we can do to square this Greek entanglement.'[5]

Churchill travelled by armoured car to visit the British Embassy and encourage the diplomatic staff, who had been holed up in the building surviving on army rations for the previous nine days. That afternoon he and Eden joined representatives from warring factions for a conference at the Greek Embassy. The meeting did not start until 6pm, and all the representatives had to endure the lack of heating, with the only light supplied by a few hurricane lamps. The Communist representatives arrived late and shabbily dressed, having argued with security guards over their wish to bring their weapons into the room. Churchill shook their hands and they took their seats around the table. The meeting was chaired by Archbishop Damaskinos, who cut an imposing figure in his flowing black robes in the dimly-lit room. Churchill was delighted to learn he had been a champion wrestler before becoming a man of the cloth and quickly warmed to Damaskinos, who he had initially claimed was 'both a quisling and a communist'. Churchill got proceedings underway with a speech, in which he said, 'Mr Eden and I have come all this way, though great battles are raging in Belgium and on the German frontier, to make this effort to rescue Greece … Whether Greece is a monarchy or a republic is a matter for Greeks and Greeks alone to decide. I wish you all that is good.'[6] Churchill and Eden then left the room and left them to it.

They repaired to the British Embassy, which at least had a few oil stoves for heating, where Churchill penned a letter to Clementine: 'We have had a fruitful day … The conference at the Greek Foreign Office was intensely dramatic. All those haggard Greek faces around the table, and the Archbishop with his enormous hat, making him, I should think, seven feet high … We have now left them together, as it was a Greek show. It may break up at any moment … At least we have done our best.'[7] The following day Churchill and Eden were told that the parties had agreed to the Archbishop as temporary regent who would form a government. Papandreou was the biggest loser, immediately being forced to resign. One faction of the Communists had remained intransigent. On 28 December Eden and Churchill flew back to London and spent almost the entirety of the following night in the company of the king of Greece, who was eventually persuaded to accept the situation on the ground and officially declare the Archbishop as regent. Communist opposition in Athens continued for a few weeks, before they conceded a truce, although a total of 90,000 British troops were deployed in the country to keep the peace.

Churchill gained a number of plaudits for his handling of the Greece situation, although the brutal reality is that the regency and administration that followed was little more than a sticking plaster for the divisions in Greek society, which would lead to a full-blown civil war in 1946. It may not have been articulated as such, but Churchill's rushed visit to Athens was primarily an effort to stop the Communists from taking power. As Churchill openly admitted to Eden, Britain had 'paid a price' to have a free hand in Greece. Four months before he hauled Eden away from his family hearth on Christmas Eve, Churchill had written to Roosevelt, 'The War Cabinet and Foreign Secretary are much concerned about what will happen in Athens … it seems very likely that EAM and the Communist extremists will attempt to seize the city … I do not expect you will relish more than I do the prospect of either chaos and street fighting or of a tyrannical Communist government being set up.'[8] Both Eden and Churchill were willing to accept the EAM as part of a broader government: Eden categorically stated to Churchill just before they departed for Athens that a broad-based Cabinet, including the EAM was what 'We desire … for the post-armistice period.'[9] But the events of Christmas 1944 demonstrated that as far as Churchill and Eden were concerned, Greece would not be permitted to turn Communist and Churchill was willing to deploy British soldiers to make sure. Officially, Stalin's Russia remained a wartime ally, but already Churchill and Eden were manoeuvring the pieces for an anticipated showdown between East and West.

Chapter 26

To Yalta

It was Churchill's idea: to get himself, Roosevelt and Stalin in a room to set the course of the world after the war. Uncle Joe agreed, but supposedly on the advice of his doctors insisted he could not travel outside of the Soviet Union and proposed meeting at the Black Sea port of Yalta on the Crimean Peninsula. It would necessitate Churchill and Eden travelling nearly 4,000 miles, while the ailing President Roosevelt would need to travel more than 6,000.

The whole idea of another meeting worried Eden, who recorded in his diary in January 1945, 'I am much worried that the whole business will be chaotic and nothing worthwhile settled, Stalin being the only one of the three who has a clear view of what he wants and is a tough negotiator.' Churchill was, he noted, 'all emotion in these matters', while Roosevelt was 'vague and jealous of others'. It did not auger well. Eden was also desperate not to have a repeat of Tehran, where there was a lack of a clear agenda and, crucially, no discussion between the Allies beforehand. He badgered Churchill until the prime minister asked Roosevelt to allow the foreign ministers to meet in advance. Even Churchill was aware that the short period of time planned for the conference was unlikely to be long enough. He messaged Roosevelt that a foreign ministers' meeting would be 'very useful', adding, 'I do not see any other way of realising our hopes about world organisation in five or six days. Even the Almighty took seven.'[1]

Eden had a fairly good idea of what he expected the Russians would want, which he sent in a note to Churchill the day before they left. Top of the list was 'recognition of the Lublin [Polish] Government.' He added, 'I want ... a free and independent Poland. Stalin has promised this to us, but he is not at present fulfilling his promise.'[2] He also expected some discussion over the Far East, but admitted that he had no idea what the Russians might desire in that area. The night before leaving, Eden

127

joined Churchill and Clementine to watch a film. It was 'a Californian colour fantasy with Deanna Durbin [the movie was *Can't Help Singing*, the only technicolour motion picture Durbin ever starred in]' and Eden noted, 'The scenery and sunshine did me good in our dark wartime London evening.' After the film ended, Churchill and Eden stayed up together and Churchill showed Eden a letter he had penned to the king, which outlined who should succeed them both if they were killed on the journey to Yalta. They joked together about what might happen back in Westminster in the event 'and came to the conclusion that on the whole our colleagues would lead much quieter lives.'

On the first leg, from Northolt aerodrome to Malta, Eden read a Somerset Maugham novel and arrived with a headache as the passengers had not been given oxygen on the comparatively high-altitude flight in the unpressurised cabin. Age and infirmity had finally caught up with Cordell Hull, who had been replaced as US Secretary of State. The new man was Edward Stettinius, a stocky, square-jawed, but amiable Chicagoan who made the cover of *Time* magazine on his appointment but was fired seven months later. Eden's discussions with the new appointee were helpful and he found they were on the same page, 'in agreement on all major points'. The positivity of the discussions with Stettinius lulled Eden into a false sense of security that was immediately shattered.

Roosevelt rendezvoused with Churchill and Eden in Malta on 2 February, arriving into the decked-out harbour aboard a US Navy cruiser as Spitfires flew overhead. The day before, Eden had been woken by the sound of Royal Navy bands noisily practising the *Star Spangled Banner*. Churchill, Eden and Roosevelt lunched together on 2 February, but Eden wrote afterwards that Roosevelt 'looked considerably older since Quebec; he gives the impression of failing powers.' Worse, Roosevelt was unpredictable in conversation and the lunch and then the dinner that evening finished with no plan of how the Allies would collectively approach the conference. As Eden recorded, it was an outcome that left he and Churchill feeling 'uneasy', but there was little they could do as all the parties left to fly to Crimea the following day. In all, 2,700 personnel made the trip from Malta, flying in twenty-five aircraft that took off at ten-minute intervals. The scale led one of the party to enquire whether the Russians might not think it was an invasion.

They landed at Saki and then had to drive eight hours to Yalta, which they found bathed in warm sunshine. The area had been occupied by the Germans until only ten months previously and was still visibly war-damaged. Once the leaders had been put up in the only palaces going, the rest of the delegation were mostly accommodated in houses, 'five or six people sleeping in a room, including high-ranking officers', with some even finding themselves sleeping on the floor in a local sanitorium. The Russians had gone to great lengths to renovate the palaces and install electricity and hot running water in the weeks leading up to the conference, but for many of the attached staff, the week they spent in Yalta was a rough one; a shortage of bathrooms led to long queues every morning. In their rush to import caviar and cover the walls in paintings, the Russians had neglected to even clean the palaces properly and Churchill and many others were plagued by bedbugs. At a quarter to eight on the first evening after their arrival, Churchill pulled Eden in for a chat and was in fine form, insisting he could easily do the eight-hour car journey again and 'make a speech at the end of it'. Eden simply wanted to go to bed. They both stayed in the same location, Vorontsov Palace, which had been built in the mid-nineteenth century for a Russian prince; one of the civil servants accompanying them described it in a letter home to his wife as 'a big house of indescribable ugliness – a sort of Gothic Balmoral – with all the furnishings of almost terrifying hideosity.'[3]

The conference opened the following afternoon and began painfully. The first session was taken up with each side updating the other on military progress and plans. At one point the conversation descended into a farcical episode of one-upmanship between Stalin, Churchill and the Allied generals. Stalin began by asking if the Allies had the reserves to exploit the success of their next planned offensive, adding that during the winter break-through on the front at Krakow the Soviet command had concentrated 9,000 tanks in the central sector. General Marshall replied that the Allied plan was to have one tank division for every three infantry divisions, at which point Churchill cut in to add that in the entire Western European theatre the Allies had 10,000 tanks. Stalin then stated that the Soviets had concentrated 9,000 planes during their offensive, to which the Chief of the Air Staff, Charles Portal, swiftly replied, 'The Allies had nearly as many planes, including 4,000 bombers, each of which was capable of carrying a bomb-load of from three to five tons.'[4] The first formal session closed with Churchill asking to discuss political questions the following day, particularly 'the future of Germany, if she had any'. Stalin agreed to the proposal, but replied that in his view Germany would have a future.

Dinner that evening was a dreary affair. Roosevelt was, Eden recorded, vague and seemingly very unwell, while Churchill had tried to 'get things going' by making long speeches. Stalin's attitude, meanwhile, was grim and sinister. Eden was particularly disappointed with Roosevelt's listlessness, noting 'Europe will take shape or break up while he stands by and it will be too late afterwards to complain of frontiers.'[5]

Roosevelt's ill-health at Yalta is a much talked about factor. It is frequently alleged to have been crucial in the resulting decisions, but Eden was adamant in his memoirs that it had no impact at all, writing, 'I do not believe that the President's declining health altered his judgement, although his handling of the Conference was less sure than it might have been.'[6] Stettinius himself wrote a violent defence of Roosevelt at Yalta, a book he claimed he was 'impelled' to pen from 'A deep respect of the memory of President Roosevelt and [an] unshaken faith in the rightness of his foreign policy.'[7] He asserted, 'I wish to emphasize that at all times from Malta through the Crimean Conference … I always found him [Roosevelt] to be mentally alert and fully capable of dealing with each situation as it developed.'[8] Eden had never been particularly impressed with Roosevelt's handling of foreign affairs and by insisting on health as a non-factor, chose in his memoirs to simply present Roosevelt as ineffective. Stettinius' devout defence of his former master's mental capacities, however, flies in the face of what actually unfolded at Yalta, which was that senior US staffers felt the need, wherever possible, to protect Roosevelt. During one session, Harry Hopkins told Eden, 'The President's not looking very well this afternoon.' Eden replied, 'Then we'd better adjourn now before we get into serious trouble,' which they immediately arranged. Churchill later admitted, 'at Yalta I noticed that the President was ailing. His captivating smile, his gay and charming manner, had not deserted him, but his face had a transparency, an air of purification, and often there was a far-away look in his eyes.'[9]

Whatever impact Roosevelt's failing body had on his mind, what followed at Yalta went on to be widely viewed as the moment Britain and the United States sacrificed the future of Europe to appease the Soviets. In the eight days of discussions at Yalta – the Allies did, as Churchill had prophesied, take slightly longer to formulate their agreement than the Almighty had to create the world – the conversations covered two areas that were of great import to Churchill and Eden: what to do with the territory of the Allies' empires and the future of Poland.

Chapter 27

'We have been deceived'

Each day of the Yalta Conference the 'Big Three' met at 4pm, prior to which were lunches and conversations between the different delegations, with the foreign secretaries meeting for discussions every morning. Outside of the orbit of the formal meetings there were informal, discussions, including between Roosevelt and Stalin, who took the opportunity of private meetings to outmanoeuvre Churchill and Eden.

When Churchill had set sail across the sea to secretly agree the Atlantic Charter with Roosevelt, he had perhaps not envisioned how the words would come back to haunt him. The Charter's third principle, that all people 'had the right to self-determination,' was one that Roosevelt and Churchill viewed very differently. To Roosevelt, it applied the world over. To Churchill, it did not apply to the territories of the British Empire. The planned role of the United Nations was to be as international arbiter and in discussions the foreign secretaries – Eden, Stettinius and Molotov – came to an arrangement. The five members of the UN Security Council would consult each other on the matter of trusteeships, but at Yalta no specifics were mentioned. Stettinius recorded, 'I explained [to Eden and Molotov] that the United States did not contemplate detailed discussions of particular islands or territories to be placed under international trusteeship.'[1] Eden agreed the principal, although claimed in his memoirs that he thought the 'wider applications' of the idea 'suspicious'. When the topic came up for discussion with the 'Big Three', Churchill took the idea considerably worse than Eden. He was livid and gave an impassioned, uninvited speech, declaring he would not consent 'to forty of fifty nations thrusting interfering fingers into the life's existence of the British Empire,' adding, 'After we have done our best to fight in this war and have done no crime to anyone I will have no suggestion that the British Empire is to be put into the dock and examined by everybody to see whether it is up to their standards.'[2]

Stalin applauded, while Roosevelt appeared embarrassed. Churchill was partially mollified by Stettinius, who insisted, 'We have had nothing in mind with reference to the British Empire.' However, the Americans very much did have in mind the French Empire.

In a private conversation with Stalin on 8 February, Roosevelt told the Soviet leader that he 'had in mind a trusteeship' for Indochina. Roosevelt was scathing of the British and told Stalin that they were anxious to rehabilitate France in Asia only because they were worried about Burma. The French, he added, had 'done nothing to help the natives' since taking over Indochina.[3]

Roosevelt went on to secure a private agreement with Stalin in which Russia would enter the war against Japan in exchange for territory lost in the war of 1904, a wafer-thin veneer of respectability for the territory-grabbing the president claimed to be so against. He only revealed the agreement to Churchill and Eden on the final day of the conference, at which point he asked Churchill and Eden to put their names to it. Eden was adamant they should not sign and the foreign secretary and prime minister got into an open argument in front of Roosevelt and Stalin. Churchill won out, insisting 'whether we like it or not, our authority in the Far East would suffer if we were not signatories, and therefore not parties to any further discussions.'[4]

When it came to the French, Roosevelt was completely dismissive. The French, and De Gaulle specifically, had not been invited to Yalta, although Eden had tried to secure their attendance, only to face rebuffs on all sides. They were, therefore, not even in the room when the proposal of a trusteeship for Indochina was discussed one afternoon. When it came up, Churchill vetoed the suggestion outright. At a later press conference Roosevelt claimed, 'Stalin liked the idea ... The British don't like it. It might bust up their empire.' The president added that Churchill was 'mid-Victorian on all things like that.'[5] Roosevelt was correct in his assertion. Churchill later noted that he opposed trusteeship in principle, as it 'might well be pressed upon nations like Britain, France, Holland and Belgium who have had great colonial possessions by the United States, Russia and China who have none.' Less than a month after Yalta the Japanese overthrew the Vichy French administration which had run Indochina under Japanese supervision. Some soldiers from the French administration resisted, and Churchill succeeded in arranging for them to receive ammunition and medical supplies from the US Air Force.

Churchill informed Roosevelt, 'It would look very bad in history if we failed to support isolated French forces ... or if we excluded the French from participation in our [future] councils as regards Indochina.'[6] Churchill at least had fully grasped that if France could be denuded of Indochina, then Britain's territories would be next.

What to do with Germany occupied a number of the sessions. Stalin had been pressing the question since Eden's visit to Moscow in December 1941, but finally the moment for discussion had arrived. The problem was that the Allies did not agree. Stalin and Roosevelt were both in favour of the complete 'dismemberment' of Germany into separate states, but Churchill was more cautious. Stalin also wanted to set it as part of the 'unconditional surrender' terms; his concern was that a united Germany would soon be strong enough to attack Russia again, and at one point he even felt the need to ask Churchill outright whether he would leave a Nazi government in power if it surrendered. Because Churchill had discussed and agreed in principal to the breaking up of Germany into separate states with Stalin when he had visited Moscow, Stalin successfully backed him into a corner. Roosevelt supported Stalin, insisting that dismemberment was an 'essential condition of surrender' and asked the other two, 'Should the Allies tell the Germans that Germany was to be dismembered?'[7] Churchill did not want to commit. In his view the Germans should be told to 'await our decision as to your future' and dismemberment, as determining the fate of eighty million people 'could not be decided in eighty minutes'. Harry Hopkins headed off a Churchillian outburst by passing a note to Roosevelt, proposing that the foreign ministers should devise a procedural approach to dismemberment the following day. The idea was agreed, but Stalin refused to let the issue lie. He continued to push Churchill, finally directly stating, 'I want it agreed (1) to dismember and (2) to put dismemberment in the surrender terms,' and afterwards waited for Churchill to respond. Churchill conceded that he would agree to the 'principle' only. The next day the issue became Eden's problem.

Eden sat down with Molotov and Stettinius on the morning of 6 February. Molotov wanted to agree a formal commitment to the dismemberment of Germany, while Eden, following Churchill's lead from the previous afternoon, wanted to agree as little as possible. Stettinius played at being moderator, suggesting that they could insert the word 'dismemberment' into the terms they planned to force Germany to agree to, while also stating that it would be necessary to conduct a study before any agreement could be made on implementation. Eden adopted the diplomat's approach of changing the wording, proposing 'measures for dissolution', which was entirely shut down by Molotov. In the end, Eden had no choice but to accept, as Churchill had done the previous evening. The foreign ministers ran out of time and afterwards shared what Stettinius claimed was an 'informal and friendly' luncheon in the sun room of Lividia Palace, looking out through the bay windows at the Black Sea. It was clear from the earliest days of the conference at Yalta that Churchill and Eden were unlikely to secure many concessions from the Russians, especially when Roosevelt was in Stalin's camp.

The other central issue at stake at Yalta was the future of Poland. Eden was desperate not to see Poland dragged into the Soviet orbit and had written to Churchill on the eve of the conference, 'The essential thing for us is that there should be an independent Poland. The danger is that Poland will ... to all intents and purposes [be] run by the Russians behind a Lublin [government] screen.'[8] A month before Yalta, the Soviets had recognised the Lublin Poles as the official government, suggesting that the best the London Poles could even hope for would be some form of involvement in the administration, given that Poland itself was increasingly under Russian control. Negotiations were difficult, as evidenced by the notes Eden made in his diary: 'February 6th: First talk over Poland. President and P.M. [Roosevelt and Churchill] were both good, but Stalin gave us a very dusty answer ... February 8th: Not such a good day. Stuck again over Poland ... February 9th: ... heavy day of little progress on Poland.'

Technically, the Polish question remained an open one, although the reality was anything but. The Russians had accepted and helped install the Lublin Government and Russian soldiers were inexorably advancing further and further into the country. Rather laughably, Lublin itself was west of the 1920 ceasefire line that had been so often debated as the post-war Polish-Russian border. Churchill's position was that he still accepted that line as the border of Poland, but he was now focused on democracy, not on demarcation lines. He insisted to Stalin that the Lublin government did not represent the will of the nation, to which Stalin retorted that they were as representative of the Polish people as De Gaulle was of the French. Roosevelt appeared tired and indifferent, and sought to end the meeting, muttering 'Poland has been a source of trouble for over 500 years,' and that 'coming from America,' he took 'a distant point of view of the Polish question.'[9] In another meeting he said the differences with the Russians were 'largely a matter of the use of words,' a position which Eden later wrote was 'deluding himself'. Churchill insisted that Britain had gone to war over Poland and that Britain wanted her to be 'mistress of her own house and captain of her own soul.'

The days and the debate dragged on and Stalin eventually agreed to monitored elections in Poland at the sixth session of discussions, which would decide who would govern the country. The joint communiqué issued after the conference called for the Polish government to be 'reorganised on a broader democratic basis' – effectively a weakening of former British support for the Polish London government – while also asserting that there would be 'free and unfettered elections as soon as possible'. Churchill seemed to accept Stalin's assurances, although in reality there were few alternative options. The decision about borders was postponed, to be decided upon at a later date, although in practice it had already been determined on the ground by advancing Russian troops. In a message that seems in hindsight to have been either deeply naïve or a product of a hangover from excessive caviar and vodka consumption, Churchill told Cabinet on his return that he was sure Stalin 'meant well to the world and to Poland'. Even during the Yalta conference Eden harboured no such delusions. It was the fulfilment of ominous words he had written almost exactly a year before: 'I confess to growing apprehension that Russia has vast aims and that these may include the domination of Eastern Europe and even the Mediterranean and the "Communising" of much that remains.' Perhaps Churchill was vainly hoping against his own premonition, which he had stated to Eden around the same time when he had despondently told his foreign secretary, 'I fear that a great evil may come upon the world … The Russians are drunk with victory and there is not a length they may not go to.'[10]

The Yalta conference ended on 11 February and produced an official joint communiqué that the Allies had coordinated plans for the defeat and future of Germany, had agreed to the creation of the United Nations, and a declaration on 'liberated Europe' that would protect all peoples the principles of the Atlantic Charter. At the same time they had settled their differences – as it was officially worded – over Poland. Entirely without sarcasm, that section of the communiqué stated that 'a new situation' had been created in Poland as a result of the 'liberation by the Red Army'.[11] The issue of the border was sidelined again, but an undefined 'Polish Provisional Government of National Unity' would hold 'free and unfettered elections' as soon as possible.

By 6 March the agreement struck with Stalin was irrelevant. The Russians ordered that only Moscow-nominated representatives would be permitted to be part of the Polish government and began rounding up priests and intellectuals: 200 were sent to Soviet labour camps by the end of the week. The moment when the Allied armies would meet was also drawing close, as Eisenhower's forces had crossed the Rhine. Eden gloomily recorded in his diary a few weeks later that there was little they could do to counter Russian control, 'Altogether, our foreign policy seems a sad wreck'. Churchill responded by sending a series of desperate telegrams to Roosevelt, including one that stated, 'we have been deceived and that well-known Communist technique is being applied behind closed doors in Poland.'[12] However, the prime minister's messages were not being read by Roosevelt in Washington, because the president was dying.

Chapter 28

The final act

Franklin Delano Roosevelt passed away on 12 April 1945. Churchill recorded that he felt 'a very painful and personal loss, quite apart from the ties of public action which bound us so closely together. I had a true affection for Franklin.' Eden had already planned a trip to San Francisco to attend the founding conference of the United Nations and became the British representative at the president's 'simple but moving ceremony' which followed the procession of Roosevelt's flag-draped coffin through the sombre, crowded streets of Washington.

After the service Mrs Roosevelt introduced Eden to Roosevelt's successor, the sixty-year-old vice president, Harry Truman. The seemingly mild-mannered, spectacled son of a Missouri farmer made a good first impression on Eden, who wrote to Churchill, 'I was struck by the [new] President's air of quiet confidence in himself.'[1] Churchill had wanted to instantly travel to the States following Roosevelt's death, but was eventually prevailed upon to stay in London and deal with a number of parliamentary commitments. He telegrammed Truman with his apologies, adding, 'I am looking forward earnestly to meeting with you at an early date. Meanwhile the Foreign Secretary knows the whole story of our joint affairs.'[2]

Truman's insight into events was, Eden conceded, rather limited and even Harry Hopkins quietly admitted to Eden during his visit that it would have been an error for Churchill to have visited Washington as he had first suggested. Truman, Hopkins said, 'knows absolutely nothing of world affairs, [and] would have been terrified'.[3] Truman did, however, know his own mind. As a young man he had been turned down for West Point because of his poor eyesight, which was so bad he should not have been allowed even to join the National Guard, although he learned the eye test by heart and managed to get in anyway, later captaining an artillery unit on the Western Front in the First World War. In his talk with Eden, the new president told the foreign secretary, 'I am here to make decisions, and whether they prove right or wrong I am going to take them.'

In Western Europe another decisive military man had taken a unilateral decision for which he would forever be condemned. In April Eisenhower ordered American forces not to drive directly for Berlin, but instead to loop south and focus on taking the Ruhr. Eisenhower had not even informed Montgomery or the British Chiefs of Staff. Churchill was livid at what he called 'the idea of neglecting Berlin and leaving it to the Russians' and personally cabled Eisenhower that the decision had 'important political bearing', which made it desirable to 'shake hands with the Russians as far to the East as possible.'[4] Eisenhower refused to budge. The power Churchill had exercised over military operations early on in the war now had become more of a meddling annoyance, especially where the Americans were concerned. Eisenhower told a colleague, 'The PM [Churchill] is increasingly vexatious. He imagines himself to be a military tactician.'[5] On 21 April Russian soldiers reached Berlin. It would take them nearly ten days to fight through the rubble of the city to raise the Red Banner over the Reichstag.

Churchill wrote to Eden on 4 May, 'I fear terrible things have happened during the Russian advance through Germany to the [river] Elbe.' He was right, but the horrors meted out by the Russians to German soldiers and civilians alike were worse than he could have imagined. Countless German soldiers who surrendered, particularly those from SS units, were simply murdered. Thousands of Germans, some of whom were known Nazis, others who simply feared what would happen to them, committed suicide. Figures are widely disputed, but in Berlin it has been estimated that 7,000 people took their lives in the final months of the war. Rape became not just a weapon of war but a form of collective punishment meted out to female members of the German population in the name of historical German crimes, or simply because men could. Helga Braunschweig, a nineteen-year-old from a village just outside of Berlin, cowered in a cellar with her mother and twenty other women. When they were discovered, the Russian soldiers first stripped them of their jewellery and then an officer selected women to be raped. Helga's mother offered herself instead, but her protestations were ignored and her teenage daughter was led upstairs to where a Russian had found a bed. Her experience was at least less violent than that of many others. A trail of looted homes, scorched earth and traumatised civilians followed the Soviets to Berlin.

Even approaching from the west, the ravages of war were visible for all to see. The Australian war correspondent Alan Moorehead wrote that it was 'almost beyond human comprehension. Around us fifty great cities lay in ruins … Many had no electric light or power or gas or running water … Like ants in an ant-heap the people scurried over the ruins.' On the map, the picture was a sinister one. The proposed lines of withdrawal of the Allied armies, according to the plans for 'zones of occupation', would leave a Russian frontier from Norway to Austria. A dispirited Churchill wrote to Eden, 'Thus the territories under Russian control would include the Baltic Provinces, all of Germany to the occupation line, all Czechoslovakia, a large part of Austria, the whole of Yugoslavia, Hungary, Roumania [*sic*], Bulgaria … This constitutes an event in the history of Europe to which there has been no parallel.'[6] The future of Eastern Europe was already mapped out. Churchill sent a final, direct appeal to Stalin over Poland, telling him, 'There is not much comfort in looking into a future where you and the countries you dominate, plus the Communist Parties in many other States, are all drawn up on one side, and those who rally to the English-speaking nations … on the other. It is quite obvious that their quarrel would tear the world to pieces … Even embarking on a long period of suspicions, of abuse and counter-abuse, and of opposing policies, would be a disaster hampering the great developments of world prosperity for the masses.'[7] Churchill's words were prescient. He would not live to see the end of the Cold War.

In late April Himmler had contacted the Allies via the Swedish government. He said that Hitler was gravely ill, or might be dead already – Hitler in fact shot himself a few days later – and Himmler offered to surrender the entire Western Front to Eisenhower. In a moment of final Allied unity, his offer was communicated to Stalin and then turned down. Churchill cabled the Soviet leader, 'There can be no question, as far as His Majesty's Government is concerned, of anything less than unconditional surrender simultaneously to the three major Powers. We consider Himmler should be told that German forces, either as individuals or in units, should everywhere surrender themselves to Allied troops or representatives on the spot.'[8] Elsewhere, unity was less in evidence. Although Eisenhower had not pursued a rush to Berlin, there was a push to beat the Russians to the German Baltic town of Lubeck, to ensure that Denmark and Norway did not end up in Soviet hands. Churchill recounted to Eden that Montgomery's forces made it to the city 'with twelve hours to spare'. He gleefully reported that Copenhagen had also been taken, concluding, 'I think therefore, having regard to the joyous feeling of the Danes and the abject submission and would-be-partisanship of the surrendered Huns, we shall head our Soviet friends off at this point too.'[9] Just over a week later, representatives of the German armed forces signed the declaration of unconditional surrender; Himmler was captured by the Russians while trying go into hiding, but managed to commit suicide by taking cyanide. Wednesday 8 May was declared Victory in Europe (VE) Day.

Churchill and Eden had been together when the war in Europe began, but were on opposite sides of the Atlantic when it ended. On 8 May Eden wrote to Churchill from San Francisco, where the UN founding conference was being held, 'All my thoughts are with you on this day ... It is you who have led, uplifted and inspired us though the worst days. Without you this day could not have been. I hate not to be with you.'[10] He received Churchill's reply the next day: 'Thank you so much for your charming telegram. Throughout you have been my mainstay.'[11]

On 13 May Churchill gave a radio broadcast to the nation from Downing Street. In contrast to the wild jubilation on the streets, he struck a sombre tone for much of the address. He admitted his concerns, albeit carefully phrased, about Soviet influence, telling the British people, 'On the continent of Europe we have yet to make sure ... that the words "freedom", "democracy" and "liberation" are not distorted from their true meaning ... There would be little use in punishing the Hitlerites for their crimes if law and justice did not rule, and if totalitarian or police governments were to take the place of German invaders.' Churchill's mind was already turning to new challenges ahead: 'I wish I could tell you tonight that all our toils and troubles are over. Then indeed I could end my five-years' service happily, and if you thought that you had had enough of me and that I ought to be put out to grass I would take it with the best of grace. But, on the contrary, I must warn you ... that there is still a lot to do.' His listeners would shortly be given the opportunity to pass their own verdict on Churchill and Eden's five years together. Great Britain was to have its first general election since peacetime.

Chapter 29

The worst form of government

Churchill and Eden tried to avoid an immediate general election. They made an offer to Attlee and the other Labour Cabinet members to continue the coalition until the defeat of Japan, but it was refused. The wartime parliament had stood unchanged for nearly a decade and the sentiment was that democracy should resume. Eden admitted in his diary, 'I never thought there was much chance of it [Labour accepting], though I very much want it.' In Churchill's words, as the end of the war loomed, 'Instead of being comrades-in-arms, we became rivals for power.'[1]

Throughout the war the coalition had been both a logical step and a powerful non-partisan statement of unity. But the end of hostilities in Europe witnessed the resumption of party politics. In May 1945 Churchill basked in an approval rating of eighty-three percent. The war in the West was won and his visionary leadership had guided Britain through its darkest hour. He assumed the vote would be a mere formality, telling the king, 'It is very likely that there will be a substantial Conservative majority in the new Parliament.'[2] The date of the election was decided as 5 July, although the requirement to collect and count the ballot papers of serving soldiers around the world would mean that the result would not be known until twenty days later.

The pending election once again prompted Eden to consider his own future. He recorded in his diary, 'Am beginning to seriously doubt whether I can take on F[oreign] O[ffice] work again. It is not work itself which I could not handle, but racket with Winston at all hours! He has to be headed off so many follies.' There was another potential option open to him. The conference in San Francisco had been a success for Eden. His diplomatic skills had played a significant part in laying the groundwork for the later establishment of the United Nations Charter, with one British representative reporting to the king 'the main credit goes to Anthony Eden … the new organisation is a very much better and more hopeful one than the League of Nations ... If the member states really mean to work it, it should be a considerable contribution to future peace.'[3] Multilateral conferences suited Eden's skills, and Labour leader Clement Attlee, who had accompanied Eden to San Francisco, reported to Churchill that Eden received 'a very fine reception at the Conference. His speech was excellent.' It was therefore a possibility that Eden could be offered the role of the first Secretary General of the UN, an idea that appealed both to him and his wife.

Ahead of the election, Beatrice returned from France where she had been assisting the running of a forces' canteen and also living with an American publisher. They had, Eden wrote in his diary, 'good talks' and came to an accommodation. If Eden remained in politics and there was a chance he would become prime minister she agreed to stay with him, but if that were not the case, or if he was offered the Secretary-Generalship, they would divorce. Eden was clearly still fond of her, privately recording, 'I hope that all will be well. She is very restless.' However, the couple's marriage had long been sustained more out of duty than reciprocal love. Even though Beatrice was in love with another man, she was still committed enough to Eden not to want to be the cause of scandal. They were spared having to hit the campaign trail together, as Eden was laid low with a flare-up of his duodenal ulcers and was confined to bed for much of the election campaign. It suited them both: Beatrice did not have to pretend to be enthused at the prospect of her husband remaining in politics and Eden did not have to pretend to enjoy elections. When presented with a collection of election campaign literature, he scrawled a note on the top page which read, 'Please keep all this muck together for me somewhere out of sight, until I have to splash into election manure.'[4]

Churchill launched himself into the electoral maelstrom with typical enthusiasm and campaigned vociferously against Labour's socialist policies. Attlee cleverly positioned Labour not against Churchill's wartime record, but against the pre-war government, which he painted as having presided over a period of mass unemployment and poverty. He pushed now-traditional socialist policies that at the time were a radical departure for British politics. They included a national health service, social security and the nationalisation of a number of key industries. Churchill's response was to lurch violently towards his own prejudices. In a profoundly ill-judged first radio address of the campaign, Churchill stated, 'My friends, I must tell you that a socialist policy is abhorrent to the British ideas of freedom. There can be no doubt that socialism is inseparably interwoven with totalitarianism and the abject worship of the State. No socialist government conducting the entire life and industry of the country could afford to allow free, sharp or violently worded expressions of public discontent. They would have to fall back on some form of Gestapo.' It was a watershed moment and harsh words aimed at Labour members who had been part of Churchill's war-winning coalition only a few weeks before. Labour was already ahead in a few early polls, but Churchill's 'Gestapo' remark was a gift. Attlee seized upon it as irrefutable proof that Churchill was not a peacetime leader.

Churchill was also distracted. On 1 June Truman informed him that Stalin was agreeable to another meeting of the 'Big Three' in Berlin around 15 July. Churchill tried to move the date, but was forced to concede and cabled the president, 'Although I am in the midst of a hotly contested election I would not consider my tasks here as comparable to a meeting between the three of us.'[5] Eden also had other matters on his mind. In late June he was informed that his son, Simon, serving as pilot in Burma, was missing. With an election result and the fate of Simon unknown, Churchill and Eden travelled to Berlin. The Potsdam Conference began on 17 July.

On arriving in Berlin the day before the conference started, Eden was struck by the damage to the Potsdam suburb caused by Allied bombing: '[The] Devastation of Potsdam [is] terrible and all this I am told in one raid of fifty minutes. What an hour of hell it must have been.' For the first time at a wartime conference, Beatrice travelled along with him. Eden was obviously affected by the strain he was under, having only partially recovered from his recent bout of illness to then receive the uncertain news about Simon. The election also loomed large and he confided in his diary, '[I am] Depressed and cannot help an unworthy hope that we may lose, or rather have lost this election.'

When Churchill reached Berlin he went straight to see Truman, who he had still not met in person. Churchill seemed desperate to make his own good impression. Unusually, he was 'on time to the dot' and Truman recorded in his own notes that evening, 'He is a most charming and a very clever person – meaning clever in the English not the Kentucky sense. He gave me a lot of hooey [nonsense] about how great my country is and how he liked Roosevelt and how he intended to like me etc etc.'[6] Truman did not warm immediately to Churchill's advances, perhaps seeing in

Churchill's instinctive pro-Americanism a whiff of insincerity. However, the two would go on to become friends; when Churchill sent Truman a signed copy of the first volume of his war memoirs three years later, Truman replied with a handwritten note that ended, 'thanks a million'.[7] At their first meeting Churchill was impressed with Truman's 'precise, sparkling manner and obvious power of decision.'[8] Truman also made a similar impression on Stalin, who he first met the following day. Stalin appeared with Molotov at the doorway of the room in which Truman was working and the surprised president got to his feet and advanced to shake hands with the Soviet leader. Truman said, 'I am no diplomat,' but added that he 'usually said yes or no to questions after hearing all the arguments.'[9] Stalin seemed pleased.

As they had at Yalta, the foreign ministers met in the morning and the 'Big Three' in the afternoon. The initial intention was to end discussions by 25 July, when Churchill, Eden and Attlee – who also attended the conference in an observatory role as a precaution – would have to return home for the general election results. A significant change to the feeling of the meetings was the presence of Truman, who was much more business-like than Roosevelt. Officially, Potsdam continued the work at Yalta to thrash out the position of post-war Europe, but was intended to settle matters permanently now that active hostilities had ended. A number of borders, including Germany's western border with Poland, were still undefined, but Eden discovered ahead of the conference that the issue of Poland itself had been entirely removed from the agenda. As with Yalta, Eden was concerned that Stalin would use the opportunity afforded by Potsdam to gain the upper hand. On the eve of the conference he wrote a memorandum to Churchill which stated, 'Russia tries to seize all that she can and she uses these meetings to grab as much as she can get.' He went on to outline further concerns over Russian policy, concluding, 'Forgive this sermon ... but reading through our briefs and documents again last night I am deeply concerned at the pattern of Russian policy, which becomes clearer as they become more brazen every day.'[10] A fortnight before the conference Truman had ordered Eisenhower to begin the process of withdrawing US troops to the pre-agreed zone of occupation in Germany, although Churchill had done his level best to stop it happening. He messaged Truman that he had 'profound misgivings' about any withdrawal, even to the agreed positions, which would have the effect of 'bringing Soviet power into the heart of Western Europe and the descent of an iron curtain between us and everything to the eastward.'[11] Truman gave the order regardless. On 18 July Churchill had a private dinner with Stalin in Berlin. The Soviet leader was positive about Churchill's election prospects, telling him he anticipated Churchill would win by a margin of around eighty seats, and at the same time reassured him that he was 'against Sovietisation' in central Europe and that the countries there would have free elections. It is unlikely either of them believed it.

The tripartite meetings at Potsdam produced further agreements on Germany. It was decided it would become a demilitarised state, but would still be required to pay reparations. The Allies also decided on how much of German territory would be given to Poland as the official compensation for the Poles' agreement to move the frontier with Russia back to the line that had been set in 1920: the fact that the only Poles who had agreed to it were the Lublin government was ignored. Potsdam was also the final nail in the coffin for the London Poles. Stalin told Truman that Russia had earned a friendly Poland 'by the blood of the Soviet people abundantly shed on the field of Poland in the name of the liberation of Poland,' and again pointed out that the Allies had recognised De Gaulle without any election.[12] Eden still pushed against any formal recognition of the 'Government of National Unity', which had been agreed at Yalta but would in practice mean recognition of the Lublin Poles. Despite his efforts, 'recognition' of the government on the ground in Poland was another of the outcomes of Potsdam.

On 20 July, in a break between meetings, Eden had returned to the villa in which he was staying and was working in the garden. A messenger arrived with the news that Simon had been confirmed killed. His plane had crashed; a Ghurkha patrol had found the burned-out wreckage on a mountainside. Among his personal affects that were later returned to the family was a copy of Shakespeare's *Henry V*; Simon had inherited his father's passion for the works of England's greatest playwright. Eden recorded that night, 'They have found his aircraft & him. Told poor B.[eatrice]. Life seems desperately empty.' Eden had now experienced the indescribable sadness of the death of two of his children. When Churchill found out the news he wept, tears streaming down his face. In a demonstration of incredible stoicism, Eden and Beatrice attended the evening dinner function that night as planned, with Eden requesting that none of the guests be informed of their personal tragedy. Afterwards he wrote a private letter to the parents of each of the other young men who had perished along with Simon.

Five days later the results of the general election were announced. Churchill, Eden and Attlee all returned home, although one of Eden's final notes at Yalta was to Attlee, after the Labour leader questioned the cost of maintaining Britain's overseas interests now that the war was won. In a comment that was a portent of what Eden would be remembered for by future generations, he told Attlee, 'You express the fear that we may run ourselves into an intolerable burden of defence expenditure by seeking to maintain our special interest in places like Gibraltar and the Suez Canal area. It does not seem to me, on the showing of this war which has proved them vital to our national existence, it is unrealistic to hold that we should continue to maintain our special position in these two areas.'[13] Churchill and Eden would never return to Berlin. Although Eden won his own seat with a strong majority, overall the Conservatives suffered a catastrophic loss and Labour won a landslide victory. It was one of the most shocking election results in British history. Eden drove from his constituency back to London through pouring rain. Arriving at Downing Street, he found that Churchill had already tendered his resignation to the king. That evening Eden ate dinner with Churchill, Clementine and the family. Churchill's youngest daughter recorded, 'everyone [was] trying to help and say the right thing', while Eden remembered, 'We did not speak much of the future, it hardly seemed possible. My own feeling was one of overwhelming sympathy for this man, to whom this country owed so much and for whom this was a devastating, and especially personal defeat.'[14]

Two days later Churchill chaired a final Cabinet meeting. Eden was on his way out of the door when Churchill called him back. They spent a quiet half hour together. Churchill told Eden that he did not feel any more reconciled to the result and that 'on the contrary, it hurt more, like a wound which becomes more painful after first shock.' He looked around the room and said to Eden, 'Thirty years of my life have been passed in this room. I shall never sit in it again. You will, but I shall not.'

PART THREE

Chapter 30

Licking wounds

Eden was aware of the incredible blow the election defeat inflicted on Churchill. He recorded in his diary on 1 August 1945, 'It is a staggering change of fortune from a week ago when at his nod came running secretaries to Chiefs of Staff and behind this was real power.' Churchill received letters of commiseration from his own party members and from around the world. The king wrote Churchill a personal note, stating, 'I was shocked at the result and I thought it most ungrateful to you personally after all your hard work for the people.' Throughout history, the leaders of democracies have had similar experiences, overnight finding themselves cast aside by the voters who previously elected them, suddenly discarded and powerless. For Churchill, however, the fall was even more acute. The criticism of his leadership in the summer of 1942 was largely predicated on the fact that Churchill led the executive in a decidedly presidential manner. A number of future prime ministers of the United Kingdom have done the same, but none have simultaneously had such a direct role in a conflict. Hitler was dead and the Germans had surrendered, but the war was still being fought against Japan, while the post-war settlement in Europe was still in flux. Nowhere was the instantaneous loss of influence clearer than at the Potsdam Conference. The precaution of taking Clement Attlee along to observe proved a wise one, as he now stepped into Churchill's shoes, while Eden was replaced as foreign secretary by Ernest Bevin. Truman described the election result as 'a shock' and was not enamoured with Churchill and Eden's replacements, writing to his daughter from Potsdam, 'I did like old Churchill ... and these two [Attlee and Bevin] are sourpusses.'

Eden was more sanguine than Churchill about his fall from power and the sudden changing of the guard. He wrote in his diary, 'I don't change my view that God takes care of England, and that, even in this it may later mysteriously so appear.' He enjoyed not having the worry of work and on a weekend in late August one friend described him as 'blooming with health' after spending several hours gardening followed by three strenuous sets of tennis. He had always gotten on well with his successor and when Bevin gave his first statement in the House as foreign secretary Eden responded kindly, adding that he 'represents a foreign policy on behalf of which he can speak for all parties in this country.' In fact, Bevin's foreign policy was so much of a continuation that it was later joked that Eden had simply 'grown fat', a reference to Bevin's more portly frame. Eden was still kept in the loop and was regularly in touch with Bevin. He suffered none of Churchill's isolation after having been wrenched from power. At the end of the Potsdam Conference Attlee wrote personally to Eden and assured him, 'We have, of course, been building on the work you did here and there has been no change of policy.'[1] Churchill's isolation was self-imposed to some degree – a few weeks after the result he fled the country to spend his time painting – but the brutal truth was that his manner meant that he was not the kind of man one invited to contribute to a discussion. Churchill invariably railroaded the room until he got his way.

Following the election defeat, Churchill's friend, Field Marshall Alexander, offered him the use of his villa on Lake Como in Italy, along with access to his own Dakota plane so Churchill could get there. In the first week of September Churchill wrote to Clementine, who had stayed behind to oversee extensive renovations that were being completed at Chartwell: 'We have had three lovely sunshine days, and I have two large canvases underway … An air of complete tranquillity and good humour pervades these beautiful lakes and valleys … There is not a sign to be seen in the countryside, the dwellings or the demeanour or appearance of the inhabitants which would suggest any violent events have been happening in the world.' The isolation seemed to do him good. He added, 'We have had no newspapers since I left England, and I no longer feel any keen desire to turn their pages. This is the first time for many years I have been completely out of the world … I feel a great sense of relief, which grows steadily.'[2]

While Churchill painted his way towards acceptance of the outcome of the election, Eden had already begun to rationalise why they had lost. He recorded, 'Before the campaign opened I thought Labour would quite likely win … But I never expected such a landslide as this,' adding, 'It was foolish to try to win on W.[inston]'s personality alone instead of on a programme.' The perception of Churchill as solely a wartime leader, which Attlee had so cleverly capitalised upon, was a weakness Eden acknowledged: 'Mr Churchill did not like to give his time to anything not exclusively concerned with the conduct of the war. This seemed to be a deep instinct in him and, even though it was part of his strength as a war leader, it could also be an embarrassment.'[3] Eden's final summation of the loss, which he confided in his diary a few days after the defeat, was that Attlee had been right: 'while there is much gratitude to W[inston] as war leader, there is not the same enthusiasm for him as P.M. of the peace. And who is to say that the British people were wrong in this?'

Before they had left Potsdam, Churchill and Eden had been informed of the first successful atomic bomb test; Churchill received the news through a coded message which read, 'Babies successfully born'. Throughout the war, Churchill and Eden had been told of the development of the research, which they only referred to under the innocuous codename 'Tube Alloys'. The day Churchill and Eden left Potsdam to return home for the election result was the day Truman gave the order for the bomb to be used on Japan. The president wrote in his diary, 'The target will be a purely military one and we will issue a warning statement asking the Japs to surrender and save lives. I'm sure they will not do that, but we will have given them the chance. It is certainly a good thing for the world that Hitler's crowd or Stalin's did not discover this atomic bomb. It seems to be the most terrible thing ever discovered, but it can be made the most useful.'[4] On 6 August the atom bomb was dropped on the Japanese city of Hiroshima. The final death toll from the blast itself and effects of radiation sickness has been calculated at 135,000 people, most of whom were civilians. Churchill later confided in a friend that he thought Truman should have used the bomb as a threat to deter the Russians and that he would have utilised it to initiate a 'show down' with Stalin, to make him 'behave reasonably and decently in Europe'.[5] A second bomb was dropped on the port of Nagasaki on 9 August. Japan surrendered five days later. Churchill invited a number of friends, including Eden, to dine together in a private room at Claridge's. Eden found it strange to hear Attlee announcing to the nation that the war was over: 'There was silence. Mr. Churchill had not been asked to say a word to the nation. We went home.'[6]

Even after the defeat Churchill was still leader of the opposition, although two key party members raised the question of Churchill's position with Eden in early August. 'Much discussion of leadership and W[inston]'s future. Edward [Halifax] has apparently thought that W[inston] would retire to write books, make only occasional great speeches and hand over leadership of the opposition to me. I told him this was not W[inston]'s idea at all.'

Churchill's ideas and actions were diverging, however. He spent nearly the whole of September on holiday, first at Lake Como and then elsewhere in the Mediterranean, and in practice it was Eden who took on most of the day-to-day leadership of the opposition, while Churchill travelled, painted, and started planning his war memoirs. At one meeting of backbenchers that Churchill did chair, an exasperated MP recorded that he 'seemed totally unprepared, indifferent and deaf'. The hard work to make the Conservative party electable again fell to Eden and other party members, while the Conservative leader increasingly only involved himself in matters that piqued his interest. As one of Eden's foremost biographers has noted, 'the more successfully the ground was laid for Conservative revival by Eden … the more certain it was that Churchill would delay his eventual retirement.'[7]

The turn of events again made Eden consider his own future. He was still attracted to the idea of becoming the Secretary General of the nascent United Nations, admitting to a friend that he was tempted because he would 'really care about the work'. 'I feel that I can do, perhaps, some good in UNO [the United Nations Organisation]; none, I think, here – Winston is very keen I should take it … though he may not know this himself … he would be relieved to see me settled elsewhere and then he would feel easier in his mind about keeping on the leadership of the Tory party as he clearly wants to do.'[8] It transpired that Eden was never offered the UN role, although he later wrote in his memoirs that he would have gladly accepted it. As the year 1946 began Eden found himself still shackled to Churchill, but neither were in government. They could only watch as the new reality of the post-war world unfolded.

Chapter 31

Old friends, new enemies

Much of Europe and the Far East was still shell-shocked from the war: cities remained shattered ruins and industries that had employed people before the war no longer existed; millions of husbands, brothers and sons would never return home, while many of those who had not fought on the front line had endured deprivation and bombardment. For soldiers who had survived, the process of demobilisation was not immediate, and in any event, the Allies had committed to occupying significant areas previously controlled by their enemies. The end of the war did not mean their immediate reunification with loved ones.

Politically, Great Britain now had the most openly socialist government in its history. It was enacting major domestic reforms, including the nationalisation of the coal and steel industries, but for all Churchill's dire warnings during the election campaign, Attlee was not turning out to be a Communist sympathiser. During his premiership he even harangued the more left-wing members of his own party in Parliament 'who shut their eyes to the absence of human rights when they look to Eastern Europe,' and in response to goading by Churchill, stated in the same speech that Stalin, 'should give up that idea that somehow or other this country is going to turn to Communism.'[1] The realities of Soviet occupation or satellite control in Europe were already beginning to become clear, but it would be Churchill who articulated them most memorably.

In January 1946 Churchill travelled to the US aboard the *Queen Elizabeth*, arriving in New York after giving an impromptu speech to a few hundred Canadian soldiers who were returning on the voyage. He travelled to Miami and holidayed for a few days, from where Clementine reported he had survived the scare of a high temperature by taking 'no remedies at all or several conflicting ones at the same time,' and had finally settled down and 'started two not very good pictures.' Truman lent him a plane for the duration of his trip in the States. Churchill caused some consternation in Conservative Party ranks by being absent for a by-election, but he was barely bothered by it. When asked for his criticism of the Attlee government by an American journalist, he sidestepped the question, but added, 'in my country, the people can do as they like, although it often happens later that they don't like what they have done.' After visiting Cuba he went to Washington at the start of March, briefly stopping by the White House on 4 March, before he and Truman boarded a train for Missouri. Churchill was about to give one of the most historic speeches of his life.

On the twenty-four-hour train ride west, Churchill and Truman played poker and Churchill completed the finishing touches to his address, which he showed to Truman. The president described it as 'admirable' and said it 'would make a stir'. It did. When Churchill spoke at Fulton he decried the rise of Communist parties in Eastern Europe, which he said was 'certainly not the Liberated Europe we fought to build up. Nor is it one which contains the essentials of permanent peace.' He spoke of his regard for his 'wartime comrade' Marshall Stalin, but asserted that he had to state the facts and utilised a turn of phrase that he had used in a message to Truman just prior to the Potsdam Conference: 'From Stettin in the Baltic to Trieste in the Adriatic, an iron curtain has descended … Warsaw, Berlin, Prague, Vienna, Budapest, Belgrade, Bucharest and Sofia … lie in what I must call the Soviet sphere, and all are subject … [to] an increasing measure of control from Moscow.' His most brutal assessment was reserved for the state of democracy: 'Police governments are prevailing in nearly every case, and so far, except in Czechoslovakia, there is no true democracy.' His conclusions were more nuanced than is often credited – he stated the Soviet Union did not want war and that what should be sought was a settlement – but he added, 'I am convinced there is nothing they [the Soviet Union] admire so much as strength, and there is nothing for which they have less respect for than weakness.'

Crucially, Churchill's words were spoken only a few short weeks after George F. Kennon, the US Chargé d'Affaires in Moscow, had dispatched his 'long telegram' to the State Department. In it, the diplomat asserted that the Soviets were 'impervious' to the logic of reason, but 'highly sensitive to [the] logic of force.'[2] It was an argument that the State Department agreed with and Truman himself embraced wholeheartedly. Churchill and Kennon between them articulated the theoretical basis for what would become known as the 'Truman Doctrine': a policy of 'containment', in which the US actively worked to counter the geopolitical spread of Communism.

At first, Churchill's speech was not widely praised. Several American newspapers – and even *The Times* in Britain – criticised it, with the *Chicago Sun* declaring that it was proposing 'world domination, through arms, by the United States and the British Empire.'[3] It proved so controversial that Truman himself gave a press conference in which he stated he had had no prior knowledge of the contents of Churchill's remarks, even though he had read through them on the train ride to Missouri. The decidedly mixed reception led Churchill to write to Attlee and Bevin defending his words. He told the men who had replaced him and Eden, 'Naturally I take complete and sole responsibility for what I said ... I am convinced that some show of strength and resisting power is necessary to [achieve] a good settlement with Russia. I predict that this will be the prevailing opinion in the United States in the near future.'[4]

Churchill eventually returned to London on 26 March, eighty-five days after he had left. Shortly after his return, he discussed the future leadership of the party with Eden. He explained that he had decided to continue as leader of the opposition 'for a while', but added that he wanted Eden to have freedom of action in his absence 'so as to make the formal transference, when it occurs, smooth and effectual.' On the face of it, Eden took it in good grace, replying, 'You can count on me to play my part,' but he was increasingly exasperated by Churchill's insistence on clinging on to the leading role and hogging the spotlight. He asserted that it was not the same as Churchill leaving him in charge when he had been Leader of the House and Churchill prime minister, pointedly telling Churchill in a hand-written note, 'It is only the leader of the opposition who can guide and father the party in the House, and take the day to day decisions. To do this he must be constantly in the House and in touch with the rank and file of the party.' Eden refrained from stating the obvious fact that Churchill had just been absent from the country for the better part of three months. His private comments were far less restrained. To a friend he confided, 'Oh God, I do wish the old man would go.'[5]

In spring 1946 Eden was already desperate to see Churchill hand over the leadership. However, for all Eden's professional frustration he still remained personally extremely close to Churchill. One of the liaisons that Eden engaged in following his agreement with Beatrice that the two would separate was with Dorothy Beatty; she was the wife of a Tory peer, who, on initially finding out about his wife's affair with the former foreign secretary and Deputy Leader of the Opposition, took the news surprisingly calmly, on the assumption it would lead to Eden granting him a position in the Shadow Cabinet if he stayed quiet. When no such advancement was forthcoming, the peer hired private detectives to watch his wife in order to acquire evidence for divorce proceedings. For Eden to appear as a named party in a divorce would likely have been a scandal that would have ruined his political career, and on discovering his lover was being watched he panicked. He appeared unannounced at Churchill's London home and told him, 'I must see you at once.' The two repaired to Churchill's study, where an agitated Eden explained his situation. Churchill took charge, gave his own address for correspondence with Eden's solicitor and an officer in the Coldstream Guards was persuaded to incriminate himself with the private detectives. The obliging soldier was later named in divorce proceedings instead of Eden. When it was all over, Churchill commented to one of his secretaries, 'Anthony must be more careful in future.'[6]

The year 1946 witnessed a key political moment in the history of the British Empire, as parliament moved to grant India dominion status, an act that would be the precursor to independence and partition into the separate nations of India and Pakistan the following year. In December Churchill spoke on the subject in the House. He acknowledged the march of history, 'There was, and there still is, a general measure of consent here and throughout the island to the final transference of power from the House of Commons to Indian hands.' But added, 'if it is to take place, [it] must be based upon the agreement and the co-operation of the principal masses and forces among the inhabitants of India. Only in this way could that transference take place without measureless bloodshed out there, and lasting discredit to our name in the world.'[7]

Violence between Hindus and Muslims was already breaking out across the country. Officially, 10,000 people had been killed since Jawarharlal Nehru's administration gained power in August, a situation Churchill contrasted with British rule: 'more people have lost their lives or have been wounded in India by violence since the interim Government under Mr Nehru was installed … than in the previous 90 years.' In his rather selective use of statistics, he neglected to mention the loss of life during the Bengal famine. But the violence was real and deadly. The most shocking took place in August 1946, when days of street clashes in Calcutta left at least 5,000 people dead, although some estimates put the number killed at more than twice that. The rioters used whatever they could get their hands on to attack the other side: 'Iron rods used in reinforced concrete building works were all stolen and sharpened at both ends,' stated one military report, 'and the butchery that these crude weapons did has got to be seen to be believed. Men, women and children were slaughtered by both sides indiscriminately.'[8] After the violence subsided, vultures crowded on the roofs and feasted on the corpses that littered the streets, and it was not until a nearly a week later that a British military recorded that most of the bodies had been 'cleaned up'. An Indian anthropologist who witnessed the appalling loss of life wrote to a friend in Delhi, 'The fear and distrust on both sides is intense. People are shifting from one quarter to another; but God knows if that is any solution.'[9]

Churchill had watched India's journey towards independence glumly over the preceding decades. His objection was not against democratic rule, but against Hindu rule, primarily because of the cultural caste system. Speaking at a meeting organised by the Indian Empire Society in 1931, Churchill had claimed, 'To abandon India to the rule of the Hindu would be cruel and wrong. The Hindus who talk about democratic principles are the same Hindus who discriminate against nearly 60 million of their fellow Indians whom they call Untouchables.'[10] In contrast, Churchill appeared to have a level of admiration for the Muslims who were in the minority and who he also claimed were discriminated against by Hindus. His view was unchanged fifteen years later when he stood to speak in the House on the granting of dominion status: 'We must not allow British troops or British officers in the Indian Army to become the agencies and instruments of enforcing caste Hindu domination upon the 90 million Muslims and the 60 million Untouchables.' Although Churchill insisted that 'British power in India, even in its sunset, [must not] be used in partisanship on either side,' he harboured a long-nurtured dislike of Gandhi and the entire Hindu independence movement and secretly kept in touch with the Indian Muslim leader, Mohammad Ali Jinnah. By the time Churchill was again in a position of power, British India had wrought itself into two separate nations, but he would forever hold the view that the manner of Britain's departure was a great embarrassment.

Eden was less reactionary to Indian independence, even though only a few years before he had contemplated the viceroyship. He described Churchill's speech as a lament, which he remarked 'did no good'.[11] As before, when Churchill had been in exile from government, he appeared to be becoming the prophet of doom and gloom: this time it was not European war with Hitler, but an escalating confrontation between the United States and Britain's former wartime ally, the Soviet Union. He also claimed to foresee bloodshed in independent India. In 1946 his messages still seemed melodramatic, but the events that unfolded in Europe and Asia the following year proved Churchill's premonitions to be correct.

The year ended on a sad note for Eden. In December he sailed to America aboard the *Queen Elizabeth*, accompanied by Beatrice and his youngest son, Nicholas. Beatrice did not return, finally deciding to permanently separate from Eden. Eden had had multiple affairs, but the separation seemed to affect him more greatly than it did her. He attempted to persuade her to make another go of their relationship, but Beatrice wrote to him from New York the following year, on Eden's fiftieth birthday: 'I find that I am still very happy in this fantastic country … I'm afraid I won't change my mind now – but I really do hope you find happiness, peace and contentment – I'm sure you will before too long – Anyway many many much happier returns of the day.'[12] Several years later Churchill lunched with Beatrice on a trip to the States and recorded, 'She seems as young and attractive as she was when I saw her last about ten years ago ... She says Anthony has no heart – she does not seem to have much herself.'[13]

Chapter 32

A changed world

The next three years witnessed a series of dramatic events which altered the political landscape in Europe, the Middle East and Asia: Mao swept to power in China; India, Pakistan and Burma became independent; British forces left Palestine, precipitating a war which created the state of Israel; and the Cold War in Europe escalated with the Soviet-backed coup in Czechoslovakia, the creation of the North Atlantic Treaty Organisation (NATO) and the beginnings of integration in Europe. It was a breathless three years of international events. And it began with one of the harshest European winters on record.

The winter of 1946-47 was bitterly cold across Europe. A fuel crisis in Britain led to electricity cuts in London of up to five hours a day, with the BBC even halting television broadcasting to conserve power. The government was forced to cut the meat ration and import whale meat and tinned 'snoek' fish, although both proved unpopular. Churchill and Eden led criticism of Attlee's administration in the Commons, pointing out how they had ample warning of the impending shortage of coal, which now meant there was not enough to fire electric power stations or heat homes. Eden delivered a number of searing short speeches in the House aimed at Labour ministers, pointing out that his own constituents were queuing up for their coal ration in the snow and then typically receiving only thirty percent of the allotted amount. The undercurrent beneath the entire debate was the fact that Labour had just nationalised the coal industry, a manifesto pledge during their 1945 election campaign, claiming that the socialist model of central control of critical industries would be better for the nation. It was the first of a number of domestic crises that shattered public confidence in Attlee's government. Churchill and Eden were as affected as everybody else by the brutal winter. The Churchill's London house was entirely heated by electricity and was, Clementine wrote, 'agonisingly cold'. When at home, Churchill mostly stayed in his bed, which he had moved closer to the window to get more natural light. Much of the population seem to have used the same method to keep warm, as the following year the country had its highest number of births since 1920.

The heavy snow that had blanketed the country thawed in the spring and by the time summer arrived, coal supplies were no longer the headline political issue. Eden was now living as a bachelor at the family home, although he had Nicholas for company when his son was not schooling at Eton. A friend who spent a weekend at Eden's home in the summer of 1947 recalled a pleasant day relaxing in the garden, but noted, 'his wife and Winston seem both to be worrying him. The former appears to have gone potty about some American who has now left her and gone back to his own wife – the latter is always being tiresome about one thing or another, and shows no sign of retiring from the active leadership of the party.'[1]

The violence of partition in India in August 1947 shocked even hardened observers. At a speech in Manchester later that year, Churchill was highly critical of the handover: 'Half the British soldiers kept in Palestine under conditions of intolerable provocation would, if they had been stationed in India, have enabled the transference of power and responsibility from British to Indian hands to have been made in a gradual and organised manner, and would have averted the slaughter of at least a quarter of a million Hindus and Muslims.'[2] For all the criticism of the situation in India and of independence in Burma, which Churchill said would 'cut Burma out of the Empire altogether, and make her a foreign power', Britain's foreign policy remained little different under Attlee and Bevin than it would likely have been under Churchill and Eden. At an extended debate on foreign affairs in January 1948, Churchill said that the Labour government had, on the whole, 'maintained a continuity in foreign policy,' adding 'We [himself and Eden] have, therefore tried to give them all possible help, and thus keep the foreign policy of Britain outside the area of party controversy.' However, he could not resist mentioning, 'I was much criticised on both sides of the Atlantic for the Fulton speech, but in almost every detail, and certainly in the spirit and in its moderation, what I there urged has now become the accepted policy of the English-speaking world.'

Eden's only real criticism was that Bevin's Foreign Office was not keeping in as regular contact with the Russians. During the war Eden had sat opposite Stalin and Molotov on multiple occasions and he viewed the deterioration in relations as something that weakened Britain's hand. He confided in a friend that Berlin was the 'danger point', but he did not think there was likely to be a war, although he admitted, 'the Russians might force us to seem to take the offensive.'[3] At heart, Eden was still a diplomat, his own summation in the Commons being that 'the only wholly satisfactory basis for international peace was close friendship and collaboration between the great Powers whose joint action brought victory on the battlefield ... That policy was pursued by the Coalition Government and by the so-called Caretaker Government, and I have no doubt it is being pursued with equal sincerity by the present Government ... [but] we have failed to realise it, and that failure to reach constructive Allied agreement has paralysed European recovery.'[4]

In the context of the poverty and ruin of much of Europe, which had been cruelly exposed in the winter of 1947, Eden therefore warmly welcomed the 1948 launch of the 'Marshall Plan', which ploughed American money into Western Europe to the tune of $13 billion. When Ernest Bevin contacted Eden for his views, Eden told his successor at the Foreign Office that he strongly favoured British support and participation. He was, however, wary of the new position which Truman's administration had rapidly and gladly adopted as both the protector and generous funder of democratic nations, noting, 'We cannot become the permanent pensioners of the United States. We have a role of our own to play as the heart and centre of a great Empire.'[5] A key part of that role was in Europe. In May 1948 the first Congress of Europe meeting was held in The Hague. Churchill spoke at the meeting and told the gathering, 'Europe has only to arise and stand in her own majesty, faithfulness and virtue, to confront all forms of tyranny, ancient or modern, Nazi or Communist.'

Churchill's affirmation of the Congress' ideals at its first meeting, and his earlier famous speech in 1946, in which he called for 'a kind of United States of Europe', has led to the widespread modern assumption that he was a complete Europhile. Ahead of the referendum on the United Kingdom's European Union membership in 2016, the *Guardian* newspaper carried the headline, 'Churchill would have been a committed voter to remain in EU'. Churchill was, in fact, ardently against federalism and both he and Eden saw Britain as having a unique but separate role in Europe. Following his speech at the first Congress meeting, Churchill asserted, 'The fact that we are not only a European power but at the heart and centre of a great empire is generally recognised and indeed welcomed ... there is not for us any European advantage which could justly be weighed in the balance against this free association with our kinsmen overseas.'[6] A few years later he explicitly articulated this position in a memorandum: 'I have never thought that Britain or the British Commonwealth should, either individually or collectively, become an integral part of a European Federation, and have never given the slightest support to the idea.' He powerfully concluded, 'Our first object is the unity and consolidation of the British Commonwealths and what is left of the former British Empire. Our second, the "fraternal association" of the English-speaking world; and third United Europe, to which we are a separate closely- and specially-related ally and friend.'[7] Eden was of the same mind. He also attended the first meeting in The Hague, where a friend who spoke to him recorded, 'He is very definitely not a federalist.'[8] Eden had always supported the defence of Europe, writing in a wartime paper, 'We have to accept our full share of responsibility for the future of Europe. If we fail to do that we shall have fought this war to no purpose,' but his internationalism did not automatically mean that he, any more than Churchill, thought Britain should join in with European political integration.[9]

Both Eden and Churchill strongly approved of the creation of NATO. For Churchill, NATO represented the outworking of the stance he had articulated in his speech at Fulton in 1946, which at the time had attracted such derision. After the signing of the NATO pact he stated, 'you have not only to convince the Soviet Government that you have superior force – that they are confronted by superior force – but that you are not restrained by any moral consideration, if the case arises, from using that force with complete material ruthlessness. And that is the greatest chance of peace.'[10] Eden retained his desire to keep diplomatic channels available, but was equally convinced of the new dynamic. In a note on Soviet policy written in October 1949, he stated, 'It is a challenge to our whole way of life, from the Elbe to San Francisco, from the Balkans to China. We must never forget this in anything we do.'[11]

China's Communist takeover was an event that Eden had partially predicted during his visit to Washington in 1943, when he had told Roosevelt that China 'might go through a revolution after the war'. Instead of a revolution, China endured a four-year civil war between

Chiang Kai-shek's nationalists and Communist forces led by a farmer's son named Mao Zedong. The Communists triumphed and Chiang Kai-shek, who had so impressed Eden when the pair met briefly during the war, established a government in exile in Taiwan. In October 1949 China became a Communist People's Republic.

Churchill was still sounding off on world events, but he was increasingly an isolated political figure within his own party, carried by his past reputation. He typically spent only three days a week in London, even when Parliament was in session, and dedicated most of his attention to his memoirs, of which several volumes had already been published. As one MP privately noted, 'WSC [Churchill] does not come near the House for several days, does not attend the Shadow Cabinet, does not know what line of conduct has been decided and then arrives to say that he is going to speak. Anthony [Eden] says that WSC has aged very much and is at times almost "gaga".'[12] Even Churchill's doctor admitted in a private letter to Eden, 'There is a change to him physically and beneath the forced Herculean efforts to work and the ubiquitous gaiety there are signs of acute strain and of general break up.'[13] Clementine took it upon herself to attempt to maintain his relationships within the party and organised dozens of lunches at their London home during which Churchill met with small numbers of backbenchers. She admitted to Churchill in a letter in March 1949 that it was 'a moment of doubt and discouragement among our followers'.[14] It was more than doubt. Key party figures were at the time reading opinion polls which suggested that the Conservative Party would be more favourably viewed by the electorate if it was led by Eden.

Chapter 33

The road back to power

Attlee's government called a general election for 23 February 1950, with Churchill still Conservative leader. Four and a half years on from Labour's shock triumph, which had ousted Churchill and Eden from government, Attlee was no longer viewed as the radical domestic figure he had once portrayed himself as. His government had presided over a currency crisis (triggered by the conditions imposed on a desperately needed loan secured from the US) and the subsequent official devaluation of sterling. Overnight, on September 1949, the value of the pound went from 4.03 to 2.8 US dollars. Although the devaluation was a sensible step to respond to a balance of payments crisis that accurately reflected the practically bankrupt post-war British economy, it was easier – as Churchill did – to paint it as '[the] result of four years government by the Socialist Party'. The narrative, from the coal shortages to the crash in the pound, was one which did not bode well for Labour's fortunes.

Eden had by now been MP in the same constituency for twenty-five years, but just before the February 1950 election his constituency was split in half, as Eden's previous one had grown to more than 80,000 voters. Eden had a choice between fighting for what looked a cast-iron safe seat, or one which party analysts forecast would return a narrow Conservative majority of around 2,000. Eden generously let a new MP contest the safer seat, opting to run in Warwick and Leamington. The Conservative candidate in the newly minted Stratford-on-Avon constituency was thirty-year-old John Profumo, who would famously go on to mire himself and his party in sexual scandal. The riskier seat turned out to be less risky for Eden, who won with a majority of nearly 9,000. Churchill's own campaign was enlivened by the widespread publication of a rumour in mid-February that he had died, which he put down swiftly by releasing a press statement which read, 'I am informed from many quarters that a rumour has been put about that I died this morning. This is quite untrue ... It would have been more artistic to keep this one for Polling Day.'¹ So it proved. The weather on 23 February was foul and the election was a disaster for Labour. The result left Attlee's government in power, but with a precarious majority of six.

There was widespread speculation that Labour's effectively unworkable majority would result in another election by the end of 1950. It did not happen, but the great gains for the Conservatives had fired Churchill with new optimism. He flung himself more passionately into his writing in an attempt to complete his war memoirs – he was now working on the final two of the six-volume set – cheerily remarking to his typist late one night, 'I know I am going to be Prime Minister again. I know it.'² Any suggestions of a leadership change in the Conservatives were temporarily put to bed. Once more, the drain of working with Churchill was weighing on Eden's mind, along with his old anxieties about politics in general. He admitted, 'It is impossible to tell how long this govt. will go on ... I cannot pretend that I enjoy it all ... Altogether I am weary of the endless publicity of political life ... But I suppose that there is no life in which one is more a prisoner than politics.'³ Attlee's government improbably clung on for over a year, with Churchill and Eden now waiting in the wings. Whenever the next election happened, it seemed certain the Conservatives would get a majority and they would be back in government.

In February 1951 Churchill diverged from his and Eden's previous position of wholeheartedly backing Attlee's government on foreign policy and laid into them on defence in a debate in Parliament. The government was proposing a new White Paper on defence, which Churchill wanted to use as a moment to force a vote on the motion that this House 'has no confidence in the ability of His Majesty's present Ministers to carry out an effective and consistent defence policy.' Churchill's hand was weakened by the fact that the Conservatives had initially supported the government's plans and were now committing a *volte face*, allegedly because planned expenditure had gone up. Churchill asserted, 'Evidences and examples of the ineptitude and incompetence of the Government are brought almost daily glaringly before us. We are convinced that the mismanagement exhibited in civil and domestic affairs extends also to the military field, and that that is the growing opinion of the nation.'⁴ The problem was that Churchill was now demanding a vote against a government proposal which he had previously supported and which at first glance seemed to comprise entirely necessary measures to increase the capacity of Britain's armed forces in the face of the new Cold War, which had turned 'hot' in Korea.

In June 1950 forces from the Soviet-backed Democratic People's Republic of North Korea had invaded South Korea. Truman sent US troops to support the South Koreans, who were joined by British soldiers as part of a United Nations' task force in August. By the time Churchill was criticising Attlee's government on defence early the following year, British soldiers were once again dying in battle, this time against Communists. Churchill had supported the government's action to join the Americans in the fight in Korea and this made his attempted dismantling of Labour's defence policy seem even more cynical. Eden was utterly unimpressed with Churchill's parliamentary manoeuvre, which led to an embarrassing defeat; the government won the no confidence vote by twenty-five, with six Liberal MPs joining Labour. 'Politically things are going well for us,' Eden wrote to his son, Nicholas, two days later, 'but I think we made a mistake to divide the House on defence this week. I tried to persuade W.[inston] of this before the event, but in vain. As a result we suffered our worst defeat, and gave [Ernest] Bevin an opportunity he used very well.'[5]

Churchill recovered from the misstep of forcing a vote of no confidence on defence issues and articulated his own thoughts on world affairs a month later, when he gave a radio broadcast after Ernest Bevin was forced to retire from his duties as Foreign Secretary because of illness (which would prove to be fatal). Churchill was mostly complimentary about Bevin – Eden too described his departures as 'a loss' – but struck a downbeat tone when he spoke of the situation the world now faced following the war: 'we thought we had won … [but] we are again in jeopardy … no home in the war-scarred democracies of Western Europe or in our own islands we have guarded so long, so well, or far across the Atlantic in mighty America – no household can have the feeling after a long day's faithful toil that they can go to sleep without the fear that something awful is moving toward them.'[6] The spectre of another world war was now discussed, even in Parliament. Churchill described it as 'a sad, sombre period of world history'.

When the political year wound to a close, Eden escaped to the United States during the summer recess, but it was a work trip rather than a holiday and he went to Los Angeles, Chicago and Colorado. His visit shared many similarities with his successful trips in 1938 and 1943 and again he was touted as a prime minister in waiting, with tickets for one dinner he spoke at in Chicago selling out, even though they were $100 each. He gave a well-received speech in Colorado, in which he revisited the theme of Britain's role in the world: 'The boundaries of British responsibility and influence may seem to have shrunk in recent years, but are they so changed after all?' He pointed out there were British troops in Korea, Hong Kong, Malaya, the Middle East, Austria and Trieste, adding, 'it is a salutary reminder … to those who underestimate our present endeavour.'[7] It was an ideal Eden would return to again and again: that Britain was still great and not a spent force on the world stage.

Churchill holidayed in Europe over the recess, making a trip to Venice by train. At one point he was hanging his head out of the carriage window only to be pulled back smartly by one of his bodyguards as a concrete pillar rushed past. It would probably have decapitated Churchill, who turned to his saviour and joked, 'Anthony Eden nearly got a new job then, didn't he?'[8] By the time both men were back in the country, Attlee had announced another election.

During the October 1951 election Eden took part in the first televised election broadcasts in history, in which spokesmen from each party had a pre-planned sympathetic interview followed by a moment to address the camera. At one point Eden's interviewer described the economic issues surrounding devaluation of the pound as 'too big for the man in the street to understand,' to which Eden responded, 'Put it this way: the pound which would buy twenty shillings worth when the Socialists came into office will buy about fourteen and sixpence today.'[9] It was a simple summary and it hit home. Eden ended his broadcast – for which he had dressed immaculately in a three-piece suit with a pocket handkerchief – speaking to camera on the international situation and addressing the voters directly. 'First of all, I'm not a defeatist,' he asserted, 'I'm convinced that peace can be preserved.' To achieve it, he told the voters three things were required: to strengthen the unity of the Commonwealth family, which he said was 'the only really successful experiment in international affairs there's ever been'; to maintain a close relationship with the United States, but not play 'second fiddle'; and to maintain 'unity across the Channel with our neighbours in Europe'. Fulfilment of those three objectives would enable 'negotiation with the nations behind the Iron Curtain.' He concluded by stating, 'I haven't the least doubt that Mr Churchill would endorse every single word of what I've said,' and lastly offered the electorate 'Opportunity and incentive at home, peace and stability abroad.'

Churchill did not do a television broadcast, but he did speak almost every day of the campaign and travelled up and down the country. Foreign affairs featured more prominently than had been expected, as the election coincided with a crisis in Iran and a rise in tensions in Egypt.

Iran was a crucial oil supplier to Britain. The British government retained a controlling stake in the Anglo-Persian Oil Company, which had secured a long-term agreement to exploit Iran's oil reserves during the First World War. The agreement itself had been negotiated by none other than Winston Churchill. At the end of the Second World War Iran's oil was being eyed up by both the Russians and the Americans, but a revised concession with the British remained in place, which granted them rights until 1993. The cosy exploitation of Iran's oil resources was abruptly ended in 1951, when an Iranian nationalist, Mohammed Mossadeq, became prime minister and the country's parliament voted to nationalise the Anglo-Persian Oil Company. At the end of September the British staff at the world's largest oil refinery in Abadan were ordered to leave the country within a week.

Attlee's tenuous grip on power and the level of agreement on foreign affairs between the government and opposition was demonstrated by the fact that Attlee called Churchill and Eden to Downing Street on the evening of 27 September to tell them the news from Iran. Churchill was typically bullish, telling Attlee that if he responded to the expulsion of British workers with force he would have Churchill and Eden's full support, regardless of the impending election. Attlee explored diplomatic channels and appealed to the United Nations at the same time as assembling a carrier strike force that could take control of Abadan, but his Cabinet backed down from military action. Suddenly, foreign policy was front and centre in the election. In a campaign address in Liverpool on 2 October, Churchill damned the response of the Attlee government to Mossadeq's action, which he said had exposed 'the will-power of the men in Whitehall,' who Mossadeq knew were only bluffing despite 'all their cruisers, frigates, destroyers, tank-landing craft, troops and paratroops, sent at such great expense.' He told his listeners, 'Presently it will be my duty and that of my trusted friend and deputy, Mr Anthony Eden, to unfold and expose the melancholy story of inadvertence, incompetence, indecision and final collapse, which has for six months marked the policy of our Socialist rulers.'[10]

Egypt was also in turmoil during the 1951 election. In a pattern that was to become increasingly familiar in countries across Britain's far-flung territories, the end of hostilities saw a rise in nationalist sentiment in Egypt, exacerbated by the presence of more than a million Allied soldiers in the country. Egypt had been granted independence in 1922, although the British retained control of military interests and foreign relations. Attlee and Bevin had struck an agreement in which they would evacuate all troops by the end of 1949, while retaining military personnel to guard the Suez Canal, but the plans were put on the back burner when Egypt joined other Arab states in going to war with Israel in 1948. A new proposal for an Allied Middle East Defence Command, in which British, US, French and Turkish soldiers would all help to provide security in Egypt, was flatly rejected by the Egyptian government on 15 October 1951. Violence and riots broke out in the Canal Zone the following day, with an unnamed spokesperson admitting to the Australian press, 'The Egyptian police, instead of trying to prevent this, actually helped the looters.'[11] The situation over the Suez Canal would come to be one of the dominant foreign policy issues of the coming years, but for now Churchill linked events in Egypt with Iran, telling his own constituents ahead of the vote that because of the 'major loss and disaster' in Iran, 'we must expect that Egypt will treat us more roughly still, and many other evils will come upon us in the near future unless the Ministers who have shown themselves to be utterly incapable are dismissed from power.'[12] At home and abroad the Labour government appeared to be presiding over a shambles.

Predictably, the Conservatives won the election. Overall they secured 321 seats to Labour's 295, with the Liberals holding only six. On 26 October Churchill travelled to Buckingham Palace to be received as prime minister for the second time. He immediately appointed Eden to the Foreign Office. Eden's new private secretary, Evelyn Shuckburgh, would go on to record the lowest points of Eden's political career, but his initial impressions of his new boss were very favourable. He noted in his diary, 'His return to office seemed to be everywhere greeted with delight and relief, as if a popular cricket captain had returned to the field.' The observation was apposite, except in one respect: Eden was not the captain, Churchill was.

PART FOUR

Chapter 34

Side by side

When Churchill became prime minister for the second time he was seventy-seven years old. Even Clementine admitted to a friend after the election victory, 'It will be up-hill work, but he has a willing and eager heart.' When Lord Ismay arrived at Churchill's London house the morning after the election to be offered the post of Secretary of State for Commonwealth Relations, he found Eden and a number of wartime colleagues busy working on draft policy in the dining room and remarked, 'The years rolled back. It was like old times.'[1] Churchill appeared to be going about his business as if it was a mere resumption of where they had left off in 1945 and initially took on the additional role of Minister of Defence, as he had during the war, although he was forced to hand it over five months later.

Eden found the Foreign Office workload even greater than it had been during wartime, in part as a result of the new institutions such as the NATO and the Council of Europe. Again, he found himself working before breakfast and into the early hours, but this time he was not able to commit to the same rigorous routine of exercise. His return to the role was welcomed by many. Before the election result was announced, an academic at Moscow University let slip to a British listening ear his predictions for the upcoming poll. The Conservatives, he stated, would be back in power with a small majority. At the suggestion that Eden would return to the Foreign Office, the professor said, 'There is a man we like. Mr Eden has been to Moscow and we understand him.'[2] Understanding was the order of the day in Churchill's first speech in Parliament referencing foreign affairs, which he gave on 6 November. He told the House, 'I and my right honourable friend the Foreign Secretary, who have acted in the closest, spontaneous accord in all these matters, still hold to the idea of a supreme effort to bridge the gulf between the two worlds, so that each can live its life, if not in friendship at least without the fear, the hatreds, and the frightful waste of the Cold War.'[3] The elusive idea of a Yalta-style summit that would put Churchill, Eden and Stalin in the same room again, this time to try and agree an easing of East-West tensions, was already formulating. For Churchill, it would become a preoccupation and another reason for him to cling to power.

Eden was once more struggling with his health. He seemed to live in genuine fear of flare-ups of his ulcers. Before giving a speech at a UN meeting in Paris in November, Eden got 'nervous' and in the middle of the night a doctor had to be fetched to give him an injection for a stomach spasm, which he had thought was a return of his painful ulcers. Eden's private secretary slept in the room next door during the trip and heard him groaning through the night, recording, 'It is discouraging that his health should be so bad.'[4]

One of the first notable events of Churchill and Eden's resumption of their former roles in government was a joint trip to the United States only nine weeks after the election. It was a watershed moment in the history of post-war Britain.

Churchill and Eden travelled from London to Southampton late on the evening of 29 December and boarded the *Queen Mary* for the transatlantic voyage. The ship was due to sail the following morning, but the captain and a sheepish-looking local Cunard representative made their way to Churchill's cabin to explain that the anchor was stuck and they would not depart for another twenty-four hours. Churchill was at first annoyed and then dispatched a rather exaggerated telegram to President Truman which read, 'The anchor is fouled. We cannot proceed.' They set sail the following day and ploughed through bad storms for most of the voyage. Churchill railed against the lack of newspapers and refused to read briefing notes from the accompanying civil servants, at one point exclaiming he was 'going to re-establish relations, not to transact business'.[5] In Churchill's mind he seemed to be reliving past voyages to meet and chat with Roosevelt, but both he and Eden would be sorely disappointed with how events unfolded once they crossed 'the pond'.

Much to the annoyance of five journalists who had booked on the passage to 'cover' the trip, Churchill barely left his cabin during the crossing, except to pop along the corridor to see Eden. Shuckburgh recorded, 'The most amusing thing was to see Winston in a very short silk dressing-gown with white knobbly legs sticking out below, and large beetroot head above, toddling down the passage to A[nthony].E.[den]'s stateroom for a morning talk.'[6] The delegation welcomed in the year 1952 in Churchill's suite, with Eden joining a crammed gathering drinking champagne and listening to the BBC on the radio. After the final chime of Big Ben, Churchill stood, champagne glass in hand, swaying slightly from the movement of the ship and the consumption of alcohol. He surprised everyone present by not giving a speech and instead raising his glass and simply toasting, 'God save the King'. For the final two days of sailing, the *Queen Mary* cleared the storms, arriving in New York on 5 January.

Churchill and Eden travelled straight to the airport and flew to Washington, dining that night with Truman aboard the Presidential yacht, *Williamsburg*. Churchill was in a jocular mood and during the dinner asked Lord Cherwell, a physicist and government scientific advisor who was along for the trip, to calculate 'how high a tide the combined total of alcoholic beverages he had consumed during his lifetime would make, if poured into the wardroom.'[7] Churchill was disappointed to learn, after Truman had found out the dimensions of the salon and Lord Cherwell had fetched his slide rule, that the party would only have been sloshing about up to their knees, but then the *Williamsburg* had a generously proportioned salon.

They talked together of the Soviet threat. Churchill said that since the end of the war 'they [the Soviets] had gained half of Europe and China without loss,' but praised Truman's decisiveness in intervening in Korea. In the following days, discussions moved to Truman's offices in the White House, which one member of the British party recorded were decorated 'in the worst possible taste … with the most frightful cartoons of Mr Truman and relics of his past political campaigns, and the main feature of his study – apart from the Stars and Stripes – is an enormous television set.'[8] Churchill continued his complimentary theme, and when discussion moved to the Middle East he insisted Britain's position in Egypt was one of international duty, not of imperialism, and asked for American support, which he also wanted to face down Mossadeq in Iran.

Churchill's complete disregard for his briefings left him exposed during a discussion on raw materials trade. Britain needed American-made steel and it was proposed to exchange it for tin and other metals, which were mined in parts of Africa and the Far East under British control. Churchill seized upon the notion of expanding copper production in Africa, where he said there was 'plenty', although Eden quietly stated that it was more complicated than it appeared. There were a number of occasions where Churchill was waxing lyrical and Truman cut him off, curtly stating, 'Thank you, Mr Prime Minister. We might pass that to be worked out by our advisers.'[9] Churchill's assertion that it was merely a visit to re-establish relations between friends was proving to be misguided. Truman rattled through the agenda with a disarming smile and played a good host, but increasingly it seemed the British were being entertained and little else.

For Eden, the visit shattered the hopes he had articulated in his widely-praised US visit the previous year, in which he had spoken of the abiding close relationship between the two nations. He later admitted that he had been 'forcibly struck' and 'horrified' at the way he and Churchill were treated. 'They [the Americans] are polite; listen to what we have to say, but make (on most issues) their own decisions.'[10] The new attitude was most obvious in US Secretary of State Dean Acheson. The Harvard law graduate had little regard for the high esteem in which Roosevelt had appeared to hold Churchill, remarking in later life, 'The qualities which produce the dogged, unbeatable courage of the British, personified at the time by Winston Churchill, can appear in other settings as stubbornness bordering on stupidity.'[11] Acheson was not diplomatic and made no secret of his own view that the world had changed and the sun had set on the British Empire, telling Eden's private secretary, 'You must learn to live in the world as it is.' Shuckburgh wrote in his diary that he thought it 'a very offensive remark, as no doubt it was meant to be.'[12] Eden and Acheson clashed repeatedly during the trip in January 1952 and forever after. As one observer noted, Acheson 'was a master of the brilliant, biting phrase, but Eden's assumption of Oxonian, Foreign Office superiority never faltered.'[13]

Shortly after Eden and Churchill returned, the situation in Egypt flared up again. Fighting erupted in Ismailia, which British troops put down using force, while violence and looting broke out in Cairo with known British institutions being targeted. While lambasting the Egyptian government, Eden also extended an olive branch: 'It is the aim of His Majesty's Government to reach agreement on arrangements for the adequate defence of the Canal Zone which would meet legitimate Egyptian aspirations. We fully accept that this is by no means exclusively an Anglo-Egyptian interest, but one in which we have an international responsibility.'[14] He again offered to negotiate with the Egyptians, asserting, 'I have always believed that it should be possible to find a solution of the differences between this country and Egypt.'

All considerations of the international situation were put on hold, however, on the morning of 6 February 1952, when it was announced that King George VI had died. Churchill was found that morning sitting in his bedroom, ignoring the newspapers, with tears in his eyes. Eden was almost equally moved. He had got to know the king well having been invited to Buckingham Palace on a number of occasions; although he considered his views on foreign affairs to often be preoccupied with the positions of other royals, a situation that had been obvious during the wartime Greek crisis, Eden had a genuine affection for him. In his public tribute Eden quoted his beloved Shakespeare: 'What infinite heart's ease must King's neglect that private men enjoy!' The succession passed to Princess Elizabeth, who at the time of the king's death was touring Kenya with her husband, Philip. She was twenty-six. Churchill's first response when it was suggested he would get on well with Elizabeth was to say 'he did not know her and she was only a child'.[15]

Churchill and Eden met the new queen the following day, when she landed at Heathrow airport. They waited alongside Clement Attlee on the tarmac as Elizabeth walked down the aircraft steps. Churchill was the first in line, black hat and stick in hand, Eden one along, his back straight, heels smartly together as if he were back in the military and on parade. The now iconic photograph of the young monarch descending to meet her heads of government stood side by side was later printed in *The Times*.

Chapter 35

Commitments

Eden's experience in Washington in January 1952 cemented in his mind the need for a new clarity of purpose in British foreign policy. In June he wrote a paper for the Cabinet on 'Britain's overseas obligations'. In the top-secret memorandum he assessed whether Britain's commitments could be reduced anywhere 'to bring them more in line with our available resources.'[1] He ruled out any reduction of the NATO commitment in Europe, as it would 'seriously compromise the Western policy of seeking peace from strength,' but when it came to the Middle East, and specifically Egypt, Eden admitted, 'it is clearly beyond the resources of the United Kingdom to assume the responsibility alone for the security of the Middle East. Our aim should be to make the whole of this area and in particular the [Suez] Canal Zone an area of international responsibility.' He exasperatedly noted that the Americans were refusing to commit any forces to the region or discuss a Middle East 'defence organisation', concluding, 'so long as there is no settlement with Egypt and no international defence organisation we are obliged to hold the fort alone.' Eden was much more a foreign policy realist than many of his critics have given him credit for. His paper ended with a statement which flies in the face of the claim that Eden never accepted Britain's change of role in world affairs, concluding, '[we] will only be successful with the United States in so far as we are able to demonstrate that we are making the maximum possible effort ourselves, and the more gradually and inconspicuously we can transfer the real burdens from our own to American shoulders, the less damage we shall do to our position and influence in the world.'

The dynamic of Eden and Churchill's working relationship was altered by the fact Britain was no longer at war, however much Churchill spoke of the 'Cold War'. In peacetime, as it officially was, responsibility for diplomacy resided squarely with the Foreign Office. An outgoing Labour minister remarked that Eden's political position was also stronger: 'Eden is certainly very established at the Foreign Office and need not tolerate interference from the Old Man.' Such sentiment would not prevent Churchill from putting his oar in, but it did strengthen Eden's hand to steer the Foreign Office more in his desired direction. That did not mean that Eden operated on his own, or did not consult with Churchill, as he still communicated almost every decision. In one typical exchange that year, after Eden met an Indian government representative, he passed on the notes of the meeting to Churchill. There were a number of revealing points, including the assertion by the Indian representative that Stalin did not want to start a third world war and was now 'an old man, and not a very fit one,' whose 'one ambition was to hand over the great position he had built up intact.' Churchill scrawled in the margin of the typed notes from Eden, 'I think this is true.'[2]

Churchill also still saw Eden as his right-hand man and when Eden was laid low for a few weeks with illness in the early summer of 1952, wrote to Clementine, 'Anthony's absence adds to my burdens. He has had a sharp dose of jaundice and has lost a stone and a half. His doctor wants him to rest for another week and I am pressing him to do so.'[3] When Eden returned at the start of August looking thin and frail, Churchill was concerned, but glad to have him back, noting, 'I have felt his absence very much.'

Events in Eden's personal life also tied them closer together. That summer Eden quietly married Churchill's niece, Clarissa. The two had met in 1936, when a teenage Clarissa recalled Eden wearing a matching tweed suit as a guest at a Churchill family gathering, but became friends in the late 1940s when she saw Eden at a number of parties and then began accompanying him on visits to London theatres and galleries. Their love grew out of a genuine friendship and Clarissa informed Clementine of their plans that summer in a letter: 'Anthony Eden and I want to get married as soon as possible now. I do so hope you will be pleased about this and give us your blessing. We have known each other for some time, and we decided a few months ago that we would like to be together for always. I am terribly happy about it, and only wonder and hope that I will prove capable of being some comfort and help to him in his life.'[4] Clarissa was twenty-three years younger than Eden, but their devoted marriage lasted the remainder of Eden's life. Churchill was delighted by the news and offered the couple 10 Downing Street as the venue for their wedding reception luncheon, which they accepted. They married on 14 August and in response to a telegram of thanks, Churchill replied to the newlyweds, 'We too have enjoyed it so much. All good luck. Winston and Clemmie.'[5] Privately, Churchill and Eden maintained a strong personal friendship despite all the travails of working together. Both seemed able to accomplish the not insignificant balancing act of largely separating their day-to-day frustrations from their personal warmth for each other, but the contention over the leadership remained.

In July a number of senior Conservatives, not including Eden, dispatched the Chief Whip to Number 10 to enquire if Churchill had set a date for his retirement, but he was sent away without an answer. The assumption within the Conservative party was that Churchill would hand over to Eden within a year, but Churchill often turned the succession into a joke. During a visit by Dean Acheson to London, Churchill, Eden and the Secretary of State dined at Downing Street. Churchill took the American over to the window and remarked that he was planning to have the poplar trees along the garden wall taken down, as they obscured the view of the Trooping of the Colour. The annual military parade takes place every year and had already happened in 1952; Churchill was teasing Eden by suggesting he would still be in Number 10 the following year. Eden protested at Churchill's suggested felling of the trees, to which Churchill replied, 'Why not? I live here don't I?' Eden pointed out that living there 'did not mean owning the place', but Churchill responded with mock sadness, 'Ah, I see what you mean. I'm only the life tenant.'[6] When Eden confronted Churchill on his retirement plans a few months later during a visit to Chequers, Churchill solemnly stated he intended to hand over authority with 'utmost smoothness and surety'. Eden replied. 'Yes, but the point was when would that be?', to which Churchill responded, 'Often I think there are things I could say … more easily if I were not Prime Minister.'[7] This was followed by a long silence.

Eden and Churchill's views were not entirely aligned on foreign policy, particularly over Egypt. Churchill did not appreciate Eden's insistence that Britain needed to organise a negotiated withdrawal from her position in Egypt, claiming that such action was an 'ignominious surrender of our responsibilities,' and a 'blow to British prestige throughout the Middle East'. He disregarded completely that under the terms of the 1936 treaty with Egypt, which at the time was still in force, all British troops stationed there would be required to leave by 1956 anyway. On one occasion he angrily exploded in private about Eden's plans, describing it as 'appeasement', adding that 'he never knew before that Munich was situated on the Nile.'[8] It was a cruel statement in the heat of the moment; Churchill seemed to have entirely forgotten that decades before, Eden had resigned as foreign secretary over Neville Chamberlain's attempts to appease Mussolini. At a Cabinet meeting in December, Churchill demanded a discussion on Egypt, even though it was not on the agenda. One of Eden's Cabinet colleagues passed him a commiseratory note, apologising for not saying anything to stem the verbal tide from Churchill, but ending, 'the whole Cabinet is with you save only the P.M.' Eden scribbled in reply, 'Nobody can ask me to go on like this.'[9] Eden subsequently backed up his position with a memo which stated, 'In the second half of the twentieth century we cannot hope to maintain our position in the Middle East by the methods of the last century. However little we like it, we must face that fact.'[10] Churchill simply did not want to, but was forced to concede in the face of strong Cabinet support for attempting negotiation. He later bitterly wrote to Eden that it left no alternative 'except a prolonged, humiliating scuttle before all the world without advantage, goodwill, or fidelity from those Egyptian usurpers to whom so much is being accorded.'[11]

Behind the scenes, Churchill continued to object to the Foreign Office policy and he was supported by senior civil servants at Number 10. Shuckburgh found himself enduring an uncomfortable half-hour one afternoon with private secretaries from Downing Street who all openly criticised Eden's policy on Egypt, which would 'be another stage in the policy of scuttle which began in India and ended at Abadan [Iran].'[12] Churchill then performed one of his swift changes of mind and decided that the eventual evacuation of the Canal Zone was a sensible military operation and started sending messages about it to the Americans. Eden was reportedly, 'half glad, half angry that he [Churchill] should thus be taking the matter out his hands.'[13] Despite Churchill coming round to the idea of eventually reducing Britain's commitment in Egypt, the Suez situation was destined to deteriorate.

The start of 1953 saw Churchill once more crossing the Atlantic. But there was to be a new occupant in the White House. Dwight D. Eisenhower had moved from war to politics and the former general had won a resounding victory for the Republicans in the November 1952 election. Churchill was again heading to Washington, this time by himself, in a single-handed effort to reignite the special relationship by meeting with the president-elect. Churchill sailed on the *Queen Mary* again and during his voyage he and Eden exchanged messages on the latest crisis in Britain's territories: the Mau Mau uprising in Kenya.

The uprising had started in 1952 and although it was far more complex than simply a revolt against British imperialism, it began with raids on the farms of white settlers and it was the murders of whites that attracted international attention. On 24 January 1953 a thirty-eight-year-old British doctor, his pregnant wife and their seven-year-old son were hacked to death by Mau Mau, along with their African employees. Churchill was sent news of their deaths while he was in the middle of the Atlantic. The uprising rent apart Kenyan society. Mau Mau targeted Africans whom they deemed to be supporting the British administration, while the brutal response from the British – which including detaining hundreds of thousands in camps – alienated Kenyans who had formerly been broadly sympathetic. The heightened violence and fear of an unidentifiable enemy led to a number of atrocities on the British side. Most were ignored, but one British captain who ordered a sixteen-year-old African private to cut off the ear of a Mau Mau suspect was court-martialled and the case led to calls for an inquiry. Churchill was only willing to sanction an investigation conducted by the army itself, writing, 'I am in favour of a military enquiry in closed court … I am opposed to such wide terms of refence as "the general conduct of the army in Kenya".'[14] He did, however, criticise the actions of the authorities in Kenya, later telling them, 'You must find someone [from the Mau Mau] to negotiate with,' and deploring 'the bad odour that the shootings, the brutalities and the detention camps gave Britain to the world.'[15] Sporadic violence continued until 1957 and a State of Emergency was in place in Kenya until 1960, but in 1953 Churchill and Eden faced more pressing problems elsewhere.

Churchill's trip to the US was, he insisted, unofficial. He held several meetings with Eisenhower and a number of his staff and found that, despite Eisenhower's military background and Republican politics, he was open to meeting Stalin. Churchill reported in a telegram to Eden, 'Eisenhower opened yesterday with much vigour about direct contacts with Stalin … He thought of making it plain in his inauguration speech that he would go to, say, Stockholm to meet him … Evidently he did not want Britain.'[16]

Eisenhower was cagey about taking on any new commitments and when Eden went on his own trip to visit the president a couple of months later he noted in his diary, 'General discussion of everything especially Egypt. Ike was very friendly but still rather vague on ideas and finds Winston's messages tiresome.' Afterwards, the president cabled him, stressing that the two nations of America and Britain 'must avoid the appearance of attempting to dominate the councils of the free world.' Eden replied, seemingly misunderstanding Eisenhower's word of caution: 'Together we cannot help wielding immense influence … I believe Egypt is the test case. If we can get a settlement there, which the world will see has been achieved by our united efforts, the benefits both in the Middle East and elsewhere will spread out like ripples in a pond.'[17] In reality, Eisenhower had no intention of shouldering any of the 'burdens' Eden had hoped to 'inconspicuously' pass to the Americans, particularly that of the security of the Suez Canal. He was less keen for the US to be the partner that Eden hoped for and Churchill desperately desired, writing in his diary that Churchill had 'an almost childlike faith that all of the answers are to be found merely in British-American partnership.' The president added, 'Much as I held Winston in my personal affection, and much as I admire him for his past accomplishments … I wish he would turn over the leadership.'[18]

Chapter 36

Frailties

In the eight years since Churchill and Eden had last seen him at the Potsdam conference in Berlin, Stalin had changed considerably. His health had deteriorated, while his paranoia had increased; when one doctor had suggested the seventy-three-year-old should rest more, Stalin had him arrested. He had become lonely and easily depressed, and often on an evening would summon a few politburo members to his *dacha* outside Moscow to keep him company into the small hours watching a movie and drinking together. Accounts of what happened following the night of 28 February 1953 differ slightly, but what is certain is that when Stalin collapsed in his bedroom his guards refused to go into the room, as they were under orders never to enter unless invited. When Stalin's unconscious figure was discovered sprawled across the carpet by a maid some twelve or more hours later, the terrified staff propped him up on a sofa and covered him in a blanket. Too scared to call a doctor, they instead summoned two senior party figures who thought Stalin seemed asleep. It was not until the next day that he was finally examined by a physician and found to have had a massive stroke. Stalin died a few days later.

Eden heard the news while travelling to America to meet Eisenhower: 'My mind was crowded with memories. I thought of an incident in my first meeting with Stalin in 1935, when at a point in our talks he walked across to a map of the world and pointed to Britain, remarking: "It is strange that so much should depend upon one small island." I remembered also the hours of discussion with Stalin in Moscow in the dark months of December 1941. The Germans were almost near enough for the sound of their guns to reach us … the scale of Stalin's achievement was stupendous, dwarfed only by its cost in human suffering.'[1]

For Churchill, the death of Stalin was an opportunity. Although Eden's view was that 'the permanent challenge of Communism transcends personalities,' Churchill saw Stalin's death as a moment for an East-West rapprochement. Stalin's successor was Georgy Malenkov, but the former Soviet foreign secretary Molotov had weathered the storms of multiple purges and remained in a senior position, which gave Churchill reason for optimism. He telegrammed Eisenhower, advocating a meeting, concluding, 'I have the feeling that we might both of us together or separately be called to account if no attempt was made to turn over a leaf ... I do not think I met Malenkov, but Anthony and I have done a lot of business with Molotov.'[2]

When Eden returned to London, he and Churchill discussed the matter. Churchill had been sparked into action by the news and was very optimistic that either he or Eden would soon find themselves across the table from the Soviets, telling Eden, 'If it is Mol[otov], you go, but if it is Mal[enkov], it's me.'[3] Eden managed to convince Churchill to agree to proceed carefully, but the following day when Eden telephoned him, he did not remember their discussion. 'He had entirely forgotten yesterday's conversation', Eden wrote in his diary. 'I went over it again with him carefully and he appeared to agree and begin to recollect. However his telegram to Ike [Eisenhower] ... showed that he hadn't really understood.' It was not simply obstinacy on Churchill's part. Increasingly, he was becoming more difficult to work with. He was hard of hearing and struggled to work through the same amount of papers as he had in his first term in office. Churchill's secretary recorded, 'The bright and sparkling intervals still come, and they are still unequalled, but age is beginning to show.'[4]

In April 1953, with Churchill's powers now more obviously waning, Eden's health deteriorated. His stomach pains had worsened and an X-ray revealed he had serious gallstones. He was rushed in for surgery. In his memoirs Eden succinctly stated, 'the operation did not go well,' although his typically English understatement glossed over the fact that he was lucky to survive at all. In an expression of concern that did far more harm than good, Churchill personally messaged the hospital to remind the staff of the eminence of the patient who was going under the knife. The pressure had such an effect that, after Eden was put under anaesthetic, the senior surgeon had to spend an hour calming himself before his nerves were in a state for him to operate. Eden lost considerable amounts of blood, and during the investigation of his gallbladder, his bile duct was accidentally severed, a mistake that guaranteed he would have problems with infection and inflammation for the rest of his life.

A second operation had to be carried out, as the surgeons had only been able to patch up Eden's bile duct in the first operation. Eden again came close to death and the surgery only provided a partial fix. His future career, and potentially even his life, was saved by the fact that an American surgeon and renowned gallbladder expert happened to be attending a conference in London at the time of Eden's operation. Dr Richard Cattell immediately offered to operate on Eden, but explained that his chances of success would be better if the surgery was undertaken in his own hospital in Boston. Eden agreed to travel for a third operation, writing later, 'Despite some protests, I do not consider that medicine or the arts have national frontiers.' Churchill arranged for the Conservative Party to cover the costs of Eden's chartered flight, operation and convalescence.

While Eden was out of action Churchill took over again at the Foreign Office, just as he had done when Eden was unwell during the war. One of his first acts was to make a speech in Parliament on foreign policy, having not informed the Foreign Office or the Cabinet in advance. His sweeping assessment of events in the world was sobering. The Korean War, which had started three years previously, appeared to be headed for a truce, with neither side able to achieve a decisive breakthrough. The impasse in ceasefire negotiations he blamed entirely on Russian-backed North Korea: 'It is obvious that, if at any time, there is a wish among the Communists to reach an agreement as between rational human beings, the matter could be instantly, or almost instantly, settled.'[5]

Churchill was similarly critical of the Egyptian government, which had been taken over by a general who had forced the abdication of the king; the monarchy had been installed in power by the British some thirty years previously. Churchill noted, 'There has followed a period of tension in Egypt during which the new dictator and his comrades have found it convenient, or necessary, to gain as much popularity as possible by the well-known process of "taking it out of the British", which included a resurgence of small acts of violence.' The Egyptians themselves had sought to open a negotiation over a British departure a few weeks previously and then had promptly walked out of the talks. Having initially brutally criticised Eden's position on Egypt, Churchill was now, publicly, squarely behind it and told the House, 'Naturally, we do not wish to keep indefinitely 80,000 men at a cost of, it might be, over £50 million a year discharging the duty which has largely fallen upon us, and us alone, of safeguarding the interests of the free nations in the

Middle East, and also of preserving the international waterway of the Suez Canal.' But in spring 1953, the situation was at an impasse.

In Europe, Germany was divided between East and West, with the Soviet-controlled side enduring what Churchill described as 'great misery and depression'. For this, he openly blamed the US for prematurely withdrawing forces to the 'zones of occupation' in 1945 after Germany had been defeated, 'If our advice had been taken by the United States after the Armistice with Germany, the Western allies would not have withdrawn from the front line which their armies had reached ... Our view was not accepted and a wide area of Germany was handed over to Soviet occupation.' In part, Churchill was blaming Eisenhower, the man who had been in overall command of Allied forces at the time and who was now in the White House. Churchill had not discussed any of what he was planning to say beforehand with the new president either.

Churchill concluded his world survey with a suggestion that 'in spite of all the uncertainties and confusion in which world affairs are plunged, I believe that a conference on the highest level should take place between the leading Powers without long delay ... At the worst the participants in the meeting would have established more intimate contacts. At the best we might have a generation of peace.' Private discussions about a potential meeting between the Americans, the British and the Soviets were one thing, declaring it before the world from the platform of Parliament was another entirely, especially as Churchill had warned no one in advance. Eden was appalled and angry and thought Churchill's statement was a major miscalculation. He bitterly recorded months later in his diary, 'It must be long in history since any one speech did so much damage to its own side.'

On 28 May, when a friend asked Churchill 'how he was weathering the storm', he replied, 'I'm getting older. I miss Anthony. He's going to Boston on the 5th of June in a special Canadian aircraft for his operation. Poor fellow.'[6] Churchill and Clementine personally went to see Eden's plane off, although the timing of his surgery meant that he was absent for the coronation of Queen Elizabeth, which he deeply regretted. The operation in Boston was incredibly risky: the British Ambassador was informed that there was a fifty-fifty chance Eden would die on the table and at least one newspaper in England prepared his obituary.

Despite the odds, the eight-hour surgery was largely successful, although Eden would never make a full recovery. He was convalescing at a hotel on Rhode Island on 26 June, when he received deeply disturbing news. The letter from Churchill's Principal Private Secretary was officially addressed to Clarissa Eden, but clearly intended for her husband. It began, 'Last Tuesday the P.M. gave a dinner party for De Gaspari [the Italian Prime Minister] (one of those dreary Government hospitality affairs, at which for once the food was surprisingly good!). He made a little speech at the end in his very best style and humour and left the dining room … suddenly, due as we now know it to an arterial clot, he lost control of his legs and his articulation became slurred and indistinct … We got rid of the guests as fast as we could and more or less helped him to bed.'[7] Winston Churchill had had a serious stroke. Initially, he had seemed to partially recover and insisted on chairing Cabinet the following morning (24 June), where 'his mouth was drooping badly and he found it difficult to use his left arm'. Remarkably, few of the Cabinet noticed anything amiss. He was confined to bed and reflectively told his doctor, 'I have stretched out my hand to grasp the paw of the Russian bear. Great things seemed within my grasp.'[8] Under doctor's orders, Churchill went to Chartwell to rest while civil servants scrambled to deal with the possibility of the imminent death of the prime minister and the potential death of his anointed successor; Eden at that precise moment was still under anaesthetic and being operated on. Eden did not die on the table, but he was still in no physical condition to take on the leadership if Churchill deteriorated. In reply to the letter informing him of the details of the stroke, he wrote, 'If all goes normally with convalescence, as so far it has, I should be fit … in October … I am so sad that this should have happened in this way and at this time, and I feel a horrible guilt that FO work must have, of course, added to PM's burdens these months. It is when something like this happens that one realises how wide the Atlantic is. We feel very far away.'[9]

A frail Eden returned from Boston and saw Churchill at Chequers on 26 July. Churchill's condition had improved dramatically, but for several days he had been partially paralysed and confined to a wheelchair. He was already back working, however, and seemed once more intent on carrying on as prime minister. In Eden's absence he had continued to foster the idea of a summit between America, Britain and the Soviets and it became his rationale for holding on to the leadership. Eden still disagreed with the whole idea, leading Churchill's secretary to note that his attitude 'depressed' Churchill, 'because he thinks it consigns us to years of more hatred and hostility.'[10] Eden meanwhile was still not well enough to return to work and spent the early autumn recovering on a Mediterranean cruise. He received lots of letters from colleagues, some encouraging him to come home to cement his position as successor, which, he noted, he found 'troublesome,' adding 'I don't want to. I cannot feel it to be really necessary, though this may be due to my lack of enthusiasm for politics which remains constant.' Eden had often talked of retirement or a change of station, but he never seemed to be able to summon the courage to step out of Churchill's shadow and away from politics, even when presented with opportunities to do so; Clarissa had suggested prior to his being taken ill that he retire at the coronation. Perhaps through a sense of duty, or still quietly harboured ambition, Eden returned to work in October 1953.

During Eden's absence, momentous events had taken place in the Middle East. The Abadan oil refinery crisis in Iran, which had defined the 1951 election campaign, had ended embarrassingly for Britain with the expulsion of British oil workers who were shortly afterwards followed by British diplomats. Churchill and Eden arrived back in office too late to do anything, but the insult festered. Instead of the military action Churchill had told Attlee he and Eden would have 'fully supported', attention moved to covert operations while formal attempts at a compromise solution were offered and then rejected by Tehran. In November 1952 the Assistant Secretary to the Department of State in Washington noted in writing, 'The British Foreign Office has informed us that it would be disposed to bring about a coup d'état in Iran, replacing the Mossadeq Government by one which would be more "reliable", if the American Government agreed to cooperate.'[11] The Truman administration had slapped down the proposals, but Eisenhower's State Department was a more willing ally, especially when it was suggested Iran might fall to the Soviets; Eden personally held meetings with State Department officials, who he persuaded that the Iranian leader was a 'source of instability'.[12]

In August 1953, while Eden was on his sick bed, the CIA orchestrated protests in Tehran. The chaos did not go entirely as planned but the end result was still the downfall of Mossadeq's government. The CIA field officer who choreographed the coup stopped by in London on his way back to Washington. Churchill was still recovering from his stroke and the spy was ushered into the prime minister's bedroom. Churchill reportedly dozed off a few times during the narrative but was alert enough by the end to allegedly tell the spy, 'Young man, if I had been but a few years younger, I would have loved nothing better than to have served under your command in this great venture.'[13] Churchill then dispatched a message to Iran's new military leader, congratulating him on 'coming to the rescue of your ancient land and preserving its constitutional monarchy.' He added, 'You may be sure that Britain will welcome the revival of our centuries old friendship. We ought to be able to find ways of helping each other'.[14] Eden arrived back to work that autumn in time to witness the Anglo-Iranian Oil Company resume operations in Iran.

Eden's first act was to meet with Churchill at Downing Street. Eden asked Churchill about his 'plans', to which Churchill replied that he wanted to see if he was able to cope with the upcoming Conservative Party conference and to then speak in the House of Commons. They dined together that night with a few colleagues. Eden wrote in his diary it was a 'depressing evening'. Churchill did not appreciate Eden's 'lack of enthusiasm' for his foreign policy speech in May, but Eden noted, 'I had to make it clear that I did not regard four power talks at the highest level as a panacea. He maintained that in the war it was only the Stalin Roosevelt Churchill meetings that had made our Foreign Secretaries' work possible. I said this was not so.' On his very first day back in the job, the old contentions had resurfaced: Churchill had no plans to hand over to Eden in the immediate future and had now found a quasi-legitimate reason to refuse to step down. As Eden's private secretary unsympathetically phrased it, 'It seems an example of the hubris which afflicts old men who have power.'[15]

Chapter 37

Bermuda and Berlin

The Conservative Party conference in October 1953 was a crucial test for Churchill and Eden, where both men had to prove in front of their party that they were, literally, fit to lead. Churchill wrote to Eden after his first Cabinet meeting back, ahead of their departure to the small seaside town of Margate where the conference was to be held: 'It was a great pleasure to me to see you in your place [at Cabinet] today ... I hope you will not over work yourself by trying to read up all the back papers.' He added, 'The important thing for you (and me) is to make a good impression on the Margate Conference and on Parliament when we meet.'[1]

Just before the party conference began, Churchill demonstrated again his propensity for changing his mind. He had asked Eisenhower if he would be agreeable to meeting in the Azores to discuss engagement with the Soviets, but the president politely declined, claiming he was too busy with other engagements in the proposed week. He suggested Secretary of State Dulles could take part in discussions in Washington instead. Churchill was offended and at first proposed moving the date to the week that clashed with the reopening of Parliament and calling Eisenhower's bluff. Eden twice went to see Churchill to try and persuade him to tone down his response, instead recommending that Dulles be invited to London for preliminary discussions. Churchill refused to be moved and Eden and his staff were braced for the despatch of a 'terrible second message' to Eisenhower, when Churchill halted the telegram while it was halfway through being encoded. Shuckburgh recorded in his diary, 'An eleventh-hour victory. Back to A.[nthony] E.[den]'s plan. In fact twelve solid hours of wholly unnecessary labour and pain for many people simply to suppress (momentarily) a fleeting whim of this old man.' He concluded that Eden 'was remarkably patient throughout it all. Much more so than he would have been before his illness.'[2]

Churchill and Eden's conference speeches both went well. Eden received a warm welcome and came across as informed and insightful despite his more than four-month absence. Churchill stood and talked for fifty minutes and, although he had to use large-print prompt cards, he also carried himself well. He ended on a personal note, addressing the question that Eden had still not directly asked him. 'If I stay on for the time being bearing the burden at my age it is not because of love for power or office. I have had an ample share of both. If I stay it is because I have a feeling that I may through things that have happened have an influence on what I care about above all else, the building of a sure and lasting peace.'[3] His stroke had not been officially confirmed, although rumours were circulating wildly, but Churchill's performance at the conference helped his cause. In the euphoria of his successful speech Churchill confided in a friend the following day that he still had great reservations about Britain reducing its commitment in Egypt: 'He hates the policy of "scuttle" which the Foreign Office and Anthony have persuaded him to accept about the Suez Canal ... The Foreign Office, he thinks, "is an excellent institution for explaining us to other countries, but when its head is weak it seems to spend its time seeking agreements abroad at our expense."'[4] Whether the remarks were Churchill's considered opinion or just his reaction in the moment is difficult to decipher. If they truly reflected his personal state of mind then it provides another reason for Churchill's reluctance to pass on the torch to Eden: despite their genuine friendship, he considered him the 'weak' head of the Foreign Office. The delegates in the hall were not the only ones watching Churchill closely. His decision to continue as prime minister also caused Clementine concern and she admitted to a friend that October, 'He promised me he would retire when Anthony was fit to carry on, and now when Anthony is perfectly fit he just goes on as before.'[5]

Churchill did not give up on the idea of a get-together in the Azores, and on 5 November messaged Eisenhower, 'We are confronted with a deadlock. So why not let us try Bermuda again? I suggest four or five days during the first fortnight in December. ... If you want the French, I am quite agreeable ... I hope you would bring [John] Foster [Dulles]. Anthony would be all for it and would come with me.'[6] This time Eisenhower accepted and preparations got underway, with Dulles making a preliminary visit to London. Churchill's aim for the meeting was simply going to 'see Ike' as the first step towards fulfilling his ambition of sitting across the table from Malenkov, but Eden sought to broaden the discussion. Churchill, however, stopped him from circulating papers to Cabinet by what Eden's secretary described as 'the usual process of sending for him and talking him out of it.' Both men's plans had to change when the Soviets suddenly proposed a four-power meeting of the Soviet, American, British and French foreign ministers in Berlin. The offer – and whether it genuinely represented a change of Russian attitudes – was the first thing discussed in Bermuda.

Churchill and Eden arrived in Bermuda on 2 December to be greeted by an honour guard of Welsh Fusiliers, accompanied by the regimental goat. It rained after their arrival and the weather proved an apt harbinger of events over the following days. The Bermuda conference demonstrated Churchill at his worst, his waning powers almost an embarrassment. He had refused to have any agenda in advance and Eden tried to make sure that their positions were aligned before they went into the room with the Americans and the French. One civil servant accompanying them recorded, 'He [Churchill] starts confused and wrong on almost every issue. He is raring to be rude to the French, [Churchill had spent the flight to Bermuda reading C.S. Forrester's 1932 novel *Death to the French*] to ask the Americans to join us with troops in the [Suez] Canal Zone, to bring the [West] Germans straight into NATO ... He hardly listens to argument and constantly reverts to wartime and post-war analogies.'[7] Eden wrote to his wife, Clarissa, that Churchill was 'amiable but completely vague'.[8] The actual meetings began in a troubled atmosphere, not aided by a sudden power cut, which left them holding discussions by candlelight.

On 6 December Eden recorded in his diary, 'The worst day yet ... W.[inston] late and President [Eisenhower] annoyed ... W. indulged in a tirade ... a catalogue of calamities.' No one was going to turn down the Soviet offer of discussion between the foreign ministers, but there was no accord over how it should be interpreted. Churchill was still proposing a grand rapprochement following Stalin's death, for which the Soviet offer of discussions in Berlin was, in his mind, proof of like-minded intention from behind the Iron Curtain. Eisenhower meanwhile was convinced the change of leadership in Russia was meaningless. He replied to a long speech by Churchill on the subject with rather coarse phrasing and asked if there 'had been any change in the Soviet policy of destroying the Capitalist free world by all means, by force, by deceit or by lies.'[9] In sum, Eisenhower concluded, 'Whether her dress was new or just the old one patched, it was certainly the same whore underneath.'[10] One British diplomat noted, 'I doubt if such language has ever before been heard at an international conference. Pained looks all round.' The US president was happy for the planned Berlin meetings to go ahead, but told Churchill he would not participate in any meeting of heads of government until after the foreign ministers' meeting and then only if the Soviets demonstrated 'good faith'. Uncomfortably, the French leaked the goings-on at the conference to the press, and newspapers in the following days carried stories of a rift between Churchill and Eisenhower.

Throughout the conference in Bermuda Churchill was troublesome. At one point he suggested they should discontinue any plan of negotiations with Egypt 'and announce that we will leave in our own time, taking away or destroying the [Canal military] base.'[11] Eden had to spend the whole day putting the idea to bed. Churchill seemed to be returning to his past obstructive position on Egypt, even drafting a never-published memo suggesting the British Governor-General in Egypt should 'be asked to provide evidence that order needed to be restored in order that we could send our troops in.' For Eden, the only real positive from his time in Bermuda was that he built a stronger relationship with Dulles. The two went swimming together early each morning. On another afternoon they were seen chatting together on the beach, Dulles vibrantly clad in a canvas hat and flowery shorts while Churchill sat on the sand, writing, twenty yards away. Bermuda resulted in some frank conversations between Western leaders and an official and cordial acceptance of the plan for a foreign ministers' conference involving the Russians, but little else.

When the foreign ministers convened in Berlin a month or so later, Eisenhower's caution was vindicated. The setting was picturesque, the city dusted in occasional snowfalls which gave way to crisp sunshine, but at the end the first day Eden noted, 'Opening was much as expected. Molotov produced nothing new. The same old gramophone record with scarcely a variant.' The Soviet foreign minister was personally friendly, but refused to compromise in any way over Germany and was incredulous at the intention of the Americans, British and the French to have full and free elections. In the open meetings he used every mention of Germany to mount an attack on NATO, but privately over dinner with

Eden appeared to find the notion of elections baffling, telling Eden that Hitler had come to power through free elections. Despite the Soviet Union's successful development of the atom bomb, Molotov seemed unable to shake his wartime fear of the Germans. Over dinner one night Molotov told Eden that he thought his intentions were good, but asserted that as NATO did not include the Soviet Union it was clear it was an organisation of European nations against her. Eden responded that the Soviet Union had built its own military and political bloc in Eastern Europe, but this, Molotov categorically insisted, was only directed against a renewal of German aggression. On Germany, it was clear they would achieve nothing and that the Soviets would block reunification at any cost, so Eden telegrammed Churchill, 'I do not think we do any good by discussing Soviet demands for the abolition of NATO in public, and I am more than ever convinced that the sooner this conference ends its discussion of the German side of our affairs the better.'[12]

The conference needed some visible achievement, if nothing else to justify the hype that had surrounded it. The achievement all parties settled on was an agreement to hold another conference at Geneva, with the intention of resolving a situation in the Far East that had embroiled the British, the Americans, the French, the Chinese and the Soviets: Indochina.

Chapter 38

Eden's finest hour

At the end of the Second World War, the French had hoped to calmly reclaim Indochina. Instead, they found themselves at war. By early 1954 they had already been fighting a Communist nationalist insurgency for nearly eight years.

Opposition to French rule was led by the diminutive, wispy-bearded Ho Chi Minh who had founded the Indochina Communist Party in 1930 and then created the Viet Minh nationalist movement in 1941. His movement took advantage of the power vacuum created by the defeat of Japan in 1945, and in September 1945 he declared the independence of Vietnam in front of adoring crowds in Hanoi, opening his speech by quoting the US declaration of independence. The future of the region might have been remarkably different. The Viet Minh had opposed the Japanese and in doing so had received support from US operatives working for the organisation that later became the CIA. Not entirely illogically, given Roosevelt's frequent assertions over Indochina and the Viet Minh's US-supported attacks on the Japanese, Ho Chi Minh looked to America to disavow the French of any notion they would be allowed to reclaim their colonial possession. He even telegrammed President Truman, warning that '[the] French population and troops are making active preparations for a *coup de main* in Hanoi and for military aggression.'[1] His plea fell on deaf ears; negotiations between the Viet Minh and the French stalled and the situation rapidly deteriorated into armed conflict in northern Indochina. Communist China came to the aid of the Viet Minh, while the French sought assistance from the US, who by mid-1953 were paying just under half the cost of the conflict.[2] Indochina was fast becoming the next proxy battle in the Cold War. Churchill found the situation exasperating, but Indochina was deemed critical in the wider context. When the famed war-time general, Bernard Montgomery, dined with Churchill in July 1953, Churchill angrily asserted, 'Indochina ... does not

matter. We gave up India. Why shouldn't the French give up Indochina?'
Montgomery replied, 'Indochina matters strategically. If Indochina goes,
Siam [Thailand] goes too. And then Malaya would be in danger.'[3]

At the start of 1954 the conflict was threatening to escalate. French
military efforts had succeeded in securing southern Vietnam and taking
the fight to the Communists in the north, but the initial success proved
a false dawn. The French adopted a strategy of holding heavily fortified
bases and encouraging the Viet Minh to attack, while deploying aerial
bombing, including the use of napalm. One fortified defensive position
was created in the Dien Bien Phu valley, around 180 miles west of Hanoi,
on what today is the border between Vietnam and Laos. The anonymous
dip between the jungle-clad hills, where the French established an
airstrip, would become synonymous with notions of colonial hubris.

The Americans, and Dulles in particular, took a similar view to
Montgomery. Speaking at the Overseas Press Club of America in March,
Dulles declared that the imposition of Communism on South-East Asia
'should not be passively accepted but should be met by united action.
This might involve serious risks, but these risks are far less than those
that will face us in a few years from now if we dare not be resolute today.'[4]
From early 1954, US officials conducted feasibility studies on American
intervention in Indochina. A plan was put together to assist the French at
Dien Bien Phu. Codenamed Operation Vulture, it involved undertaking a
massive air strike against the Viet Minh artillery which was bombarding
the French position from the surrounding hills.[5] There was even open
talk about the potential deployment of nuclear weapons, an idea to
which Eisenhower seemed not entirely unsympathetic. At Bermuda he
had discussed hydrogen bomb production with Churchill and Eden over
lunch one day, explaining that atomic weapons 'were now coming to
be regarded as a proper part of conventional armament,' and a 'sound
concept'.[6] He had also privately expressed the wish that the Communists
should 'take a good smacking in Indochina'.[7] In spring 1954 *The Times*
declared Indochina to be the most dangerous crisis facing the world since
1945. The prospect of Chinese direct military action in support of the
Viet Minh against the French – in addition to the guidance, training and
Soviet-made weapons already being provided – would seemingly leave
the US with no choice but to intervene too, an act that would likely have
led the Chinese to invoke the Sino-Soviet Pact. The conflict over who
should control France's former colonial possession had the potential

to cast the world once more into the abyss of a global war, with one side already openly speculating on the use of the hydrogen bomb as a battlefield weapon. *The Times'* assessment was fairly accurate.

On 25 April, with the French now surrounded and under siege at Dien Bien Phu, Churchill chaired an emergency Cabinet meeting to consider a request from the US government for joint Anglo-American military action. Eden was adamant that Britain should refuse to join in any 'precipitate military action in Indochina,' a stance Churchill wholly supported. The following day Churchill informed the Americans, 'The British people would not be easily influenced by what happened in the distant jungles of South East Asia.'[8] Dulles was upset by Churchill and Eden's failure to align themselves behind the US position and cabled Washington, 'UK attitude is one of increasing weakness. Britain seems to feel that we are disposed to accept present risks of a Chinese war and this, coupled with their fear that we would start using atomic weapons, has badly frightened them.'[9] Eden was not so much frightened as appalled by the noisy banging of the drums of war, writing in his diary that he was doubtful the American people or government would have the guts to 'ever see the business through' if they did directly intervene militarily. It would turn out to be a prophetic private observation. Just before leaving for Switzerland, Eden wrote an extended note to Churchill on Indochina, explaining how Dulles had read out to him a telegram from Eisenhower that implied the British were 'indifferent' to the plight of the French at Dien Bien Phu, which now looked almost certain to become an embarrassing defeat unless they received eleventh-hour assistance from the US. Eden drew on their past collective experience, telling Churchill that the whole situation was 'all too reminiscent of the French demand for our last R.A.F. squadrons in the 1940.'[10] The result was that Eden set off for Geneva with Churchill's blessing, having resisted calls to support direct US action and determined instead to find a diplomatic solution.

The British delegation began their lengthy stay in Geneva at the Hotel Beau Rivage, an elegant white-stone building that looked out across the lake, and which, traditionally, had for decades been the residence of the British foreign secretary during talks at Geneva. It proved to be a rather unsuitable location as the dining room had a direct line of sight to the Chinese delegation's hotel across the lake. During Eden's first evening meal they had to bang on the table while they were speaking, to provide covering noise in case the Chinese were attempting to listen in with a long-range microphone. Keen not to spend the coming weeks enduring a loud cacophony at every mealtime, Eden transferred himself and his immediate staff to a villa on the outskirts of the city. The US delegation had impressive protection, but even that was outdone by the Russians and Chinese who travelled *en masse*. As one diplomat recorded, 'They form up a solid phalanx with strong-arm men in front, behind and on the flanks – fellows like guerrillas with their right hands menacingly in their coat pockets.'[11] They also used bullet-proof cars, precautions which Eden made look rather farcical by travelling between the venues in an unaccompanied car with his female driver and a single detective.

Preliminary conference discussions began rather unpromisingly on 26 April, with Eden engaging in extended conversations over who should sit where: the French did not wish to be anywhere near the Viet Minh delegation and the Americans, and Dulles in particular, had not wanted the Chinese to be invited at all.

The sixty-six-year-old Dulles was the Washington-born son of a Presbyterian minister, a successful lawyer and, in the words of Churchill, 'a dull, unimaginative and uncomprehending man'; on another occasion Churchill stated there was 'dull, duller and Dulles.'[12] Dulles may not have been imaginative, but he was firm in his opinions. Although he and Eden had struck up a decent enough working relationship while chatting on the beach at Bermuda, it was already beginning to sour. Dulles cared little for mincing his words and appeared much of the time to speak first and think later, a trait that grated with Eden who, in public, carefully watched his words. In conversations with Eden before the conference began, Dulles claimed that the situation in Indochina was analogous to Hitler's occupation of the Rhineland in 1936, which would have been a laughable comparison had the Secretary of State not been entirely serious. Dulles seemed to hardly care if the conference produced anything at all, as long as the battle was won on the ground. To the relief of almost everyone, Dulles departed after the first week to return to Washington, leaving the more mild-mannered Walter Bedell Smith, who had formerly been Eisenhower's wartime Chief of Staff, in his stead. Eden went to see Dulles depart and while they waited on the steps of Dulles' hotel for the arrival of a car to take him to the airport, Eden turned to him and said, 'The trouble with you, Foster, is that you want World War Three.'[13]

Molotov and Eden dined together on 5 May and Eden found Molotov in a very different mood to that which he had demonstrated at Berlin. They chatted about the film of the Queen's coronation and it quickly became apparent that Molotov shared Eden's concerns over Indochina. He agreed with Eden that the situation had 'dangerous possibilities' and even risked another world war. Eden was initially wary, cabling London that it might be an 'adroit exercise in "wedge-driving" intended to emphasise the difference of opinion between the British and the Americans,' but Eden added that he had 'formed the impression that there was more substance than that.'[14] Eden's judgment was right. When discussion began, the representative for the Viet Minh, Pham Van Dong, stunned almost everyone in his opening statement by expressing a willingness to consider the partition of Indochina. It was an idea Eden had circulated before the conference, but remarkably the Vietnamese Communists had stated straight away that they would consider it, although in all likelihood the acceptance of the idea came in part as a result of pressure from the Russians. It signalled that, for the first time, it might be possible to achieve a breakthrough at Geneva.

The plenary sessions at which all the delegations and the international press were present proved a nearly complete waste of time, consisting of the exchange of written questions, which were typically answered by each side repeating their grievances. On 7 May Dien Bien Phu was overrun, an acute embarrassment for the French and an event that riled the Americans. With the public talks now going nowhere, Eden proposed meeting different delegations outside of the stifling atmosphere of official discussions, to try and make progress. Dulles had objected to the idea when Eden had suggested it as a potential method of getting a result before the conference, leading Eden to write to a colleague, 'They [the Americans] like to give the orders, and if they are not at once obeyed they become huffy. That is their conception of an alliance.'[15] But with Dulles in Washington and Eden and Molotov both keen to make progress, private conservations went ahead.

The spanner in the works came on the morning of 16 May. On reading the newspapers, Eden discovered that the French government had apparently asked the US what their preconditions would be for direct military intervention in Indochina. Eden cornered Bedell Smith and the French prime minister, Joseph Laniel, who were both evasive but could not deny what the newspapers were printing. It transpired that the

French government had approached Dulles via the French ambassador in Washington. Dulles had been only too glad to state the US would intervene if the French government could get the support of the United Nations and if they also invited Britain, although British participation was not required. Churchill was forced to admit in the House of Commons that the British government had had no prior knowledge of what was being published in the newspapers and dismissed them as informal exchanges of an 'exploratory nature'. He also told MPs, 'The immediate object of the discussions about Indo-China is to bring the fighting to an end on terms acceptable to both sides. My right hon. Friend the Foreign Secretary is doing all in his power to help in finding an agreed basis for this, and I am sure the House would not wish that anything should be said which might make his task more difficult.'[16] The awkward truth was that while Eden was attempting to negotiate peace, Dulles was trying to fan the flames of war and placing Eden in a very difficult position with the Russians and Chinese, who he now had to convince that there was still interest from the West in a genuine settlement. A frustrated Eden told his private secretary, 'All the Americans want to do is replace the French and run Indochina themselves. They want to replace us in Egypt too. They want to run the world.'[17] Eden left everyone to cool down and briefly returned to England from Geneva. He and Clarissa joined Churchill for a meal at Chequers. Churchill wrote afterwards to Clementine, who was away at the time, 'Anthony and Clarissa enjoyed themselves ... I have very good talks with Anthony and we are in pretty close agreement on the Geneva issues.' But he added, 'though I of course do not want to have a break with the Americans. They are the only people who can defend the free world even though they bring in Dulles to do it.'[18]

The eventual outcome of the Geneva conference was remarkable. As Churchill noted: 'The French are paralysed and the Americans very difficult. [While the] Communists are playing their winning hand with civility,' a position that did not seem conducive to achieving any result. But Eden managed to navigate the minefield, displaying what one witness described as 'almost inhuman good humour and patience'. He charmed the Chinese premier, Chou En-lai, by revealing his art-collector's knowledge of Chinese porcelain, and secured the crucial commitment from the Chinese and the Russians that Laos and Cambodia would be permitted to be free and neutral, as long as the Americans would agree to the same, a move that enabled the focus to shift to ending the actual fighting. More than twenty days after the conference began, the French and Viet Minh delegations finally agreed to sit down in the same room to discuss a cessation of hostilities. The meeting was painful, with the Americans causing the worst disruption. Eden recorded that night, 'Back exhausted and not very pleased with what should have been a relatively happy day.'[19] At the start of June the talks were on a knife-edge. Eden cabled London that the chances of securing a favourable outcome were not good, but Churchill sent him a private message, encouraging him to ignore the problems being caused by the US, 'The chance of preserving world peace should not be prejudiced by irrational American inhibitions against making any contact with Communist representatives.'[20]

After months of discussion, on 20 July 1954 agreement was reached on an armistice. Eden had even managed to secure a commitment from the Americans by cornering Dulles (with French support) during a trip to Paris. 'After all,' Dulles conceded, 'Russia was enemy number one, China was enemy number two, and the Viet Minh were only a bad third.'[21] The Geneva Accords agreed the end of fighting in Laos, Cambodia and Vietnam and provisionally divided the country along the seventeenth parallel; the French had wanted the eighteenth parallel and Viet Minh the thirteenth. The final declaration also included the outline of a political settlement that within two years elections were to be held to unify Vietnam. Eden had achieved what, at the outset, had seemed impossible: an end to the immediate conflict and the basis of longer-lasting peace. It was a victory for old-fashioned diplomacy in which what mattered most was what could be achieved by the men in the room. As one delegate noted, if Eden 'had not set himself out to meet Molotov and Chou En-lai in private as much as possible, nothing would have been achieved at all.'[22]

One writer has stated that British actions may not have diverted, but they did delay the march of history: Vietnam never had its election and war came anyway. On 23 October 1954 President Eisenhower offered the South Vietnamese leader the military support of the United States. President Lyndon Johnson later singled out that moment as the beginning of the American commitment to defend Vietnam, which escalated into the bloodiest entanglement in US history.[23] Eden did not prevent a war, but his efforts at Geneva certainly stopped Indochina becoming the trigger for open confrontation between East and West that could have resulted in nuclear Armageddon. But in the midst of Eden's finest hour, he and Churchill had once more come to blows over Churchill's long-delayed retirement.

Chapter 39

The end of the road

At the start of June Churchill ventured to suggest that he might consider stepping down in July 1954, following a planned trip to the US. Churchill was coming under increasing pressure from within his own party. The occasional good speech and polished performance at the dispatch box could no longer disguise the fact that he had given up making an effort in relationships with party colleagues and was increasingly enlivened only by policies that interested him. Following their initial conversation, Eden wrote to Churchill, 'Thank you for listening so patiently ... As it seems to me, a new administration must have the chance once formed to face Parliament for, I would suppose, at least two weeks before the [summer] recess begins.' Eden was pushing Churchill to bring forward his retirement date to only a few weeks away. He was courteous but firm, adding, 'I realise this may be a more difficult time-table for you.'[1] Churchill replied in his own hand a few days later, painting himself as a lone statesman fighting against the dying of the light and batting aside his own proposed July timetable: 'My dear Anthony, I am not able to commit myself to what you suggest ... I am increasingly impressed by the crisis and tension which is developing in world affairs and I should be failing in my duty if I cast away my trust at such a juncture or failed to use the influence which I possess in the causes we both have at heart.'[2] He concluded, 'I am afraid this may entail a longer period than your letter contemplates. It will not I hope extent beyond the autumn ... I am most anxious to give you the best opportunity to prepare for an election at the end of 1955.' He ended with a comment on their friendship, 'My personal regard and affection for you will ever weigh with me. I am always ready to talk these matters over with you with all the frankness which our friendship makes possible between us.' Once again Churchill was clinging on, hoping to personally be the man to bring about a rapprochement with the Soviets. Churchill was drawing line after line in the sand and then acting as if the tide of events was conspiring to wash each away, just as they came within Eden's reach. As a columnist in the *Observer* newspaper noted at the end of June, there was 'no reason, at least in theory, why he [Churchill] should not lead his party at another General Election.' Such public utterances were a bitter pill for Eden to swallow, who wrote to Clarissa, 'I cannot go on like this with this old man. I must escape somehow.'[3]

For all Churchill's words about friendship between the two of them, Churchill's litany of broken promises over the leadership had hurt and worn down Eden to the point that he began to question whether he even wanted the role. Like an old married couple, the two men knew each other so well that they could easily annoy one another. Eden, having carefully avoided clashing with Churchill for much of his career, seemed to have reached the point of no longer caring, instead rising to the bait. As one Cabinet member recalled at the time, 'When Anthony was about, he and Winston had constant arguments ... Egypt was the first bone of contention, in the end Winston gave way. On Summitry [Churchill's plan to meet the Russians], Winston got his way.'[4]

Churchill was so obsessed with his desire for a summit with the Russians that he now acted on his own initiative to try and make it happen. On 3 July he privately messaged Molotov. While Churchill's message came out of the blue for the Russian, the idea of a potential summit did not. Eden had even mentioned the possibility during one of his many conversations with Molotov at the Geneva Conference, with the Russian responding that he would mention to his government the idea of meeting outside of the Soviet Union. Eden was with Churchill at the time of his communication to Molotov, but when the Cabinet found out, Churchill faced open revolt for one of the first times in his prime ministerial career. The nub of it, as Macmillan told the Cabinet, was that the message 'was an important act of foreign policy which engaged the collective responsibility of Cabinet and that Cabinet should have been consulted before it was sent.' Churchill protested that he should not be stopped from contacting other heads of state and that Eden had agreed to sending the message, to which Eden responded that it 'had been his view' that Cabinet should have been consulted and that he had made that clear to Churchill at the time. Churchill then implied Eden was to all intents and purposes lying: the minutes of the stormy Cabinet meeting on 23 July record Churchill asserting that 'he had gained the impression that, while he [Eden] would not himself have initiated this project, he did not disapprove it.' Churchill defended himself at length, but the conclusion of the meeting was that any future messages from Churchill to Molotov would only be sent after 'full discussion' with Cabinet and would engage 'the full collective responsibility of Ministers.' Churchill had been dressed down by his colleagues and three days later he withdrew his plan to personally meet Malenkov.

The idea of a face-to-face meeting with the Russians at the highest level had consumed Churchill from almost the moment he had heard of Stalin's death. Now, the idea was dead and with it Churchill's oft-repeated argument for refusing to step down and allow Eden to become prime minister. At the start of August 1954 Churchill was contemplating the end and wrote a melancholy note to Eisenhower, 'One has one's duty as one sees it from day to day and, as you know, the mortal peril which overhands the human race is never absent from my thoughts. I am not looking about for the means of making a dramatic exit or of finding a suitable Curtain. It is better to take things as they come … Forgive me for bothering you like this, but I am trying to explain my resolve.'[5]

For the summer recess both men finally had some time off. Eden holidayed in Austria while Churchill secluded himself away at Chartwell, writing to Clementine when she was on a trip to France that he 'stayed in bed most of the time and only got out to feed the fish.' He did play cards with a few friends but confessed he was 'brooding' about life. Having finally told Eden before the recess that he would hand over to him in September before the party conference, alone with his own thoughts, Churchill changed his mind. Instead of stepping down he planned to stay on as leader for as long as he could. In response to a letter from Eden on 10 August that enquired again about the handover, Churchill penned a shattering response. It was not a spur of the moment decision – Churchill even discussed the text of his message to Eden with a number of colleagues, including Harold Macmillan, who disagreed with the entire idea – but the final communication was still brutally phrased:

My dear Anthony, I have been pondering over your letter of 10 August … I have been oppressed by a series of suggestions that I should retire in your favour. I have done my best to discharge the commission I hold from Crown and Parliament, and am glad to say that I have not missed a single day in control of affairs, in spite of my temporary loss of physical mobility a year ago. Now I have good reports from my doctors and I do not feel unequal to my burden. I have no intention of abandoning my post at the present crisis in the world … I trust therefore I may count on your loyalty and friendship during this important period, although it will not, as I hoped in my letter to you of June 11, be ended by the autumn.[6]

Eden sent a polite note in reply, asking to meet in person a few days later.

Eden met with Churchill at Downing Street on 27 August. After beating about the bush discussing Foreign Office matters, Churchill finally asked Eden 'what he thought of the position.' Eden rather bitterly replied, 'I have your letter. What more is there to say?' In his diary that night Eden noted, 'He then launched into a long rigmarole as to how he felt better (he didn't look it) and his argument was often confused.' Churchill appeared bemused at Eden's impatience, telling him, 'You are young. It will all be yours before you are sixty. Why are you in such a hurry?'[7] In a telling admission, Eden angrily told Churchill that he would have been glad of the chance to take over in 1953, but it meant less to him now and would 'mean much less still next year', if he was 'still there'. Churchill suggested Eden lead a rebellion as an 'alternative'. Eden angrily wrote in his diary, 'he knew perfectly well that I was the last person to want to do this after our many years of working together.' Despite the raised tempers of the moment, the confrontation ended with Eden backing down and Churchill getting what he wanted.

Eden was still deeply troubled by the turn of events and oscillated between the desire to hold out for the day Churchill would at last hand over the reins as he had so long promised, and the desire to throw in the towel and retire from politics. After a phone call to Macmillan in which Eden was 'distressed', Macmillan wrote to Churchill, 'I feel the most important thing now is Anthony's position … After all that has happened, I hope you will find it possible to come to a clear and definite arrangement with him about the hand-over … Otherwise I fear we may lose him now, as well as the Election, when it comes.'[8] But the party conference in Blackpool came and went and by November it seemed that Churchill intended to carry on in post beyond his eightieth birthday. That month, Churchill gave an address for the fifteenth year in a row to the boys at Harrow, his old school. He told them, 'You must not let the ordinary flow and ebb of political affairs interfere with loyalty and friendship.'[9] He might have been wishing his words upon Eden.

Chapter 40

'I am going'

In many ways 1954 had been Eden's year. The *Daily Mirror*, a previous a critic, named him 'politician of the year' and another critic noted that 'middle-of-the-road voters', for whom Churchill's bulldog wartime image seemed an anathema, 'had no such qualms about Anthony Eden … the perfect peace-maker.'[1] With the next election likely to be in 1955, it would have been a ringing endorsement for a party leader, except that five years after returning to government Eden was still waiting in the wings.

Churchill conducted a reshuffle of his Cabinet and suggested to Eden that he might like to be deputy prime minister and Leader of the House instead of foreign secretary, so he could 'look after the home front'. Eden flatly refused, recording in his diary, 'The reshuffle was mainly a device to enable him to carry on longer while doing even less.' During December 1954 Churchill was not present at five Cabinet meetings, leaving Eden to chair. As one civil servant noted, when Churchill was present, Cabinet meetings were often 'slow, waffling and indecisive … The only trouble is, the old boy is feeling rather well at the moment … though it seems he sleeps most of the day.'[2]

The inexorable march of time was finally beginning to catch up with Churchill, who had maintained remarkable health for most of his life, considering his decidedly unhealthy lifestyle. He smoked, drank to excess and barely exercised, but all the while seemed stronger than Eden, whose efforts to stay in a good physical shape had not held off his now chronic stomach problems. Churchill's own Principal Private Secretary admitted, 'He was reluctant to read any papers except newspapers or to give his mind to anything he did not find diverting … it was becoming an effort even to sign letters and a positive condescension to read Foreign Office telegrams.'[3] When the artist Graham Sutherland unveiled his specially commissioned portrait of Churchill – a present from Parliament for Churchill's eightieth birthday – the subject dismissed it as 'malignant' and 'filthy'. Churchill despised the work, but was eventually persuaded to publicly accept it, laughing it off with his fellow parliamentarians as 'a remarkable example of modern art'. Many of his colleagues at Westminster, however, saw a clear resemblance in Sutherland's melancholy, age-ravaged depiction of an old man slumped in a chair.

Just before Christmas Eden and a group of ministers met to discuss when they should plan to call the next General Election. Unofficially, they were attempting to discuss when Churchill would resign. It was a painful meeting, at which a bullish Churchill suggested stepping down in July 1955. Now it was not just Eden calling for him to stand aside but a cabal of ministers from his own Cabinet. Eden wrote in his diary that night, 'What the result of all this may be I cannot tell except that the old man feels bitterly towards me, but this I cannot help. The colleagues are unanimous about drawling Cabinets, the failure to take decisions, the general atmosphere of "après moi le déluge" [devil-may-care attitude] and someone had to give the heave.' Churchill was increasingly resenting the pressure that was being brought to bear, telling his secretary that he 'would not be hounded out of office merely because his second in command wanted the job,' melodramatically stating that Eden had 'hungry eyes'.[4]

Eden was in rude political, if not physical health. He was well-regarded by much of the general public and his stock had risen considerably since Geneva. He was still as impeccably dressed as ever, but he was no longer just the dandily-attired up-and-comer. As the *Spectator* commented after his efforts at Geneva, 'Mr. Eden's gifts as an emissary are an international asset which we are apt to take too much for granted, forgetting how delicate and exacting such missions must be and how easily they could be fumbled. The Americans seem to have no one in quite the same class.'[5] The situation over the Suez Canal in Egypt also appeared to have been resolved; another of Eden's successes in 1954. In October a new Egyptian government led by Gamal Abdel Nasser had signed the Suez Canal Agreement which committed Britain to withdrawing all troops by 1956 – the same year in which the original 1936 agreement would have expired anyway – but left the canal itself still under control of the joint British and French company that had owned and operated it since its construction in 1869. Churchill publicly supported the agreement while privately hating it, but it was the conclusion of Eden's very logical argument that Britain could no longer afford the cost of policing the waterway, especially since guerrilla attacks on British forces had increased. With no assistance forthcoming from the Americans, the only realistic option was for the British to leave. As Eden later phrased it in his memoirs, 'The Suez Canal remained of supreme importance, the base was yearly less so. The tangled mass of workshops and railways in an area the size of Wales was cumbersome and dependent upon Egyptian labour. It did not seem likely that in this nuclear age we would ever need a base on the past scale.'[6] The agreement with Egypt saved the exchequer millions of pounds while giving Egypt's nationalist government a 'win', despite the fact the British would have been required to leave anyway if they had adhered to the original treaty regarding the canal.

In February 1955 Eden travelled to Egypt to meet Nasser for the first time, but before he left he called on Churchill. He asked him to set a date for the handover of power. Finally caving to the inevitable, Churchill admitted to his long-serving foreign secretary that he 'could not carry on'. At Eden's suggestion, Churchill sent for a calendar and settled on resigning in the last week before Easter. For Eden, the decades of waiting were finally over and he departed for Cairo with a spring in his step. When Eden's former private secretary heard 'in great secrecy' a few days later that a date had been set for the handover, he confided in his diary, 'As I have observed before on similar occasions, I shall believe it when I see it.'[7]

Eden's encounter with Nasser was not, as has been alleged in popular television programmes, a moment when Eden deeply offended the Egyptian leader. Eden did surprise Nasser with his ability to speak fluent Arabic, but the two men spoke at length, exchanged Arabic proverbs and Nasser told Eden his 'interest and sympathy were with the West.' Eden thought Nasser was friendly, while Nasser felt Eden was a man 'with whom he could do business.'[8] But there was still a stark contrast between them. Nasser was the latest victor of the infighting within the military coup-plotters who had attained power in Egypt in 1952 and he had only recently survived an assassination attempt. Eden, for all his language skills and ability to make diplomatic small talk, still presented the persona of the arrogant imperialist. He gave Nasser a signed copy of the treaty, while recounting to the Egyptian leader how he had also signed the earlier agreement in 1936. As one Egyptian observer noted, 'It was a glamorous performance. He was the star of Western diplomacy who knew all the answers, talking to an unknown colonel with an uncertain future.'[9]

Shortly after his return to London the plans for the handover came awry. On Friday 11 March Eisenhower cabled the Foreign Office about a pending visit to Paris. Buried in the middle of the message was a note that he might be open to a discussion to 'lay plans for a meeting with the Soviets in a sustained effort to reduce tensions and the risk of war.'[10] When Churchill saw the message he suddenly questioned his decision to resign. Seizing on the single line, he rattled off a cable to Eden from Chequers, where he had gone to spend the weekend. Churchill told Eden that the message 'must be regarded as creating a new situation which will affect our personal plans and time-tables,' because it was 'the first time President Eisenhower has responded to my appeals [for a summit] since May 11, 1953 [when Stalin died].' The long dead and buried summit with the Soviets was, in Churchill's mind, undergoing an unexpected resurrection. Eden replied, bluntly, asking to discuss it at Cabinet the following week.

At midday on 14 March 1955 the Cabinet assembled. The first item on the agenda was the Washington telegram. Churchill stated that Eisenhower's message was of 'primary importance,' and 'a new and significant initiative'. Eden completely disagreed, pointing out that there was nothing in the message to suggest that Eisenhower had in mind anything more than a possible repeat of the Berlin Conference, which had only involved foreign ministers. The Cabinet discussed the potential of another Four Power meeting, but it was clear Churchill viewed it as an invitation for the summit between the heads of government which he had so long championed. The 'dramatic moment', as one minister described it, came near the end of the meeting. To the complete shock of nearly all his Cabinet colleagues, 'Eden said, slowly and without evident emotion, "Does this mean, Prime Minister, that the arrangements you have made with me are at an end?"' In response to a muttered reply from Churchill, Eden burst out, 'I have been Foreign Minister for ten years, am I not to be trusted?'[11] Only a few of the Cabinet were aware of the planned 5 April departure date, although everyone now knew something was going on. But Churchill outright refused to discuss it. The 14 March Cabinet meeting was the moment of complete breakdown in Churchill and Eden's already severely fractured political relationship, laying bare Churchill's inability to let go of the reins of power and Eden's deep personal insecurity. Churchill wrote to Clementine afterwards, 'The poor Cabinet, most of whom knew nothing about the inner story, seemed puzzled and worried.'[12] Churchill said the 'only thing' that influenced him was the meeting with Eisenhower and the Soviets, insisting, 'Otherwise I am very ready to hand over responsibility.' If no meeting were forthcoming, he told Clementine that it would relieve him of the duty to continue and 'enables me to feed the hungry', an apparent reference to Eden.

Eden's own state of mind is more problematic to gauge. At the 14 March Cabinet meeting he was clearly angered and upset at the prospect that Churchill might once more go back on his word. However, his reading of the telegram from Eisenhower had been right: the president was not proposing a direct meeting with Russia and communication with Dulles over the following days confirmed it. The plan was shelved. Churchill's last opportunity to prevaricate was gone. By the start of April all Eden's doubts had dissipated. His destiny was finally at hand. One civil servant noted that he seemed 'relaxed and confident, all being set for the hand-over by Winston on about 5 April. There have, however, been a number of last-minute efforts by the Old Man to escape the inevitable.'[13]

A decade after Churchill and Eden had remained behind after the final war Cabinet to contemplate in melancholy silence, they once more sat looking out over Horse Guards Parade. The early spring sun had already set. Churchill addressed his words to Rab Butler, the chancellor, who had been invited to accompany Eden. Churchill said simply, 'I am going and Anthony will succeed me. We can discuss details later.'[14] The following day Churchill informed the palace of his intention to resign. On 4 April the Queen and the Duke of Edinburgh were the honoured guests at Churchill's farewell dinner at Downing Street. At the end of the evening, after Churchill and Clementine had escorted the royals to their car, Churchill went upstairs and sat on the edge of his bed, still in his full evening dress. For several minutes he did not speak and then he looked at his secretary and said earnestly, 'I don't believe Anthony can do it.'[15]

PART FIVE

Chapter 41

Flying solo

Eden became prime minister on 6 April 1955. Six days later, Churchill and Clementine flew to Sicily for a holiday. Churchill sat on the plane clutching the now famous personal note from the Queen, which ended, 'For my part I know that in losing my constitutional advisor, I gain a wise councillor to whom I shall not look in vain for help and support in the days which lie ahead. May there be many of them.' It was not the only kind note he had received before departing. Eden and Clarissa also wrote, 'Just to send the warmest love from us both to you and Clemmie, with every good wish for the journey and for sunshine and a happy holiday.'[1] For all the fragmentation of Churchill and Eden's political relationship over the preceding months, personally there was still a warmth between them.

Eden began his tenure with the customary reshuffle, placing Harold Macmillan in his former post. Churchill's meandering Cabinet meetings were immediately consigned to history and it was agreed to call a General Election for May 1955. Even though Churchill was now officially only a backbench MP, Eden quietly informed him of the planned date of the election, adding, 'I should be grateful if you would treat this letter as between ourselves alone because I am not showing a copy of it to anybody.'[2] When the election came, Churchill was corralled in his constituency and not asked to take part in any political broadcasts. Although Churchill told a friend, 'I have at the moment a great desire to stay put and do nothing,' he was disappointed at being so swiftly sidelined.[3] It was a necessary act though, as Eden desperately needed to present himself to the voters as a new leader.

Although Eden had once admitted in his diary that he hated the 'game' of politics, he was gifted on the campaign trail. He initially got in the habit of travelling around in a car with Clarissa and a single aide, stopping frequently by the side of the road to meet and speak to voters.

In Warwickshire he shared lunch with some road workers, but security had to be stepped up after a series of anonymous threats, necessitating he carry a detective in the car and have another car following behind. Economic issues had been expected to be the primary focus of the campaign. Just before the vote Rab Butler had dished out a pre-election budget which included income tax cuts and the abolition of levies on cotton goods to boost the milling industry, which largely happened to be located in constituencies the Conservatives were targeting. The largesse was encouraged by Eden, but there were several underlying issues in the British economy: strikes by workers in a number of industries were plaguing the government; a two-week national newspaper strike that coincided with the public announcement of Churchill's resignation resulted in the *Daily Telegraph* never publishing its planned tribute, while the Bank of England had recently increased interest rates to 4.5 percent to try and curb price inflation. Internationally, the country's balance of payments was a growing problem, while efforts to ease the convertibility of sterling on international money markets were eating into the government's reserves. The pound was traded at a fixed rate of $2.80 but the government was finding itself having to periodically expend dollar reserves in the face of increasing speculation. As Eden had admitted to Churchill in his letter informing him of the date of the election, 'It is the disagreeable reality which pushes us towards a May election … I have been tempted to try and show that we can be a good Administration for at least six months before appealing to the country but I am increasingly compelled to take account of these distasteful economic factors.' For the public, the election was painted as their chance to affirm Eden as the new leader; in private, Eden wanted the vote over, in case the economy quickly worsened under his watch. Thankfully for Eden, foreign policy ended up taking centre stage.

The change occurred largely because of Eisenhower. Having repeatedly poured cold water on Churchill's bleating for a 'high level' summit with the Soviets, he suddenly changed his tune and stated he would be willing to personally attend. There was a receptive audience on the Soviet side too: Malenkov had been replaced as Chairman of the Council of Ministers by Nikolai Bulganin, whose power grab had been aided and abetted by Nikolai Khrushchev, who would go on to become one of the Soviet Union's reformist leaders. Months previously, the idea of talks had been dead and buried, but Eisenhower's change of tune led Eden to view the idea favourably. Eden's own position on the talks changed significantly once Churchill stopped using the idea of a Soviet summit as a reason to cling on to the leadership. Just before taking over as prime minister he had penned a memo to Cabinet, outlining his thoughts on what might be achieved in discussions to ease tension. He ruled out any conversation over nuclear disarmament or the situation in the Far East, but suggested a constructive conversation could be had on Europe, noting, 'The Americans will not at present agree to talks at the highest level.'[4] With Eisenhower on board and Churchill finally in retirement, the plans for a Four Power summit between the US, British, French and Soviet leaders began to take shape. When Churchill found out, he was remarkably magnanimous, publicly congratulating Eden on the plans for the conference, 'the policy for which I have faithfully striven'. It helped Eden that the announcement of a planned summit with the Soviets to ease the Cold War tension occurred at the height of the election campaign. Attlee, who was still Labour leader, had started the campaign trying to score points by claiming Eden's administration were 'dragging their feet' over meeting the Soviets to talk peace and end the war that officially did not exist. But he was suddenly made to look a fool. Instead, he ended up arguing that he would be the best person to meet the Soviets, but Eden could nonchalantly point to his distinguished diplomatic record, his success at Geneva and the fact he had dealt with the Russians during the war. Any discussion of foreign affairs on the campaign trail was a gift.

The Conservatives sailed serenely to victory in the 1955 election. Their parliamentary majority was increased from seventeen to sixty and the voters in Eden's constituency returned him to Westminster with 4,000 more votes. Eden was delighted, writing in his diary, 'Our majority staggered us … I had never thought it possible.' The outcome of the snap election was, he recorded, 'better than I had dared hope.' Churchill wrote: 'I congratulate you on the manner you fought the election. You did not put a foot wrong, and one is a centipede on such occasions.' Four days after the election, Eden penned a long and friendly letter to Churchill, confiding in him his concerns over the disruption caused by the strike of railway engine drivers which had begun the day before and was already significantly affecting food supplies. He also wrote of the planned meeting with the Soviets, giving Churchill the date suggested by Eisenhower. Churchill replied the following day, telling Eden, 'Firmness in the strike is vital … Personally, I have always had a great liking for engine drivers, and am astonished at their behaviour.' On the summit, Churchill appeared to have resigned himself to the fact that he would not be a key figure at the meeting, while still hoping it would achieve something. 'I was sorry I could not persuade Ike [Eisenhower] to test the Malenkov 'New Look' in 1953. Khrushchev has the [Russian] Army in a way that Malenkov did not … it may be more fruitful.'[5]

The reality of life at the top was brought home to Eden shortly after his arrival at Number 10 when he received a dour note from Macmillan, which congratulated the new PM on the 'wonderful job' he was doing diplomatically, but darkly added there was a 'lot of trouble' on the home front. The economic issues that had led to the election being called earlier than planned had not improved. At the start of his leadership, Eden was compelled to turn his attentions to the far less glamorous world of domestic affairs.

Many of Eden's critics have liked to paint him as a 'supposed' foreign affairs expert, who proved incapable of dealing with domestic issues as prime minister, before his hubris about Britain's place in the world led to his downfall. However, Eden was a far more rounded politician than he is often given credit for. Years later, Lord Salisbury defended Eden's domestic record, stating he was 'equally concerned with home politics and, in particular, with problems of industrial peace and better industrial relations.'[6] Even when he was out of government and in opposition, his parliamentary contributions were never just confined to foreign affairs. Eden had been acting leader of the opposition for much of the period between 1946 and 1950 before he and Churchill regained power, when Churchill spent a significant amount of time overseas or writing his war memoirs. Harold Macmillan noted that when Eden spoke opposing Labour's plan to nationalise the coal industry in 1946, 'The House listened to him attentively. It was the fashion to say that he only shone in debates on foreign affairs. In fact he often made a far more profound contribution to the solution of our many economic problems than appeared from his modest and debonair approach.'[7] Eden was certainly concerned with domestic issues when he felt he needed to be, and did attempt to understand particularly the inflationary pressures on the economy and their impact on the currency. But he was understandably always more comfortable on the international stage, where he had spent the vast majority of his political career.

Eden's style of leadership was markedly different to Churchill's. He could appear indecisive, while his natural diplomacy lent itself to the allegation that he was weak. When he lost his temper it was behind closed doors in private, sometimes over petty matters, and he pestered colleagues with endless telephone calls; one recorded they were 'on every day of the week and at every hour of the day, which characterised his conscientious, but highly strung supervision of our affairs.'[8] A number of historians have argued that Eden's style of leadership as prime minister was weak, but any man following on from Churchill was bound to appear comparatively indecisive; it was impossible to compete with Churchill's legacy, even if in his final days in office he was a pale shadow of his former self. Eden was not, and never would be, Churchill. As he delicately picked his way through the minefield of his first few months as leader, Eden frequently sought Churchill's advice, writing to him not out of politeness or necessity, but because he wanted to. What Eden's regular communication with Churchill demonstrated was that their friendship had somehow remained intact and that, once the dust had settled, Eden still valued the judgement of the leader he had stood alongside during his two tenures as foreign secretary. Soon, Eden would face the gravest crisis of his political career, and throughout he would seek Churchill's wisdom and support.

Chapter 42

Dark horizons

The Four Power summit with the Soviets took place in Geneva as planned in July 1955. In marked contrast to summits when Churchill had been in charge, Eden held a preliminary meeting with Eisenhower and the French prime minister, Edgar Faure, and tried to do as much of the summit as possible in private, adopting the same method he had used at the Geneva Summit to get an agreement over Indochina. The proposal of a demilitarised zone in Germany fell flat on its face and there was no diplomatic breakthrough, an outcome that has led many historians to conclude the summit was a failure. However, there was a less immediately obvious achievement: Eden established such a good rapport with the Russians that they expressed a desire to visit Britain, a plan Eden immediately put into motion. As one Conservative minister noted, 'Eden conducted the whole affair brilliantly. He exuded all his charm … There ain't gonna be no war.'[1]

In hindsight, it is clear that in 1955 the Soviet Union had no wish at all for the Cold War to become an open conflict. But the spectre of the hydrogen bomb, which had far greater destructive power than the atom bombs dropped on Hiroshima and Nagasaki, still loomed large. The threat posed by thermonuclear war had been the subject of Churchill's final speech in Parliament as prime minister, which he had given four months previously. In it he said, 'There is an immense gulf between the atomic and the hydrogen bomb. The atomic bomb, with all its terrors, did not carry us outside the scope of human control … [with] the hydrogen bomb, the entire foundation of human affairs was revolutionised, and mankind placed in a situation both measureless and laden with doom.'[2] The Four Power summit, largely a success because of Eden, had made that eventuality far less likely in the short-term.

After the meetings the four leaders posed on upright chairs for a photo shoot in the garden of the UN building. They laughed and joked,

Bulganin looking portly and bearded on the far left alongside a grinning Eisenhower, with the French premier, Edgar Faure, maintaining an air of bespectacled insouciance between them and Eden, who sat on the far right in a fetching cream suit. The newspapers were full of images of world leaders from East and West once more side by side in conversation, but for the first time Churchill was not present. Eisenhower had kindly written to Churchill before departing for Geneva with the encouragement that, 'I know – as does the world – that your courage and vision will be missed at the meeting. But your long quest for peace daily inspires much of what we do.' A touched and grateful Churchill replied, 'It is a strange and formidable experience laying down responsibly and letting the trappings of power fall to the ground ... I did not know how tired I was until I stopped working. I cannot help, however, feeling satisfied with the way things have turned out. I am fortunate to have a successor whose mind I know and whose abilities are of the highest order.'[3]

At home, one of the main news items of 1955 was a royal scandal. Princess Margaret had publicly expressed her wish to marry Group Captain Peter Townsend, with whom she had been engaged in a long-term affair. Townsend was divorced and the debate about whether such a union was morally proper or even constitutional split the nation. As she was in the line of succession, events could have conspired to put Margaret on the throne, and if she married Townsend she would have placed herself in the impossible constitutional position of being head of a Church which refused to recognise divorce, while herself being married to a divorcee. Much of the public and the popular press held the view that Churchill had espoused, moments after he was informed of the news by the palace: 'The course of true love must always be allowed to run smooth ... nothing must stand in the way of this handsome pair.'[4] Eden was also sympathetic to Margaret's plight and was, of course, himself a divorcee. In fact, Eden was Britain's first divorced prime minister and his multiple marriages had not proved any impediment to high office, despite his being concerned about how it would be perceived by the public. Times were changing, but Eden was placed in a problematic constitutional position. Princess Margaret herself wrote to Eden in August 1955. In her handwritten note she admitted to still being unsure of her own mind. Townsend had been dispatched overseas, while the princess was being kept out of the way at Balmoral, but she confided in Eden, 'It is only by seeing him … that I feel I can properly decide whether I can marry him or not. At the end of October or early November I very much hope to be in a position to tell you and the other Commonwealth Prime Ministers what I intend to do. The Queen of course knows I am writing to you about this, but of course no one else does, and as everything is so uncertain I know you will regard it certainly as a confidence.'[5] The final outcome was a brutal one for Margaret. Eden met with the Queen at the beginning of October and the palace and government were united: Margaret was told that it was her own decision to marry, but that if she married Townsend she would lose her right to succession and all her royal benefits and allowance, which the government was responsible for paying. On 31 October she announced her decision to call off the union. Large parts of the press and public were aghast at the outcome, but Eden was more preoccupied with other matters. That autumn, the chancellor, Rab Butler, unleashed a budget that effectively reversed all the tax cuts granted just before the election, raising the rate of the Purchase Tax on goods (now known as Value Added Tax) and expanding the items included to common kitchenware. Privately, Eden was livid at what was a terribly conducted policy U-turn and made dark notes in his diary, but it was an occasion that demonstrated his lack of an in-depth understanding of economics; he had supported Butler's foolish pre-election budget and was now paying the consequences. As one Treasury official privately noted, 'There is still quite a job of education to be done with the P.M.'[6] Eden was not illiterate in economic affairs and made a significant effort to try and understand the issues bedevilling the British economy, but he was not an expert. By the end of 1955 that fact was also painfully clear to the public.

The year that would come to define Eden's place in history began calmly enough, as he undertook his first solo trip to Washington as prime minister. The Cold War threat still exercised his attention, despite the planned friendly visit of the Russians to London, and when he spoke to Congress, Eden expressed his concern that now Europe had reached an uneasy stalemate the Russians might cause trouble elsewhere, 'Brought to a halt in Europe, Soviet expansion finds its way south and probes other lands.' At the end of February, after his return from Washington, Eden met with Churchill at Downing Street. They talked at length about Russia, the world and government. Eden wrote in his diary, 'I walked with him to the lift. He kept me there a few moments and told me how glad he was he had handed over. [And] How confident he felt that I could do the job, that now he realised how far his strength had fallen.' Eden's years of frustration with Churchill for not handing over power already appeared to have melted away. He noted, 'I was moved and sad.'

With spring came the visit of the Russians to London. They had almost been uninvited after visiting India and Burma where, in Eden's words, 'They indulged themselves in abusive rhetoric of the colonial system, ignoring their own extensive empire over subject peoples from Samarkand to Hungary.'[7] In a letter to Churchill mulling whether or not to retract the invite, Eden said, 'the bears are certainly behaving ill.'[8] The British Ambassador delivered a salutary message and received a chastened reply from Moscow, insisting that the references 'had been to the past'. Bulganin and Khrushchev arrived in Portsmouth on 18 April, having sailed from Russia on the cruiser *Ordzhonikidz*. They were met by inquisitive crowds almost wherever they went. During their trip the two Russians even greeted the Queen at Buckingham Palace; she gave them paintings of St Petersburg originally gifted to Victoria by Tsar Nicholas I, while the Russians handed over thoroughbred horses along with a bear cub called Nikki for Princess Anne.

The first evening was an informal dinner at Claridge's, where all parties scrupulously avoided mentioning anything on the official agenda. Wide-ranging discussions began at Downing Street the following day. When it came to the Middle East, Eden was quite open. He told the Russians that the uninterrupted supply of oil 'was literally vital to our economy'. Eden later recalled, 'I said I thought I must be absolutely blunt about the oil, because we would fight for it.' Khrushchev replied that Eden 'would hardly find sympathy with the Soviet Government if he said he was prepared to fight a war.'[9] Bulganin was urbane and thoughtful, while Khrushchev, although theoretically junior, was the more outspoken. The two parties were at loggerheads over Europe but came to respect each other's points of view, Eden noting, 'I found Marshal Bulganin and Mr. Khrushchev perfectly capable of upholding their end of the discussion on any subject. They did this without briefs or detailed guidance from any of their advisors.' In his memoirs, published while the Cold War still raged, Eden stated, 'It will be tragic for us, and it may be fatal, to underestimate these men and their knowledge.'

At Eden's initiative, Churchill was invited to dine with the Russians at Downing Street on one evening. It was a happy moment, which allowed Churchill to reminisce and have a lively discussion with Khrushchev on the status armaments and the pace of military technology. Khrushchev remarked that the five-year-old cruiser *Ordzhonikidz*, on which he and Bulganin had sailed to Britain for their visit, was already 'practically a museum piece' and that in the future he could not imagine surface ship engagements taking place, adding it 'must be a matter of regret for Sir Winston as a former head of the Navy.' Churchill had a marvellous evening and wrote afterwards, 'I sat next to Khrushchev. The Russians were delighted to see me. Anthony told them I won the war.'[10]

Bulganin and Khrushchev's visit did not end Cold War tensions – the nuclear threat remained ever-present – but it demonstrated the changed dynamic of the Cold War. The Soviet threat was much subtler. Eden concluded that they remained 'unshakably determined' that Communism would ultimately triumph and sent a note to the Foreign Office, 'Now that the Russian visit is over, it is necessary to review our policy … I do not believe the Russians have any plans at present for military aggression in the West. On the other hand, are we prepared with other weapons to meet the new challenge?'[11] The dinner-table bonhomie was a false dawn.

Chapter 43

Suez

In spring 1956, following a meeting with Eden, Churchill admitted his successor was 'having a hard time and the horizon is dark whichever way one looks.'[1] Eden faced long-term economic issues at home, the continuation of the Cold War and related, rising tension in the Middle East.

Under the agreement Eden had concluded with the Egyptians two years previously, British forces guarding the Suez Canal were due to leave the country in June, but their impending exit had not stemmed the tide of anti-British propaganda being spouted across the Middle East by Nasser's own radio station. Eden angrily wrote to a friend, 'The Voice of Egypt continues unchecked and pours out its propaganda ... We have simply got to take action.' More than once, Eden completely lost his cool over Nasser. In one oft-repeated example, Eden interrupted lunch between a British Foreign Office minister and an American UN official. The minister was called to the telephone at The Savoy and Eden laid into proposals he had penned to sideline Nasser on the international stage, telling him, 'What's all this nonsense about isolating Nasser ... I want him murdered, can't you understand?'[2] There was not inconsiderable apprehension at the departure of British troops; as one Conservative backbencher articulated it, 'The recent conduct of Colonel Nasser gives nobody any grounds for confidence in him as custodian of an international waterway.'[3]

Long-standing tension between Egypt and Israel was also complicating matters: the French had sold weapons to Israel, while Nasser had concluded an arms deal with Czechoslovakia, which it transpired was merely a smokescreen for the purchase of large volumes of Soviet-made weaponry. The development concerned Churchill. He gave a speech at the unveiling of a memorial to a recently deceased friend, the famous newspaperman Lord Camrose, in April, in which he maintained his faith that the United States would not stand idly by. 'They know well that both the great wars which have darkened our lives … could have been prevented if the United States had acted before they began … Now a somewhat similar case has arisen, though on a much smaller scale. Egypt and Israel are face to face … I think we can be perfectly sure that the United States as well as the United Kingdom will both intervene to prevent aggression.'[4] Eden did not share Churchill's starry-eyed view of the Americans, having told his Cabinet a few months previously, 'The British should not allow themselves to be restricted overmuch by reluctance to act without full American concurrence or support. We should frame our own policy in the light of our own interests and get the Americans to support it to the extent that we can induce them to do so.'[5] His suspicions were confirmed when Churchill forwarded a letter (theoretically a private correspondence) he had received from Eisenhower in which the president said that a collective policy in the Middle East and cooperation with the British would be 'very difficult'. Eden thanked Churchill for passing the note on: 'I am, as always, most grateful to you for your help.'[6] Behind closed doors, the Americans, and Dulles in particular, were completely scathing, with the US foreign secretary noting on a tour of Egypt, 'Such British troops as are left in the area are more a factor of instability rather than stability … The association of the U.S. in the minds of the people of the area with French and British colonial and imperialistic policies are millstones around our neck.'[7]

At 12.15am on 13 June 1956 the last British troops left Port Said. Ten days later Nasser became president of Egypt after winning elections in which he was the only candidate. The company that ran the canal was still a jointly-owned British and French concern and Nasser had extended their concession to manage and profit from the waterway, but the canal itself was effectively being left defenceless. Eden believed Nasser would keep his word and not interfere with the canal, although he was acutely aware of the risk. As he had phrased it in one previous communication with Eisenhower, the British military departure from Suez was 'an act of faith in Egypt'. Nasser was wielding Soviet weapons, but he was still sitting on the Cold War fence, as he continued to engage in talks with the Americans over securing funding for his planned marquee infrastructure project: an attempt to dam the Nile at Aswan. The plan had been that the US, Britain and the World Bank would provide a large proportion of the funding for the dam, but the money was conditional on the Egyptians prioritising building the dam, awarding contracts on a competitive basis and refusing any aid from Communists, requests denounced in Egyptian government propaganda as demands for 'the control of the Egyptian economy'. Domestic political pressure mounted against US funding and a month after the British troops had left Egypt, the Americans unilaterally withdrew their support, precipitating the collapse of the entire deal. It was Dulles who told the Egyptian ambassador in Washington that the deal was off, but he did so without telling London. As Eden recorded in his memoirs, 'We were informed but not consulted and so had no prior opportunity for criticism or comment … it gave our two countries no chance to concert either timing or methods … and the news was a wounding to his [Nasser's] pride.'[8]

On the evening of 26 July 1956 Egypt's new president strode to a trio of microphones erected on a stage in Menshiya Square in Alexandria. He waved with both hands to the crowd beyond the shadowing glare of the spotlights and then began a lengthy, passionate address. He started with past wrongs, citing Egypt's occupation by the British since 1882, lambasting Israel and ending the litany of grievances with the story of the Aswan Dam. Cutting through it all was the canal. Nasser damned the waterway and the fact that the vast sums of money it earned never ended up in Egyptian hands: 'This Canal is an Egyptian canal. It is an Egyptian Joint Stock Company. Britain has forcibly grabbed our rights … The income of the Suez Canal Company in 1955 reached 35 million pounds, or 100 million dollars. Of this sum, we, who have lost 120,000 persons, who have died in digging the Canal, take only one million pounds or three million dollars … We shall not repeat the past. We shall eradicate it by restoring our rights in the Suez Canal.'[9] While Nasser spoke, Egyptian soldiers seized control of the offices of the Canal Company. Nasser had taken over the Suez Canal. In his rapturously received speech he announced plans to use the fees earned from transiting ships to fund the construction of the Aswan Dam.

That evening Eden was in the middle of holding an official dinner at Downing Street. When an aide came in to deliver the news the dinner ended early. Eden held an impromptu meeting with key ministers which went on until 4am. *The Times* the following morning denounced Nasser's action as 'a clear affront and threat to Western interests, besides being a breach of undertakings which Egypt has freely given.' Eden was of the same view, but as he admitted to the Cabinet the following day, Nasser's actions did not provide a strong case for Britain to go to war under international law. The Canal Company was technically Egyptian, and in the midst of all his angry nationalist statements Nasser had affirmed that he would compensate the shareholders at market prices for his seizure.

Eden's long-held desire to play by the rules of diplomatic decency proved a great stumbling block early on in his response to the Suez Crisis. Instead of immediate action, there was discussion and delay. Nasser had still broken the 1954 treaty that Eden had so carefully negotiated in the face of strong objections from Churchill and it seems that Eden felt personally let down, but a swift military response was problematic; the Chiefs of Staff then informed Eden that it would take two months to plan and prepare significant forces to retake control of the canal along its entire length. He was given no choice but to sit and watch as Nasser gloated. Eden dispatched a letter to Eisenhower warning of an 'immediate threat' to oil supplies to Western Europe – Britain only had six weeks of reserves – and inviting support, adding, 'My colleagues and I are convinced that we must be ready, in the last resort, to use force to bring Nasser to his senses. For our part we are prepared to do so.'[10] Eisenhower would later publicly claim, as he sought re-election, that the US was not consulted or informed in advance about what followed.

The British press strongly condemned Nasser, with comparisons even being made between the Egyptian leader and Mussolini. It was an analogy far too close for comfort for Eden. He had been embarrassed by a dictator before and would not let it happen again. On 30 July Eden asked Churchill to come and see him. He found his predecessor in complete agreement: 'Personally,' Churchill wrote afterwards, 'I think France and Britain ought to act together with vigour, and if necessary with arms.'[11] Nasser's action riled Churchill as much as it did Eden. He had never wanted Britain to leave Suez and now the nightmare scenario was unfolding. For once, Churchill also seemed to have dropped his desire for transatlantic partnership, telling a friend that Nasser was 'a malicious swine sitting across our communications [the Canal],' adding, 'We don't need the Americans for this.'[12] To Clementine, Churchill confided, 'I am pleased with the policy being pursued about Suez … Anthony told me everything.'

Thirteen days after Nasser's shock announcement, Eden gave his first broadcast to the nation. He had no qualms about drawing an instant comparison between Nasser and other dictators he had faced: 'Why not trust him? The answer is simple. Look at his record ... Instead of meeting us with friendship Colonel Nasser conducted a vicious propaganda campaign against this country. He has shown that he is not a man who can be trusted to keep an agreement ... We all know this is how fascist governments behave, as we all remember, only too well, what the cost can be in giving in to Fascism.' Churchill and Eden were once more united in purpose, in their eyes facing down a dictator who threatened Britain and all she stood for.

Chapter 44

'A slow bleeding to death'

Even though Eden had secured agreement from Cabinet for the use of force if necessary, he insisted he did not want to restore British control of the canal, but simply to ensure the security of Britain's oil supplies. As he outlined to Eisenhower in a telegram on 5 August, 'I do not think we disagree about the primary objective; to undo what Nasser has done and set up an international regime ... to ensure the freedom and security of transit through the Canal.' Critics of Eden who claim that he saw the Suez Crisis as a moment to restore the flagging prestige of the British Empire are guilty of oversimplifying his motivations. Eden did, however, clearly feel personally affronted. In his same message to the president he added, 'I have never thought Nasser a Hitler ... but the parallel with Mussolini is close. Neither of us can forget the lives and treasures he [Mussolini] cost us before he was finally dealt with. The removal of Nasser and the installation in Egypt of a regime less hostile to the West must therefore also rank high among our objectives.'[1]

The following day, a bank holiday, Churchill set off for Chequers. He dictated his thoughts to his secretary as they drove. On arrival, he greeted Eden cheerily, 'I've prepared a little note.' It read, 'The military operation seems very serious. We have a long delay when our intentions are known ... The more one thinks about taking over the Canal, the less one likes it.'[2] The delay to British military action was unavoidable. As Eden himself later admitted, 'Unless we could fly all the forces needed, they had to swim. The nearest place from which to swim was Malta, a thousand miles away ... We had nothing like enough airborne troops for an operation of this kind.'[3] The French were better equipped, but combined, the total number of British and French paratroops amounted to less than a division. In the face of the fact that no military action was immediately possible, Eden opened the door to diplomacy.

Dulles was hauled back from a trip to Peru and dispatched to London, while preparations began for an international conference which would assess a joint British, French and American proposal for leading maritime nations to collectively operate the Suez Canal. Eden took a brief moment to escape the gathering storm, spending a weekend at a cottage Clarissa owned in Wiltshire. 'The cottage there was a haven,' Eden later wrote. 'It lies in the fields at the lane's end; its western windows overlook Gainsborough scenery in the Ebble Valley, its eastern gives on to downland … Forty-eight hours at the cottage were worth a week's holiday to me.'[4] Eden would need all his reserves of strength as events unfolded.

The London Conference opened on 16 August and included representatives of twenty-two countries, although Egypt refused to attend and Nasser denounced the proposed internationalisation of the canal as a 'conspiracy'. Eden was initially optimistic, writing to Churchill, 'We are only at the beginning, but there are some encouraging elements. Most important of all the Americans seem very firmly lined up with us on internationalism.' He also added '[military] Preparations about which I spoke to you are going forward with some modifications, which should lead to a simplification of our plan should the need arise.'[5] British and French ships were already refusing to pay their dues for transiting in the canal, but Eden's attempts to persuade US-flagged vessels to do the same got nowhere: 'Mr Dulles was not forthcoming,' recorded Eden, 'He sidestepped the point by telling us much that we already knew about the disadvantages of sailing round the Cape and the undesirability of petrol rationing.'[6] The British government also prepared an approach to the United Nations to seek legitimisation for military action. Dulles was supportive, but insisted that any such approach had to be an effort to find a solution, not 'a device for obtaining cover' for military action.

At the start of September Eden received a disquieting note from Eisenhower. 1956 was an election year in the US and the crisis was now running ever closer to the November polling day. The president informed Eden that 'American public opinion' rejected the use of force. While Eisenhower was seeking re-election, he clearly did not wish to be associated with any British attack on Egypt. Eden replied politely, stating that if Nasser accepted the proposals arising from the conference there would be no need for force, but added, 'But if the committee fails, we must have some immediate alternative which will show that Nasser is not going to get his way.' Eden used both Hitler's invasion of the Rhineland and Russian actions in Eastern Europe to stress his view that the seizure of the canal was the first in a series of actions that would lead to an increase in Soviet influence in the region, concluding, 'if the only alternative is to allow Nasser's plans to quietly develop until this country and all Western Europe are held to ransom by Egypt acting at Russia's behest it seems to us that our duty is plain.' Eden's early optimism that an international solution might emerge was now crumbling and in mid-September he told Churchill, 'I am not very happy with the way things are developing here, but we are struggling hard to keep a firm and united front in these critical weeks ... Foster [Dulles] assures me that the U.S. is as determined to deal with Nasser as we are, but I fear he has a mental caveat about November 6th [polling day in the US].'[7] American politics was holding up action against Nasser.

Churchill travelled to south-east France in late September to spend some time writing his *History of the English-Speaking Peoples* in a villa, where he confided in Clementine, 'I had a letter from Anthony ... showing robust spirit ... I must say I am very glad the burden does not rest on me.'[8] It was now two months since Nasser had nationalised the canal and Eden had come to the conclusion that Dulles was 'stringing us along at least until polling day.' A second conference discussing a US-suggested Suez Canal Users' Association was similarly rejected by Nasser, and Eden went to the UN to try and secure a resolution stating that Egypt's actions were 'a threat to peace' and that Egypt should accept the proposed Canal Users Association. The resolution was blocked by Russia who used their veto in the Security Council. The international solution was a dead end. Britain could now either go to war or accept Nasser's compensation to the shareholders of the Canal Company, an action that Eden regarded as a theft of British property which would set the stage for Russian dominance of the Middle East. Churchill wrote to Clementine from France that the delay was harming the prospects of any successful military action: 'It would be very hard to use force now.'

On the afternoon of Sunday, 14 October, eighty days after Nasser took over the canal, two French representatives, a government minister and a general visited Chequers. They presented to Eden a plan which they intimated they had been working on with the Israelis for over a fortnight. As it was being explained, Eden turned to the junior Foreign Office minister who was present and said, 'There's no need to take notes.'[9] The plan was elegantly simple: Eden needed a *casus belli* and the Israelis were willing to provide one. Israel would invade Egypt, advancing towards the Suez Canal zone, giving the British and French the opportunity to intervene as peacemakers, while also securing the canal as an international waterway. In fact, the plan for Israel to invade Egypt first was a French idea and they had not yet told the Israelis. When they did tell them, it was presented as a British idea, as Israeli prime minister, David Ben Gurion recorded in his diary, 'The English proposed that we should start on our own, they will protest, and when we reach the Canal they will come in as if to separate [the Israelis and Egyptians] and then they'll destroy Nasser.'[10] The foreign secretary, Selwyn Lloyd, attended secret discussions with the French and Israelis at Sevres outside Paris just over a week later, where all three parties signed a protocol outlining the plan. At subsequent Cabinet meetings Eden hinted at reports the Israelis might take unilateral action against Egypt, and finally, on 25 October, he told his colleagues that Israel was advancing military preparations to attack Egypt, adding the Israelis clearly felt they could 'not afford to wait for others' to curb Nasser's 'expansionist tendencies'. He then secured Cabinet agreement – although a number of ministers raised objections – to intervene in the event that the Israelis and Egyptians refused an ultimatum, adding it would provide 'ample justification' for British action. He admitted, 'We must face the risk that we should be accused of collusion with Israel.'[11] A handful of Cabinet members knew the truth, but most either fell for the deception or chose to look away, knowing something might be going on behind the scenes. Eden now carried with him the knowledge that he was scheming to go to war. Churchill did not know the details and, tellingly, Eden did not confide in him. As military action loomed, Eden clearly missed his former partner. Eden called for Churchill's secretary and asked if there was any chance Churchill, who was still in France at the time, would accept a position in Cabinet as a minister without portfolio. He was assured it was a nonstarter and Eden dropped the idea. At the time Churchill was not in a position to reply: he had suffered another stroke.

Churchill was unconscious for around twenty minutes on 20 October, during which time he lost the use of his right arm, his right leg and the left side of his face. He recovered enough to be flown back to Britain for private treatment on 28 October and was on doctor's orders to rest when, two days later, Israeli forces crossed into the Sinai Desert. The British and French issued a twelve-hour ultimatum to both sides to halt hostilities and when they duly failed to do so, conveniently prepared British and French aircraft went into action, while a British naval taskforce set sail from Malta. One observer remarked that the British prime minister displayed 'a curious serenity'. Eden faced pointed questions in the House of Commons from the Labour opposition. Labour leader Hugh Gaitskill claimed the action was a 'transparent excuse', and pointing to reports already appearing in US newspapers, he suggested 'the whole business was a matter of collusion between the British and French Governments and the Government of Israel.'[12] Gaitskill was right, but for all the accuracy of his condemnation of Eden, public opinion was still largely in support of the war. Even in November, at the height of the crisis, Eden had an approval rating of fifty-two percent. On 3 November Churchill issued a public statement in support of the Suez operation, which was published two days later as British and French paratroopers descended from the sky on Port Said. Britain, Churchill said, simply intended 'to restore peace and order to the Middle East.' In a demonstration of unquenchable enthusiasm for Britain's wartime ally, he added he was 'confident that our American friends will come to realise that, not for the first time, we have acted independently for the common good.' Eden wrote to Churchill that day, 'My dear Winston. I cannot thank you enough for your wonderful message. It has had an enormous effect, and I am sure that in the US it will have maybe an even greater influence. These are tough days – but the alternative was a slow bleeding to death.'[13] In his televised address to the nation, Eden said, 'All my life I have been a man of peace, working for peace, striving for peace, negotiating for peace … but I am utterly convinced that the action we have taken is right.'

Chapter 45

A premature end

In Washington and Moscow the perception of events was rather different. In a wonderful twist of irony, American efforts to stall any British military action for the sake of the elections actually resulted in the polls in the US coinciding with British amphibious landings in Egypt. The day before, Eden had sent a pleading message to Eisenhower, 'We do not want occupation of Egypt, we could not afford it ... But I am convinced that ... Nasser would have become a kind of Moslem [*sic*] Mussolini ... History alone can judge whether we have made the right decision, but I do want to assure you that we have made it from a genuine sense of responsibility, not only to our country, but to all the world.'[1]

From the moment it became clear that Britain and France intended to intervene as 'peacekeepers' by their issuing of the pre-agreed ultimatum to Israel and Egypt, the diplomatic pressure on Eden ramped up. The General Assembly of the UN held an emergency debate on 1 November and passed a motion for an immediate ceasefire. The idea of a UN peacekeeping force was also proposed, something the Cabinet and Eden were in favour of – it would have given Eden the multinational military defence of the canal that he had been calling for since 1954 – but Eden resolutely informed Washington that the British military effort 'must go on until we can hand over responsibility to the United Nations.' In case Eisenhower had any doubts, Eden told him, 'If we draw back now .... Everything will go up in flames in the Middle East.'[2]

Everything was threatening to go up in flames anyway. The Soviet leader Bulganin wrote to Eden that he would 'crush the aggressors and restore peace in the East through the use of force.' The Soviet note was menacing, but the context strengthened Eden's hand. In October, in response to protests against Russian influence, Moscow had permitted a new, moderate Communist leader to form a government in Hungary. The following month, when the new leader suggested leaving the Warsaw

Pact (the collective defence treaty signed by Eastern European states under the Soviet orbit), Moscow sent 6,000 tanks across the border into Hungary and violently put down all opposition. The Russian actions were not lost on Eden, although he and his Cabinet were almost entirely focused on dealing with the fallout from Suez, and in his reply to Bulganin he said, 'In the past three days Soviet Forces in Hungary have been ruthlessly crushing the heroic resistance of a truly national movement for independence … At such a time it ill becomes the Soviet Government to speak of the actions of Her Majesty's Government as "barbaric".' In reality, the Russians were preoccupied with Hungary and did not want to go to war over Suez. As the Soviet foreign minister later admitted, 'There was a firm decision not to bring the matter to the point of an armed conflict,' while in response to frantic calls for assistance from the Egyptian ambassador, Khrushchev replied, 'We are full of admiration for the way in which you are resisting aggression . . . but unfortunately there is no way in which we can help you militarily. But we are going to mobilise world public opinion.'[3] Eden's confidence in the crisis not worsening was short-lived, however. It soon became clear that the outbreak of war was hurting the position of the pound on international money markets and forcing the government to use up more and more of its now-dwindling dollar reserves. For the general population, though, the more obvious impact was the sharp rise in petrol prices at the pumps. It had also become abundantly clear that Britain and France would receive no support from the US.

On the morning of 6 November, the very moment that the naval taskforce was finally landing the troops who had, as Eden phrased it, 'swam' from Malta, the Cabinet held a crisis meeting. In the first week of November alone, Britain's US dollar reserves had fallen by $85 million and reserves were predicted to fall below the worst-case scenario ceiling of $2 billion by 1 January 1957. The two corrective options open to stop the haemorrhaging of government reserves would be to either implement currency controls or officially devalue sterling, but the latter would ramp up already high domestic inflation and the former would shatter the nation's economic credibility for a generation. It was a situation Civil Service advisors at the Treasury had warned about more than a month before the conflict started. The alternative was to get a loan from the International Monetary Fund, but to do so would be impossible without support from Washington, support which currently was not forthcoming. The Americans, instead of standing alongside Britain as Churchill had forecast they surely would, had voted in favour of the UN ceasefire resolution. The negativity across the Atlantic to Eden's military venture in Egypt was so vitriolic that the Americans played hardball, openly threatening the pound. As one US financial official phrased it, US assistance would only be forthcoming when the UK was 'conforming to rather than defying the United Nations'.[4] Almost overnight, the Cabinet was faced with the reality that international opinion had decreed Britain was fighting an illegal war, one that was placing the economy in jeopardy. Churchill in his pomp might have managed to carry the room, to rouse and cajole his Cabinet into ploughing ahead, to never surrendering, but Eden's desire to have his colleagues with him left him vulnerable. Only three of the seventeen Cabinet ministers present supported Eden's desire to carry on the military action. That day, after the French had been regretfully informed, British forces stood down.

The Egyptian military had already suffered significant losses at the hands of the Israelis, but it was as humiliating a moment for the British and the French. Worse, the Suez Canal was now blocked to all maritime traffic. The Egyptians gleefully told the world that it was as a result of ships sunk by British and French bombers, although in fact the Egyptians had deliberately scuttled vessels to block the waterway. In his memoirs, Eden claimed that the decision by Cabinet to accept the ceasefire was not done for economic reasons, but because, 'The occasion for our intervention was over, the fire was out.'[5] What he did not mention was that he was fast losing political support. He won a motion of no confidence tabled by the Opposition in the Commons, but within the party there was a growing perception that Suez had indeed become a 'crisis'. Eden's critics claimed they saw 'fear in his eyes' when he appeared at Remembrance Day commemorations at the Cenotaph on 11 November, and false rumours began circulating that he was dependent on the stimulant Benzadrine. The narrative that would come to define Eden's legacy was already being written: in the space of a few short months he had gone from being the staunch defender of fairness and British interests around the world to a leader who had overplayed his hand and brought about a national embarrassment. Eden was not, as has been subsequently alleged in numerous accounts and on television, dependent on drugs, but he was by now ill, on medication and in a state of nervous exhaustion. At least one government figure would claim afterwards they never thought Eden's health would survive Suez if the crisis became protracted.

On 19 November it was announced that Eden was cancelling all his engagements because of ill-health. Five days later, as the UN officially passed a vote of censure against the actions of Eden's government, he left for a rest in Jamaica on doctor's orders. His decision to convalesce in the Caribbean gave his critics a field day; the *Daily Mirror* flippantly invited readers to 'solve' the Suez Crisis, offering as a prize a three-week holiday in Jamaica.

Eden was therefore not present at the meetings when the Cabinet agreed the complete withdrawal of British forces from Egypt, an action that earned enough goodwill from the Eisenhower administration for the Americans to back Britain in seeking a loan from the International Monetary Fund to save what was now bordering on a catastrophic currency crisis. With Eden absent, the speculation was already beginning. *The Economist* unflinchingly asserted, 'As the dust swirls over the Middle East … there is only one subject in domestic politics. It is the Prime Minister – should he go or stay?' The British press then began printing the rumours that Britain and France had colluded with the Israelis. Eden's *casus belli* had technically hinged on the respectable notion that Britain was intervening as a 'peacemaker' to protect her interests, but the rumours shattered the already flimsy myth. By the time a tanned-looking Eden returned to London on 14 December, he was already being treated as effectively in retirement by some of his own ministers, while the impression created for the public was that he had triggered a political and economic catastrophe and then cut and run to take a holiday away from it all in the sunshine. Compounding his situation was the fact that, when he spoke in Parliament on 20 December, Eden claimed that the allegations that he had known about the Israelis' plans in advance were false: '[To say] that Her Majesty's Government were engaged in some dishonourable conspiracy is completely untrue, and I most emphatically deny it.'[6] Eden would maintain the lie to his grave, but it did not take long for the truth to out. When it was confirmed to Eisenhower that Eden had colluded with the French and Israelis he was outraged; one aide recorded, 'The President just went off the deep end. He wouldn't have anything to do with Eden at all. He wouldn't even communicate with him.'[7] The last threads of the 'special relationship' had been severed. If

Eden stayed on as prime minister, it was clear he would never have the ear of the White House again.

On 3 January 1957 Eden wrote in his diary, 'Diplomacy is a continuing process. The consequences travel on. You cannot just close a chapter if you want to and leave it at that.' But Eden's frail body, wracked by the stress of Suez, would not permit him to carry on, even if in his mind he stubbornly wished to. He was now suffering from intermittent fevers – caused by his bile duct problems – barely slept and was taking powerful stimulants to counteract the other drugs he was on, which he admitted, 'had an adverse effect on my rather precarious inside.'[8] His party and almost his entire Cabinet were also insisting that it was time. After a number of senior ministers informed Eden that he no longer had their confidence and they felt a 'new head of government' was necessary, one civil servant recorded that Churchill 'would have told them to go to the furthermost part of hell, but as you know very well, Eden has none of Churchill's pugnacity.'[9]

The die was cast. At Eden's final audience with the Queen she told him she shared his regret at having to go, remarking what a painful decision it must have been. On 9 January, just before the announcement of his resignation went public, Eden wrote to Churchill, admitting that he was once again in pain and that the verdict of his physicians was unanimous: 'In short they say firmly ... that I am endangering my life and shortening it by going on ... the immediate result is a gradually increasing fatigue: in short I shall be less and less able to physically do my job as the weeks go by ... I am very sad but I did not want you to know by any hand but mine.'[10]

Eden had spent barely eighteen months in post as prime minister. Two days before his resignation was announced he had sent a defiant memo to his Cabinet. In contradiction with nearly all the ministers in his government and much of British public opinion, he blindly asserted, 'I do not think that the events of Suez can be reckoned as a tactical defeat ... The Soviet-Egyptian air force has been destroyed. The Israelis have eliminated one-third of the Egyptian army and its equipment ... The extent of Soviet penetration in the Middle East has been exposed, with the result that the United States at last seems to be taking the action for which we pleaded in vain throughout 1956.'[11] The Americans were, finally, taking more of an interest in the Middle East, but only to fill the gaping void created by the fact that the British and French had collectively disgraced themselves.

Militarily, Britain had been capable of winning a war over Suez. Economically, the war proved a disaster. The final outcome was that Britain was forced to secure a loan from the International Monetary Fund of $561 million. The Suez Canal itself remained completely blocked to all shipping for months, and Arab countries – in solidarity with Egypt – were denying Britain oil, which had led to petrol being rationed at the pumps. Eden had arrogantly defied his critics and clung on when the Suez Crisis was a foreign policy disaster. Once it also became an economic disaster it sealed his fate. When Churchill was later asked by a friend what he would have done in response to Suez if he had still been prime minister, he replied, 'I would never have dared, and if I had dared, I would never have dared stop.'

PART SIX

Chapter 46

Out of office

Eden had not only resigned as prime minister, he had also decided to step down as an MP, citing his ill-health. He was now officially more politically unemployed than Churchill. On 18 January 1957 he and Clarissa boarded the RMS *Rangitata* at a foggy Tilbury docks to sail to New Zealand; for much of the remainder of his life, Eden would live overseas. In a painful reminder that putting distance between himself and his former life might not prove easy, the liner's journey to New Zealand took longer than usual because the ship had to sail via the Panama Canal as Suez was still closed. Eden experienced very similar emotions as Churchill had two years previously, having suddenly gone from a position of power to one of impotence, writing to a friend, 'It is a strange feeling on this ship – completely cut off after so many years.'[1]

Harold Macmillan took over as prime minister and had to confront a world in which Britain's status had apparently changed overnight. As Eden had admitted in a revealing memorandum he penned a few weeks before he left office: 'We must review our world position and our domestic capacity more searchingly in the light of the Suez experience, which has not so much changed our fortunes as revealed realities.'[2] Eden was conveniently consigned to history, but Macmillan accepted an invitation from Churchill to dine at Chartwell shortly after his appointment. The new prime minister wrote in his diary afterwards, 'He was in good form though getting very deaf. Nor does he say much now, for the first time he listens. All this is rather sad – for the fight has gone out of him. He is a very charming, courteous old man.' Macmillan's observations were not entirely correct. Churchill was still delighting in completing his work on *A History of the English-Speaking Peoples*. When the final volume was published later that year, Eden informed Churchill that the work was 'grand writing and proud reading'. Churchill was also enjoying a slower pace of life which allowed him time to paint, and he exhibited an oil painting of 'Black swans at Chartwell' at the Royal Academy that spring.

For all the good it seemed to be doing Churchill, rest did not cure Eden's health problems and it was discovered that his bile duct had become blocked again, necessitating another operation. Eden and Clarissa travelled to the US in April to see the same surgeon who had operated on him before. Following the surgery, Clarissa confided in a friend, 'The doctors say they cannot predict if and when the same complaint will not start again. They think it pretty well inevitable that it will – maybe in months, maybe years. When it does, the operation will have to be repeated. They say he will only be capable of leading a very quiet life, because of this threat.'[3]

With the exception of his subsequently published memoirs, Eden made no attempt to publicly defend himself from the storm of criticism he now received. However, Churchill made a number of interventions on his behalf. Speaking at a public event in May 1957, Churchill asserted, 'Our party and indeed our country owes him its gratitude for a lifetime of work upon the causes we all serve,' adding that those who attacked Eden's actions over Suez might 'perhaps have reason to reconsider their opinions. I do not think … the United Nations has been helpful to either the free world or to the cause of peace and prosperity in the Middle East.'[4] Eden, who was convalescing following his operation in the US at the time, telegrammed Churchill with his thanks. Eden and Clarissa returned to England in the summer, at first making their home in a cottage in the West Country lent to them by a friend, from where Clarissa telephoned her uncle. Churchill recorded afterwards on 4 June, 'This morning I was rung up by Clarissa from their tiny cottage where she and Anthony have at last fetched up after so many trials and tribulations – I think their courage and dignity in adversity are making a deep impression.'[5] For Eden, there was additional sadness upon his return, as he learned that his first wife, Beatrice, of whom he remained very fond, had died of cancer in the US, aged fifty-one. During the whole of June, Eden was confined to the cottage on doctor's orders and he had to decline an invitation from Churchill to lunch in London, replying that travelling to London or Chartwell was 'beyond my strength at present'. The two men discussed the latest developments in Westminster, but in a sign that Eden's mind was at least benefiting from the cessation of the stresses and strains of public life, he added, 'But enough of politics.

I find it pleasant to read again – books not newspapers. When we have a little more time for documents and papers, I may feel disposed to try my hand at some account of the Thirties. You have always told me what a good companion the writing of a book can be.'[6] A few weeks later Churchill and Clementine took the train from London to see Eden. He was delighted and sent a note afterwards: 'It was very kind of you and Clemmie to come and see us yesterday. Your visit gave us so much pleasure. I enjoyed every minute of it.'[7]

The following year witnessed another crisis in the Middle East. On 14 July 1958 officers in the Iraqi army overthrew the monarchy, which had been installed by the British in the 1920s. The king and his family were murdered, the prime minister's body was paraded through the streets and the British Embassy in Baghdad was ransacked and set on fire. The country, which had been a strong Western ally in the region, was now in chaos. Since Suez, Nasser had cemented his credentials as an 'anti-imperialist' leader and in early 1958 Egypt formally united with Syria to form the United Arab Republic. The aim was no less than the unification of the Arab world. It was uncertain what the outcome of the Baghdad coup would be, but cheering crowds on the streets were waving pictures of Egypt's president. Suddenly it seemed the concerns Eden had expressed to Eisenhower in September 1956 – that Nasser planned to bring down Western regimes across the region – were coming true. The US president later recalled, 'We feared the worst … the complete elimination of Western influence in the Middle East.'[8] Lebanon's pro-western, Christian president called for assistance to shore up his regime against internal unrest, and thousands of US Marines were deployed to Beirut, while Macmillan dispatched British paratroops to Amman in Jordan, the last remaining pro-British Hashemite monarchy in the region. The Labour Party opposed the action and called for a debate in Parliament. On hearing of the planned debate, Churchill wrote to Macmillan to inform him that he intended to speak. Churchill made a few short notes in preparation, including, 'Anthony Eden and Suez. He was right. These recent events prove him so. It may be that his action was premature … I do not want to take points off the US and point the finger of scorn at them. How easy to say look at the US and compare them with us at Suez. We were right.' But Churchill in the end decided not to respond and wrote to Macmillan on 15 July, 'I spent an hour or two thinking what I would say, and came to the conclusion I had nothing worth saying ... Forgive my change of plan.'[9] It eventually transpired that the Iraqis were not intending to align themselves to Nasser, but the swift arrival of nearly 15,000 US military personnel in Lebanon signalled that it was the US that was now the dominant Western power and that the age of the old empires was drawing to a close. It was not just happening in the Middle East, but in Africa too.

In Algeria a movement for independence had descended into a war of astonishing brutality, although Eden's sympathies remained with the colonial overlords. He wrote to Churchill, 'As I see it, the French are fighting for their lives, all our lives, in Algeria. The oil is there and if the French have it and can control it, the dependence on the [Suez] Canal will be less and we can be firm at last with Nasser.'[10] That same year, 1958, Ghana was granted independence from Britain. Over the next five years, half of Africa would follow, as the British, the French and Belgians were swept aside by the tide of history. In October Nasser agreed a deal with the Soviet Union to provide the finance for his long-awaited Aswan Dam.

Chapter 47

Old men

As the world neared a new decade, Churchill and Eden watched events unfold with a sense of trepidation. Eden wrote to Churchill in 1959, 'The world news seems to me to get steadily darker. Perhaps that is how retired politicians view events.' Churchill replied, 'I can only agree with you that the world picture seems to grow progressively blacker.'[1]

Both Churchill and Eden preferred Kennedy in the 1960 US presidential election, but Eden was dismayed by the tone of discussion on foreign affairs in the televised debate between Kennedy and Nixon, the first of its kind in the US. He wrote to a friend, 'I thought the experience profoundly depressing. Not one of them mentioned the word "ally" from first to last, neither seemed conscious that the US has any.'[2] Kennedy, for his part, idolised Churchill. The two exchanged a series of friendly messages following his victory and when Churchill experienced a bout of illness a few months later, one of the get-well-soon messages he received came from the White House. Kennedy wrote, 'We have been encouraged by reports … and heartened again by your display of indomitable courage in the face of adversity. The wishes of all our people, as well as those of Mrs. Kennedy and I go to you.'[3] Although Eden and Churchill personally liked the young president, Eden was less sympathetic over Kennedy's foreign policy. When the Cuban missile crisis brought the world to the brink of nuclear Armageddon, Eden declared, 'The United States has been a prisoner of its own past. If it had given us firm support in the first weeks after Nasser seized the Suez Canal he could have been called to order and international authority restored … Nasser was allowed to get away with it. This encouraged the other petty dictators … Now the United States has a life-sized decision on its hands.'[4]

Eden and Churchill both struggled with ill-health: Eden with his never-ending gall bladder problems and Churchill with more typical issues of old age, the greatest being the risk of strokes, which steadily plagued the rest of his life. The harsh truth was that Churchill's insistence in 1954, when they discussed handing over the leadership, that Eden was 'still young' had proved a false assertion. In the two decades that Eden spent away from frontline politics following his resignation he had nine operations on his gall bladder. In one of his later operations, the surgeon took two hours to make the initial incision due to all the scarring caused by the previous occasions Eden had gone under the knife. To ease his ailing body, Eden spent winters abroad and in 1961 he and Clarissa acquired a home on the British overseas territory of Saint Vincent in the Caribbean. That year, Churchill toured the Caribbean on the luxury motor-yacht *Christina*, owned by his friend, the Greek billionaire Aristotle Onassis. When he docked in Saint Vincent he invited Eden and his wife to join him for a meal. Churchill recorded afterwards, 'Have had a very agreeable voyage in [the] Grenadines and Anthony and Clarissa lunched on board. We are now bound for Jamaica and Haiti.'[5]

Churchill enjoyed the diversions of painting and cruises, while Eden returned to his first love: Shakespeare. He was made president of the Shakespeare Memorial Theatre in Stratford-Upon-Avon, and during his years in the role he demonstrated a commendable capacity to not interfere with the day-to-day running of the theatre, defending a number of more modern, creative interpretations of Shakespeare's plays when they faced criticism in the press. He still enjoyed the company of a few close friends and one noted following a birthday celebration, 'Anthony, sunburnt and wearing a marrow-coloured velvet dinner suit seemed a picture of health … Bottles of champagne popped, and the gathering was very English, understated and poignant.'

Churchill, though very deaf and losing his once prodigious memory, was still treated as a senior statesman. Eisenhower invited him to visit the White House in 1959, in what would transpire to be his last visit to the US, and on multiple occasions Churchill had lunch at Downing Street with Macmillan. He also met with David Ben Gurion when the Israeli prime minister visited London in 1961. Wherever he went he was well-received, but one proof of the advancing years was that Churchill no longer wrote the short speeches he occasionally delivered. Eden was granted some of the honours of statesmanship – he entered the House of Lords as the Earl of Avon in 1961 where he contributed to debates on thirteen occasions – but his disastrously perceived premiership had already eclipsed most peoples' memories of his achievements as foreign secretary and he was not a former politician who found himself sought out for advice.

In October 1961 Eden and Churchill dined together at Churchill's residence in London. They talked about the situation in newly independent Ghana and both men were concerned at Queen Elizabeth's planned visit to the country, which remained a member of the Commonwealth. Churchill wrote to Macmillan the following day, 'I find that he [Eden] shares the increasing perturbation with which I view the Queen's forthcoming visit there … the visit would seem to endorse a regime which has imprisoned hundreds of opposition members without trial … No doubt Nkrumah would be much affronted if the visit were now cancelled and Ghana might leave the Commonwealth.' But he added, 'I am not sure that that would be a great loss.'[6] The Queen went anyway – her planned trip had been pushed into 1961 as she had been pregnant with Prince Andrew – and famously danced with a beaming Nkrumah, the photographic highlight of a royal visit which kept Ghana in the Commonwealth fold. As Macmillan himself had phrased it, 'winds of change' were sweeping the continent of Africa, and Churchill and Eden's hankering for the Old World appeared increasingly at odds with the march of progress.

While staying in Monte Carlo in 1962 Churchill slipped off his bed and fell. Unable to call for help, he covered himself in a blanket and waited for someone to arrive. He told his secretary when she discovered him, 'I think I've hurt my leg.' He had in fact seriously broken his hip. He was X-rayed and put in a cast by a local hospital, while an RAF Comet was sent to pick him up from Nice. Churchill had to undergo surgery to pin the shattered bones back together. He recovered well enough to return to his London home, which was modified with a bedroom and bathroom downstairs, and returned to walking with a stick. That November, he was eighty-eight.

Eden accepted Churchill's advice about writing books, along with an advance from *The Times,* and spent much of the next few years working on the three volumes of his memoirs, the first of which was published in 1960 and the last in 1965. His contributions in the House of Lords during the same period have been almost entirely overlooked by historians, including Eden's biographers, but they paint an interesting picture. His attendance was impacted by his ill-health, but when he did speak, he confined his comments to the increasingly frequent moments of tribute for deceased former colleagues and to areas of foreign policy where he had past experience.

In June 1963 he spoke in a debate on the international situation, eloquently arguing that the mutually assured destruction which persisted in the context of the Cold War was, in fact, working as a deterrent:

> I know that there are many who feel, "If only we could be rid of the nuclear weapon, we should all feel much safer". That is a natural reaction, but I am not at all sure that it is a wise one ... more people were killed at Dresden [the German city fire-bombed by the RAF in the Second World War] than at Hiroshima. If we were to rid the world of the nuclear weapon, is there not a risk that we should leave in men's hands very powerful destructive forces at which they would not feel the same abhorrence as all now feel for nuclear war? ... For the present, therefore, unless and until we can work out better methods than we have yet found for maintaining an international law, I think it is as well that the nuclear weapon is there.[7]

He also contributed to discussions on Vietnam (formerly Indochina) as the prediction he had made in 1954 came true: neither the American people nor government had the guts to 'see the business through' when it became a costly, protracted guerrilla war. In his sixties, Eden had finally found a pace of politics that suited him: occasional, well-thought-out contributions to debate, without the early mornings and late nights that had accompanied working alongside Churchill for decades.

For Churchill, it was increasingly clear that his own involvement in politics was beyond his capacities. He was still a constituency MP, but he barely appeared in the House and those around him knew he would no longer be capable of the rigours of campaigning whenever the next election was called. His share of the vote in his Woodford constituency, while still an impregnable seventy-one percent, had gone down in the 1959 election and his majority had fallen by more than 4,000 since his triumphant Conservative victory of 1951. After much soul-searching, in 1963 it was announced that Churchill would not contest his seat at the next parliamentary election. It was a painful decision for Churchill, but it was the right one. The electorate of Woodford had ceased to vote for an active representative and were instead voting for a legend. Churchill's daughter later wrote, 'Mentally he had become more lethargic. Gradually the silences became longer, and he was content to sit gazing into the fire … He rarely initiated a subject … But he hated to be alone … Sometimes after a long silence he would put out a loving hand or say apologetically, "I'm sorry I'm not very amusing today".'[8] In August 1963 Churchill suffered another mild stroke and was confined to bed for the summer, and for the first time he was unable to read. Just as he was recovering, came the tragic news that his eldest daughter, Diana, had committed suicide, aged fifty-five; she had experienced several breakdowns of her mental health throughout her life. Eden was among those who sent Churchill messages of condolence.

In the final years of his life Churchill was a shadow of his former self. He struggled to concentrate on reading and spent afternoons listening to the gramophone or looking at picture books. Eden still visited him, and as with all Churchill's guests there was an understanding that even if he was silent during a meal, or spoke only a few words, he still very much enjoyed their company. In November 1964 Churchill celebrated his ninetieth birthday. It was to be his last. On 10 January 1965 he suffered a massive stroke and remained in a coma for fourteen days. Eden, who had returned from the Caribbean on hearing the news, visited Churchill before he died on 24 January.

The following day as the nation mourned, Eden joined the politicians offering tributes in the House of Lords. He called for the establishment of a 'Churchill Day' to remember the man's war legacy, telling the Lords, 'Looking back now at the war, victory may seem to have been certain. But it was not always certain; and when news is bad, it is very lonely at the top … I saw much of Sir Winston then – often many times a day, not only at official meetings but in such periods of comparative relaxation as there were, at meals and, as was his wont, late into the night.' Eden told the House he remembered those moments fondly, 'even though the argument might sometimes be sharp'. There was much about Churchill that he could have complimented, but Eden singled out the fact that, 'He saw clearly and further than most, and he spoke fearlessly and without favour of what he saw. He sensed the danger for his country with the instinct of the artist and the knowledge of the historian.'[9]

On a bitingly cold and windswept Saturday nearly a week later, Eden was one of a select group who escorted Churchill's coffin for the state funeral at St Paul's Cathedral. He walked alongside Clement Attlee; Attlee was eighty-two, Eden sixty-nine, but more than one person commentated that they looked the same age. London was stationary and sombre, the chimes of Big Ben stilled for the day, the reverent silence of the crowds only broken by a roaring flypast by RAF Lightning jets. Churchill's body was interred next to his mother and his brother at Bladon churchyard, near Blenheim Palace, later that day. A partnership that had lasted a quarter of a century, endured a world war, a bitter struggle over leadership and a dramatic alteration of Britain's place in the world had finally ended.

In 1974 Eden was interviewed for BBC television about his time with Churchill. He spoke of their years together and of their disagreements, but added that there was 'a very big, generous streak about Winston, which one couldn't help liking.' The interviewer interjected, 'You loved him really', to which Eden replied, 'I did, I did. I had a very great affection for him.'[10]

Epilogue

Eden died twelve years after Churchill, *The Times* declaring in their obituary, 'He was the last prime minister to believe Britain was a great power and the first to confront a crisis which proved she was not.' Churchill's and Eden's careers were intimately interlinked, but it is hard to imagine two leaders who are viewed more differently. Eden's own memoirs, which he spent many hours working on after his retirement from frontline politics, have not helped his cause. The first to be published was his account of his time as prime minister, in which he tried valiantly to justify his actions over Suez, while not admitting he had known in advance about the Israeli invasion plans. Eden had wanted to see the volume on his wartime experiences come out first, but *The Times*, who paid his advance, insisted on the Suez book taking precedence for commercial reasons. As Eden's foremost biographer, D.R. Thorpe, elegantly attests, Eden's legacy has been affected: 'One of the disadvantages for Eden of the sequence of his publications was that it contributed to a tendency from the 1960s onwards to assess his career backwards.'[1] Churchill meanwhile spent so much time writing, including significant periods while technically in office, that he had in part penned his own legacy before his death.

Churchill's legacy is almost always viewed singularly, akin to that of a dictator. His wife, Clementine, receives occasional credit for her support, but in most biographies Eden is relegated to the role of an also-ran, and in some he is barely even mentioned. Boris Johnson's biography, *The Churchill Factor: How One Man Made History*, rather adheres to its title by including only one indexed mention of Eden. It is an aberration of the historiography which Churchill himself would have objected to: he always maintained that he was Parliament's servant, not its master, and when Eden's ulcers laid him low during the war, he insisted his friend Eden take a rest, telling him, 'You are my right arm; we must take care of you.' Even in 1952, when the acrimonious debates about potential retirement were already underway, Churchill viewed Eden's absence through illness as something which 'added to his burdens'.

Far too many historians have glossed over Eden's contribution to Churchill's successes. Neither man was without their faults, but their strengths greatly complimented each other. As one of Churchill's biographers, Roy Jenkins, has remarked, Eden was Churchill's 'sometimes creditably unsubservient Foreign Secretary.'[2] When Churchill was without Eden he was more prone than ever to rash decision-making and pig-headed obstinacy. When Eden was without Churchill he was indecisive and unable to shake the private insecurities that had dogged him all his life. Churchill could brow-beat an opponent into submission, while Eden could charm them into the same state. Together, they were a formidable political pairing.

There were multiple occasions during the war when Eden changed Churchill's mind. He even stood up for De Gaulle time and again despite the Frenchman's flaws, because he saw what Roosevelt and Churchill refused to see: that De Gaulle was a uniting force for a liberated France. It is true that when they argued Churchill won more often than not, but on occasion he came around to Eden's perspective after the shouting, as in the case of the appointment of former Vichy ministers in North Africa. It is a testament to the close alignment of their perspectives on the world, and Britain's place in it, that Eden remained Churchill's foreign secretary when they returned to power in 1951. In their second term together it was Eden who appeared to have the better grasp of the pace of change: he accepted that there would need to be an accommodation with the Egyptians over Suez and recognised that the United States would have to take on a greater role in the world to police the Soviet threat, even if different occupants of the White House were less than keen to do so.

It would be wrong to paint Eden as a visionary reformer – he always maintained that Britain should still be great, even if it was not in her traditional imperialist role – but he proved to be far more capable of moving with the times than Churchill. Their relationship certainly grew more fractious as Churchill delayed and delayed his retirement, but only weeks after Eden finally got the keys to Downing Street he was writing to Churchill to ask for his advice. Their relationship was complex: they were simultaneously political colleagues and rivals, while also being firm friends, a situation that many casual observers of history seem incapable of reconciling. At times, the assessment of Churchill and Eden's relationship has suffered from a rather blinkered view that, in its most simplistic form, treats the war as Churchill's single-handed victory and Suez as Eden's single-handed failure, while painting Eden as a sickly, grasping princeling, desperately hoping Churchill would take a tumble down a flight of stairs.

There is no doubt that Suez was both a personal and a policy failure for Eden, but in the midst of the howls of criticism still directed at him, few people recall that Churchill backed him most of the way. If military logistics had not dictated a delay, Churchill would have gone to war just as readily. It was Eden's more diplomatic tendencies that lost him the initiative and confidence within his own Cabinet, before the economic situation and political pressure forced an embarrassing retreat. What reflects worst on Eden is his refusal to admit complicity with the Israelis. Given that the ruse was not Eden's idea – he was led to believe he was joining a plot already hatched between the French and Israelis – perhaps he was embarrassed when it came to light so quickly, but his denials only came across as arrogant lies. It was a sad end for a politician who, for the rest of his career, was deeply principled. Truman's Secretary of State, Dean Acheson, famously remarked following Suez that Britain had 'lost an Empire but not found a role,' and the statement has largely been accepted as gospel ever since. However, Eden had recognised long before that Britain could not maintain what he described as her 'commitments' overseas. It was in fact Churchill who found the bitter pill of Britain's changed place in the world harder to swallow.

The wider context to the latter part of their relationship – the Cold War – is also a crucial factor in understanding the two men's place in history. Decades since the fall of the Berlin Wall it is hard to imagine a world on the brink of catastrophic conflict, but the spectre of war between East and West genuinely alarmed both Churchill and Eden. Churchill's last speech as prime minister was on the threat of nuclear war, as were some of Eden's final speeches in the House of Lords. Churchill and Eden had sat and dined with Stalin and Molotov, and Eden had coaxed nations back from the brink over Indochina in 1954. Although Churchill could be hawkish when it came to countering Communism, he was as open as Eden to personal diplomacy. Reagan took the historical plaudits for his visit to China in 1984 and later meetings with the Soviet leader, Gorbachev, but the Americans were comparatively late adopters of the kind of in-the-room diplomacy which Churchill and Eden had carried out their entire careers.

Churchill still towers above Eden as a statesman, as war leader, and if nothing else for the length of time he served as prime minister. But while history has been generous to Churchill, it has almost uniformly been unkind to Eden. His role in Churchill's success is overlooked and undervalued and, if he could speak from the grave, Churchill himself would be the first to challenge that view. On VE Day, when Eden messaged Churchill from San Francisco congratulating him on the end of the war in Europe, Churchill's reply summed up the impact Eden had during their years together. Churchill thanked Eden and added, 'Throughout you have been my mainstay.'[3]

Acknowledgements

To my Grandpa, who would have been pleased to see at least one chapter mostly about the Royal Navy and who, along with many others, bravely lived the consequences of Churchill and Eden's decision to send military supplies to Stalin on the Arctic Convoys. And to my Commissioning Editor, Claire, for her endless enthusiasm for this book and for having the idea in the first place while watching *The Crown* on Netflix.

Endnotes

Chapter 1: Sun, sand and Fascism

1. Eden, Anthony, *The Eden memoirs: Facing the dictators*, Cassell & Company, 1962, p547
2. Ibid., p36
3. Minutes of a Conference in the Reich Chancellery, Berlin, November 5, 1937, Yale Law School, The Avalon Project, http://avalon.law.yale.edu/imt/hossbach. asp, accessed 30 March 2018
4. Carlton, David, *Anthony Eden: a Biography*, Allen Lane, 1981, p48
5. Clark, M., *Mussolini*, Routledge, 2014, p167
6. Harbutt, Fraser, J., *The Iron Curtain: Churchill, America, and the Origins of the Cold War*, Oxford University Press, 1988, p30
7. Buchanan, Patrick, J., *Churchill, Hitler, and "The Unnecessary War": How Britain Lost Its Empire and the West Lost the World*, Crown, 2007, p161
8. Mitgang, Herbert, Article Hemingway wrote for Pravda in 1938 is published in English, The New York Times archives, 1982, https://www.nytimes. com/1982/11/29/nyregion/article-hemingway-wrote-for-pravda-in-38-is-published-in-english.html, accessed 6 April 2018
9. Cabinet Conclusions, 8 September 1937, National Archives, CAB 23/89/5
10. Carlton, p110

Chapter 2: 'The complete gangster'

1. Gilbert, Martin, *Churchill: A Life*, Random House, 2000, p508
2. Barker, Elizabeth, *Churchill and Eden at War*, Macmillan, 1978, p18
3. Carlton, and Murfett, M., *Shaping British Foreign and Defence Policy in the Twentieth Century: A Tough Ask in Turbulent Times*, Springer, 2014, p116
4. Barker, p18
5. Harvey, Oliver, *The Diplomatic Diaries of Oliver Harvey, 1937-1940*, Harper Collins, 1970, p48
6. Toland, John, *Hitler: the Definitive Biography*, Knopf Doubleday, 2014

7. Faber, David, *Munich, 1938: Appeasement and World War II*, Simon & Schuster, 2009, p77
8. Carlton, p120
9. Thorpe, D.R., *Eden: The Life and Times of Anthony Eden First Earl of Avon, 1897-1977*, Random House, 2011
10. Carlton, p122

Chapter 3: Going quietly

1. Faber, p85
2. Ibid., p93
3. Thorpe, p258
4. Faber, p94
5. Adams, R., *British Politics and Foreign Policy in the Age of Appeasement, 1935-39*, Springer, 1993, p80
6. Cabinet Conclusions, 19 February 1938, CAB 23/92/6
7. Adams, R., p81; Cabinet Conclusions 20 February 1938, CAB 23/92/7
8. Peters, A.R., *Anthony Eden at the Foreign Office 1931-1938*, Gower Publishing Ltd., 1986, p361
9. MacDonogh, Giles, *1938: Hitler's Gamble*, Constable, 2009, p35
10. Faber, p109
11. Telford, Taylor, *Munich: the Price of Peace*, Vintage Books, 1979, p343
12. Churchill, Winston, House of Commons, 22 February 1938, Foreign Affairs, Hansard, https://api.parliament.uk/historic-hansard/commons/1938/feb/22/foreign-affairs, accessed 7 April 2018

Chapter 4: Wars and rumours of wars

1. British Pathé newsreel, 21 April 1938, 961.21, https://www.britishpathe.com/video/anglo-italian-pact-signed-in-rome-2, accessed 15 April 2018
2. Churchill, Winston, *The Second World War, Volume 1: The Gathering Storm*, Cassell & Company Ltd, 1948, p254
3. Thorpe, p278
4. Eden, Anthony, House of Commons, 3 October 1938, Prime Minister's Statement, Hansard, https://api.parliament.uk/historic-hansard/commons/1938/oct/03/prime-ministers-statement, accessed 15 April 2018
5. Churchill, Winston, House of Commons, 5 October 1938, Policy of His Majesty's Government, Hansard, https://api.parliament.uk/historic-hansard/commons/1938/oct/05/policy-of-his-majestys-government, accessed 15 April 2018
6. Churchill, *The Gathering Storm*, p307

7. Peters, pp377-378
8. Churchill, *The Gathering Storm*, pp361-362
9. Prime Minister Neville Chamberlain's broadcast to the nation, 3 September 1939, BBC Archive, 1939, http://www.bbc.co.uk/archive/ww2outbreak/7957.shtml?page=txt, accessed 21 April 2018
10. Churchill, *The Gathering Storm*, p363

Chapter 5: Downing Street, De Gaulle and Dunkirk

1. Churchill, Winston, statement in the House of Commons, 13 May 1940, https://www.parliament.uk/about/living-heritage/transformingsociety/private-lives/yourcountry/collections/churchillexhibition/churchill-the-orator/blood-toil-sweat-and-tears/, accessed 4 May 2018
2. Thorpe, pp299-300
3. Formation of the Local Defence Volunteers, BBC Home Service speech by Anthony Eden, 14 May 1920, http://www.bbc.co.uk/history/ww2peopleswar/timeline/factfiles/nonflash/a1057303.shtml, accessed 4 May 2018
4. Thorpe, p301
5. Gilbert, Martin, *Churchill: A Life*, Heineman, 1991, p646
6. Cooper, Artemis and Beevor, Anthony, *Paris After the Liberation: 1944-1949*, Penguin, 2007, p5
7. Carlton, p165
8. Gilbert, *Churchill: A Life,* p646
9. Barker, p35
10. Hastings, Max, *Finest Years, Churchill as Warlord 1940-45*, Harper Press, 2009, p87
11. Eden, Anthony, *The Reckoning*, Cassell, 1965, p139
12. Ibid.

Chapter 6: The home front

1. Maler, Thomas, *When Lions Roar: the Churchills and the Kennedys*, Crown, 2014
2. Thorpe, p353
3. Hastings, p17
4. Gilbert, *Churchill: A Life,* p665
5. Ibid., p200
6. Ibid., p859
7. Thorpe, p398
8. Ibid., p265

Chapter 7: Priorities

1. Eden, *The Reckoning*, p168
2. Gilbert, *Churchill: A Life,* p682
3. Hastings, p120
4. Ibid., p121
5. Harby, Jennifer, 'The Coventry Blitz: Hysteria terror and neurosis', BBC News, 13 November 2015, https://www.bbc.co.uk/news/uk-england-coventry-warwickshire-34746691, accessed 8 June 2018
6. Gilbert, *Churchill: A Life,* p684
7. Taylor, Frederick, *Coventry: November 14, 1940*, Bloomsbury, 2015
8. Eden, *The Reckoning*, pp175-176
9. Gilbert, *Churchill: A Life,* p685
10. Eden, *The Reckoning*, p183
11. Churchill, Winston, *The Second World War*, Random House, 2002, p373

Chapter 8: The dark hour

1. Hastings, p128
2. Kennedy, Ludovic, *Pursuit, The Chase and Sinking of the Bismarck*, Book Club Associates, Collins Sons & Co Ltd, 1975, p47
3. 'Germans gloat over sinking of HMS Hood', *Canberra Times*, 27 May 1941, https://trove.nla.gov.au/newspaper/article/2568506, accessed 25 May 2018
4. Kennedy, p211
5. Ibid., p212
6. Churchill, Winston, House of Commons, Hansard, War Situation, 27 May 1941, https://api.parliament.uk/historic-hansard/commons/1941/may/27/war-situation, accessed 15 June 2018

Chapter 9: 'The Prime Minister's compliments'

1. Eden, *The Reckoning*, p270
2. Gilbert, *Churchill: A Life,* p701
3. Churchill, Winston, S., 'Payment of Debts by Soviet Russia, 4 December 1920', CAB 24/116/37
4. Gilbert, *Churchill: A Life,* p701
5. Ed. Gorodetsky, Gabriel, *The Maisky Diaries, Red Ambassador to the Court of St James's 1932-1943*, Yale University Press, 2015, p372
6. For a more detailed account of the Polish-Soviet war, see *1920: A Year of Global Turmoil*, also by the author, published Pen & Sword, 2020
7. Eden, Anthony, House of Commons, Soviet Union and Poland (Agreement), Hansard, 30 July 1941, https://api.parliament.uk/historic-hansard/commons/1941/jul/30/soviet-union-and-poland-agreement, accessed 22 June 2018

8. Eden, *The Reckoning*, p273
9. Churchill, Winston, *The Grand Alliance*, Cassell & Co., 1949, p385
10. Fenby, Jonathan, *Alliance: The Inside Story of how Roosevelt, Stalin and Churchill Won One War and Began Another*, Simon and Schuster, 2015
11. Gilbert, *Churchill: A Life,* p275
12. Ibid., p707
13. Ibid., p711
14. Eden, *The Reckoning*, p286

Chapter 10: Uncle Joe and FDR

1. Maisky, Ivan, *Memoirs of a Soviet Ambassador: The War 1939-1943*, Hutchinson, 1967, p227
2. Barker, p235
3. Eden, *The Reckoning*, p514
4. Ibid., p296
5. Ibid., p303
6. Gilbert, *Churchill: A Life,* pp712-713
7. Carlton, p192
8. Barker, p212
9. Maisky, p432
10. Ibid., p435

Chapter 11: Avoiding losses

1. Roberts, Andrew*, Churchill: Walking with Destiny,* Penguin, 2018
2. Thorpe, p332
3. Carlton, p202
4. House of Commons Debate, 2 July 1942, Central Direction of the War, https://api.parliament.uk/historic-hansard/commons/1942/jul/02/central-direction-of-the-war, accessed 10 August 2018
5. Eden, *The Reckoning*, p332
6. Boyle, Peter, *The Eden-Eisenhower Correspondence, 1955-1957*, University of North Carolina Press, 2006, p11
7. Carlton, p205
8. Maisky, p448
9. Ibid, p453

Chapter 12: To Moscow

1. Gilbert, Martin, *Road to Victory: Winston, S. Churchill 1941-1945*, Heinemann, 1986, p161

2. Churchill, Winston, S., *The Hinge of Fate: The Second World War, Volume 4*, Rosetta Books, 2010, p409
3. Ibid., p435
4. Ibid., p441
5. Ibid., p439
6. Cadogan, Alexander, Foreign Office's Permanent Under-Secretary's Department, account of Operation Bracelet, FO1093-247
7. Eden, *The Reckoning*, p339
8. Churchill, *The Hinge of Fate*, p537
9. Eden, *The Reckoning*, p349
10. Barker, p65
11. Eden, *The Reckoning*, p351
12. Churchill, *The Hinge of Fate*, p568

Chapter 13: Churchill, Eden and the Holocaust

1. Eden, Anthony, Soviet Union: Foreign Office despatch to Kuibyshev, No 393. Talk with Maisky about German atrocities against the Jews, 2 December 1942, FO 954/25B/493
2. Cabinet conclusions 14 December 1942, German atrocities, CAB 65/28/38
3. W.M. (42) 168th Meeting, 14 December 1942, Notebook, CAB 195/2/7
4. United Nations Declaration, House of Commons, 17 December 1942, https://api.parliament.uk/historic-hansard/commons/1942/dec/17/united-nations-declaration, accessed 17 August 2018
5. Eden, *The Reckoning*, p358
6. Michael, Robert Marrus, *The End of the Holocaust*, Walter de Gruyter, 1989, p287
7. Gutman,Israel and Berenbaum, Michael, *Anatomy of the Auschwitz Death Camp*, Indiana University Press, 1998, p574
8. Thorpe, p359
9. Eden, Anthony, to Oliver Harvey, September 1941, quoted Collins, Joseph, Book says British ignored Jews' war plight, *New York Times*, 27 July 1979, https://www.nytimes.com/1979/07/27/archives/book-says-british-ignored-jews-war-plight-eden-i-prefer-arabs-a-few.html, accessed 24 August 2018
10. Eden, Anthony, to Gordon Vereker, 15 November 1944, FO 505/497
11. Gilbert, Martin, *Churchill and the Jews: A Lifelong Friendship*, Henry Holt and Company, 2007, p186
12. Gilbert, Martin, *The Holocaust: A History of the Jews of Europe during the Second World War*, Henry Holt and Company, 1985, p 231

13. Churchill, Winston, to Private Secretary, 18 September 1944, https://www.jewishvirtuallibrary.org/churchill-s-decision-to-not-bomb-the-concentration-camps, accessed 24 August 2018
14. Robin, Anthony and Kushner, Jeremy, *The Persistence of Prejudice: Antisemitism in British Society during the Second World War*, Manchester University Press, 1989, p159
15. Cohen, Michael J., *Churchill and the Jews, 1900-1948*, Routledge, 2013, p355

Chapter 14: Casablanca

1. Churchill, *The Hinge of Fate*, p595
2. Marsh, Richard C., 'France and the French – Churchill and Flandin', Finest Hour 157, Winter 2012-13, p22
3. Eden, *The Reckoning*, pp367-368
4. McCrea, John L., *Captain McCrea's War: The World War II Memoir of Franklin D. Roosevelt's Naval Aide and USS Iowa's First Commanding Officer*, Skyhorse Publishing Inc., 2016
5. Barker, p69
6. Churchill, *The Hinge of Fate*, p610
7. Eden, *The Reckoning*, p363
8. Hindley, Meredith, 'Allied Leaders at Casablanca: The Story Behind a Famous WWII Photo Shoot', *Time Magazine*, 16 January 2018, http://time.com/5101354/churchill-fdr-casablanca-photo/, accessed 27 August 2018
9. Ibid.
10. Holmes, Richard, *The World at War: The Landmark Oral History from the Previously Unpublished Archives*, Random House, 2008, p347
11. Churchill, *The Second World War, Volume V: Closing the Ring*, Cassell & Co Ltd., 1951, p584
12. Maisky, p473
13. Con Coughlin, Marrakesh: Where Churchill and Roosevelt played hookey, *Daily Telegraph*, 10 April 2013, https://www.telegraph.co.uk/travel/destinations/africa/morocco/marrakech/articles/Marrakesh-where-Churchill-and-Roosevelt-played-hookey/, accessed 28 August 2018

Chapter 15: East to west

1. Maisky, p477
2. Dunn, McFarlane and Donkin to the Prime Minister, September 1942, FO 371/33035
3. Maisky, p485

4. Thorpe, p345
5. Dutton, David, *Anthony Eden, A Life and Reputation*, Hodder, 1997, p227
6. Gilbert, *Churchill: A Life*, p731
7. Smith, T.O., *Britain and the Origins of the Vietnam War: UK Policy in Indo-China, 1943-50*, Palgrave Macmillan, 2007, p7
8. Eden, *The Reckoning*, p374
9. Ibid., p376
10. Ibid., p377
11. Maisky, p509
12. Dilks, David, ed., *The Diaries of Sir Alexander Cadogan, 1938-1945*, Cassell, 1971, p521
13. Materski, Wojciech, *Katyn: A Crime without Punishment*, Yale University Press, 2008, p219

Chapter 16: Second-in-command

1. Eden, *The Reckoning*, p383
2. Farrell, Brian, *Churchill and the Lion City: Shaping Modern Singapore*, NUS Press, 2011, p22
3. Amery, Leo, (ed.), Barnes and Nicholson, *The Empire at Bay: The Leo Amery Diaries 1929-1945*, Hutchinson, 1988, p873
4. Dutton, p228
5. Thorpe, p348
6. Eden, *The Reckoning*, p384
7. Thorpe, p348
8. Barker, p72
9. Ibid., p73
10. Ibid., p78
11. Carlton, p220
12. Churchill, *Closing the Ring*, p43
13. Barker, p162
14. Eden, *The Reckoning*, p401

Chapter 17: Visiting friends

1. Barker, p128
2. Eden, *The Reckoning*, p402
3. Churchill, *Closing the Ring*, p83
4. Eden, *The Reckoning*, p404
5. Ibid., p414
6. Gilbert, *Churchill: A Life*, p758

7. Thorpe, p352
8. Churchill, *Closing the Ring*, p266

Chapter 18: A very small country

1. Simpson, John, *A Mad World, My Masters: Tales from a Traveller's Life*, Pan Macmillan, 2001, p222
2. Eden to Churchill, 13 July 1943, FO 954/8/43/128A
3. Eden, *The Reckoning,* p425
4. Churchill, *Closing the Ring*, p302
5. Barker, p129
6. Ibid., pp227-228
7. Barker, p130
8. Eden, *The Reckoning*, p429
9. Smith, p4
10. Thorpe, p322
11. Beitzell, Robert (ed.), *Tehran, Yalta, Potsdam: The Soviet Protocols*, Academic International, 1970, p347
12. Thorpe, p354
13. Eden, *The Reckoning*, p427
14. Churchill, *Closing the Ring*, p340
15. *New York Times*, 4 December 1943, https://archive.nytimes.com/www.nytimes.com/learning/general/onthisday/big/1128.html#article, accessed 14 September 2018

Chapter 19: Maladies

1. Danchev and Todman (ed.), *War Diaries 1939-1945: Field Marshall Lord Alanbrooke*, Weidenfeld & Nicolson, 2001, p496
2. Moran, C., *Winston Churchill: The Struggle for Survival*, Constable & Company, 1966, p150
3. Churchill, *Closing the Ring*, p373
4. Vale, J.A. and Scadding, J.W., 'In Carthage ruins: the illness of Sir Winston Churchill at Carthage', December 1943, Journal of the Royal College of Physicians of Edinburgh, Volume 7, Issue 3, September 2017, p291
5. Ibid., p290
6. Gilbert, *Churchill: A Life,* p764
7. Ibid., p766
8. Ibid., p768
9. Eden, *The Reckoning*, p435
10. Ibid., p439

11. Ibid., p435
12. Eden, Anthony, The Future of Indo-China and other French Pacific Possessions, Memorandum by Secretary of State, 16 February 1944, CAB 66/47
13. Smith, p13
14. Lehrman, Lewis E., *Churchill, Roosevelt & Company: Studies in Character and Statecraft*, Rowman & Littlefield, 2017, p218
15. Nicolson, Sir Harry, *Diaries and Letters: 1939-1945*, Collins, 1967, p359
16. James, Robert Rhodes, *Anthony Eden*, Papermac, 1987, p304
17. Carlton, p236

Chapter 20: D-Day, De Gaulle and Doodlebugs

1. Churchill, *Closing the Ring*, p549
2. Hastings, p485
3. Barker, p106
4. Ibid., p107
5. Ibid., p108
6. Churchill, *Closing the Ring*, p556
7. Eden, *The Reckoning*, p455
8. Barker, p111
9. Eden, *The Reckoning*, p457
10. Churchill, Winston, *Triumph and Tragedy*, Houghton Mifflin Company Boston, 1953, p6
11. Ibid., p11
12. Eden, *The Reckoning*, p468
13. Churchill, Winston, House of Commons, Hansard, Prime Minister's Review, Flying Bomb Attacks, 6 July 1944, https://api.parliament.uk/historic-hansard/commons/1944/jul/06/prime-ministers-review, accessed 21 September 2018
14. Hastings, p497

Chapter 21: 'A deathless memory'

1. Barker, p252
2. Davies, Norman, *Rising '44, The Battle for Warsaw*, Macmillan, 2003, p249
3. Churchill, *Triumph and Tragedy*, p115
4. Davies, pp251-252
5. Ibid, pp116-117
6. Davies, p298
7. Ibid., p324
8. Barker, p256
9. Davies, p392

10. Ibid., p352
11. Gilbert, *Churchill: A Life,* p795

Chapter 22: The post-war world

1. Eden, *The Reckoning*, p476
2. Dutton, p172
3. Eden, *The Reckoning*, p476
4. Churchill and Roosevelt to Stalin, 'President Roosevelt and Prime Minister Churchill to Marshall Stalin', 16 September 1944, Roosevelt Papers, United States Department of State Foreign Relations of the United States. Conference at Quebec, 1944, U.S. Government Printing Office, 1944, http://images.library.wisc.edu/ FRUS/EFacs/1944/reference/frus.frus1944.i0013.pdf, accessed 1 October 2018
5. Churchill, *Triumph and Tragedy*, p138
6. Dietrich, John, *The Morgenthau Plan: Soviet Influence on American Postwar Policy*, Algora Publishing, 2013, p66
7. Gilbert, *Churchill: A Life,* p798
8. Eden, *The Reckoning*, p483
9. Moran, p215
10. Gilbert, *Churchill: A Life,* p797
11. Eden, *The Reckoning*, p486

Chapter 23: Vive la France

1. Beevor, p41
2. Churchill, *Triumph and Tragedy*, p214
3. Eden, *The Reckoning*, p494
4. Mangold, Peter, *Britain and the Defeated French: From Occupation to Liberation, 1940-1944*, I.B.Tauris, 2011, p238
5. Barker, p112
6. Churchill, *Triumph and Tragedy*, p222
7. Eden to Churchill, 29 November 1944, PRO. PM Minute, 44/732
8. Barker, p115
9. Ibid.
10. Churchill, *Triumph and Tragedy*, p228
11. Barker, p117

Chapter 24: Hands off the British Empire

1. Brendon, Piers, *The Decline and Fall of the British Empire*, Random House, 2010, p397

2. Toye, Richard, *Churchill's Empire*, Macmillan, 2010, p230
3. Dutton, pp145-146
4. Janam, Mukherjee, *Hungry Bengal: War, Famine and the End of Empire*, Oxford University Press, 2015, p128
5. Churchill, Winston, S., Note by the Prime Minister and Minister of Defence, Directive to the Viceroy designate, 8 October 1943, CAB 66/41
6. Ibid.
7. Cabinet Conclusions, 7 February 1944, CAB 65/41
8. Secretary of State for Dominion Affairs, Secretary of State for India and Burma, Secretary of State for the Colonies, Report for the Month of November 1944 for the Dominions, India, Burma and the Colonies and Mandated Territories, 29 December 1944, CAB 66/59/30
9. Dutton, p169
10. Ford, Douglas, *Britain's Secret War against Japan, 1937-1945*, Routledge, 2001, p1
11. Moran, p29
12. Smith, p14
13. Mr Dening (South-East Asia Command) telegram to Foreign Office No 14. French Mission in Indo-China, 6 January 1945, FO 954/7B/267

Chapter 25: A Greek Christmas

1. Eden, *The Reckoning*, p498
2. Churchill, *Triumph and Tragedy*, p250
3. Hastings, p525
4. Mr Cocks, House of Commons, Liberated Europe (British Intervention), Hansard, 8 December 1944, https://api.parliament.uk/historic-hansard/commons/1944/dec/08/liberated-europe-british-intervention, accessed 12 October 2018
5. Churchill, *Triumph and Tragedy*, p273
6. Hastings, p537
7. Churchill, *Triumph and Tragedy*, p276
8. Barker, p193 and Vulliamy, Ed and Smith, Helena, 'Athens 1944: Britain's Dirty Secret', *The Guardian*, 30 November 2014, https://www.theguardian.com/world/2014/nov/30/athens-1944-britains-dirty-secret, accessed, 12 October 2018
9. Eden, *The Reckoning*, p500

Chapter 26: To Yalta

1. Churchill, *Triumph and Tragedy*, p298
2. Eden, *The Reckoning*, pp508-509
3. Plokhy, S.M., *Yalta: The Price of Peace*, Penguin, 2010.
4. Beitzell, Robert (ed.), *Tehran, Yalta, Potsdam: The Soviet Protocols*, Academic International, 1970, p55

5. Eden, *The Reckoning*, p505
6. Ibid., p513
7. Stettinius, *Roosevelt and the Russians: The Yalta Conference*, Greenwood Press, 1970, pix
8. Ibid., p73
9. Churchill, *Triumph and Tragedy*, p416

Chapter 27: 'We have been deceived'

1. Stettinius, p232
2. Toye, p253
3. Clemens, Diane Shaver, *Yalta*, Oxford University Press, 1970, p249
4. Eden, *The Reckoning*, p513
5. Smith, p20
6. Ibid., p29
7. Clemens, p145
8. Carlton, p251
9. Hastings, p553; Gilbert, p818
10. Carlton, p248
11. Beitzell, p131
12. Gilbert, p830

Chapter 28: The final act

1. Eden to Churchill, 14 May 1945, AP 20/219/44
2. Churchill, *Triumph and Tragedy*, p418
3. Eden, *The Reckoning*, p529
4. Gilbert, *Churchill: A Life,* p834
5. Hastings, Max, *Armageddon*, Macmillan, 2004, p485
6. Churchill to Eden, 4 May 1945, FO954/20
7. Gilbert, *Churchill: A Life,* p837
8. Churchill, *Triumph and Tragedy*, p468
9. Ibid, p469
10. Thorpe, p374
11. Eden, *The Reckoning*, p534

Chapter 29: The worst form of government

1. Churchill, *Triumph and Tragedy*, p509
2. Churchill to King George VI, 28 January 1945, Chartwell papers, Churchill College, Cambridge, CHAR 20/193A/77
3. Thorpe, p376
4. Dutton, p255

5. Churchill, *Triumph and Tragedy*, p520
6. Truman, Harry, S., Notes by Harry S. Truman on the Potsdam Conference, July 16 1945, Truman Papers, President Secretary's file, Mr and Mrs Charles Ross, https://www.trumanlibrary.org/whistlestop/study_collections/bomb/large/documents/index.php?documentid=1&pagenumber=4, accessed 28 October 2018
7. Truman, Harry, S., to Winston Churchill, 10 July 1948, Library of Congress, https://www.loc.gov/exhibits/churchill/interactive/_html/wc0261.html, accessed 28 October 2018
8. Churchill, *Triumph and Tragedy*, p545
9. Truman, Harry, S., Diary entry 17 July 1945, National Archives Catalog, Alonzo Fields Papers, 1939-1952, https://catalog.archives.gov/id/976500?q=976500, accessed 28 October 2018
10. Eden, *The Reckoning*, pp546-547
11. Churchill, *Triumph and Tragedy*, p523
12. Neiberg, Michael, *Potsdam: The End of World War II and the Remaking of Europe*, Hachette, 2015
13. Eden to Attlee, 23 July 1945, FO 954/22/45/60
14. Eden, *The Reckoning*, p550

Chapter 30: Licking wounds

1. Thorpe, p387
2. Soames, Mary (ed.), *Speaking for Themselves: The Personal Letters of Winston and Clementine Churchill*, Transworld Publishers, 1998, pp534-535
3. Hastings, p422
4. Truman, Harry, S., Diary entry 25 July 1945, Harry S. Truman Presidential Library and Museum, https://www.trumanlibrary.org/whistlestop/study_collections/bomb/large/documents/fulltext.php?fulltextid=15, accessed 2 November 2018
5. Gilbert, *Churchill: A Life,* p857
6. Eden, *The Reckoning*, p555
7. Thorpe, p403
8. Ibid, pp406-407

Chapter 31: Old friends, new enemies

1. Lomas, Daniel W.B., *Intelligence, Security and the Attlee Governments, 1945-1951: An Uneasy Relationship?*, Oxford University Press, 2017, p.102; Prime Minister, Foreign Affairs, House of Commons sitting, Hansard, 23 January 1948
2. Telegram, George Kennan to George Marshall ["Long Telegram"], February 22, 1946. Harry S. Truman Administration File, Elsey Papers,

https://www.trumanlibrary.org/whistlestop/study_collections/coldwar/documents/pdf/6-6.pdf, accessed 4 November 2018

3. Gilbert, Martin, *Churchill and America*, Simon and Schuster, 2008, p373
4. Muller, James W., *Churchill's "Iron Curtain" Speech Fifty Years Later*, University of Missouri Press, 1999, p41
5. Dutton, p233
6. Thorpe, p411
7. Churchill, Winston, S., House of Commons, Hansard, 12 December 1946, India (Constitution), https://api.parliament.uk/historic-hansard/commons/1946/dec/12/india-constitution, accessed 4 November 2018
8. HQ, Eastern Command, Calcutta, 24 August 1946, WO 216/662
9. Quoted, Guha, Ramchandra, Divided or Destroyed – Remembering Direct Action Day, 23 August 2014, Telegraph India, https://www.telegraphindia.com/opinion/divided-or-destroyed-remembering-direct-action-day/cid/157755, accessed 5 November 2018
10. Churchill, Winston S., 'Our Duty in India', Speech at Albert Hall, 18 March 1931, Churchill Archive, CHAR 9/98
11. Dutton, p320
12. Thorpe, p406
13. Soames, pp563-564

Chapter 32: A changed world

1. Thorpe, p414
2. Gilbert, Martin, *Never Despair, Winston S., Churchill 1945-1965*, p285
3. Ed., Pottle, Mark, *Daring to Hope – The Diaries and Letters of Violet Bonham Carter, 1946-1969*, Orion, 2000, p48
4. Eden, Anthony, House of Commons, Hansard, 19 June 1947, Foreign Policy in Europe, https://api.parliament.uk/historic-hansard/commons/1947/jun/19/foreign-policy-in-europe#S5CV0438P0_19470619_HOC_328, accessed, 9 November 2018
5. Eden, Anthony, *Days for Decision*, Houghton Mifflin, 1949, p24
6. Dutton, p287
7. Churchill, Winston, S., Note by the Prime Minister and Minister of Defence, 29 November 1951, United Europe, CAB 129/48 C(51)32
8. Pottle, p50
9. Dutton, p283
10. Gilbert, *Churchill: A Life,* p883-884
11. Dutton, p314
12. Ibid., p234
13. Ibid., p235
14. Gilbert, *Never Despair,* p344

Chapter 33: The road back to power

1. Gilbert, *Never Despair,* p378
2. Ibid., p380
3. Thorpe, p425
4. Churchill, Winston, S., House of Commons, Hansard, 15 February 1950, Defence (Government Policy), https://api.parliament.uk/historic-hansard/commons/1951/feb/15/defence-government-policy#S5CV0484P0_19510215_HOC_303, accessed 12 November 2018
5. Thorpe, p424
6. Gilbert, *Never Despair,* p440
7. Dutton p323
8. McGowan, Norman, *My Years with Churchill*, Souvenir Press, 1958, p101
9. Eden with Leslie Mitchell, 17 October 1951, Party Election Broadcast BBC, http://pebs.group.shef.ac.uk/sir-anthony-eden-leslie-mitchell, accessed 13 November 2018
10. Gilbert, *Never Despair,* p467
11. British Troops In Action In Egypt, *The Townsville Daily Bulletin*, 17 October 1951, https://trove.nla.gov.au/newspaper/article/63394043, accessed 16 November 2018
12. Gilbert, *Never Despair,* p468

Chapter 34: Side by side

1. Gilbert, *Never Despair,* p475
2. Unknown author, note of Moscow meeting 16 July 1951, Miscellaneous, FO 800/803
3. Churchill, Winston, S. House of Commons, Hansard, 6 November 1951, Debate on the Address, https://api.parliament.uk/historic-hansard/commons/1951/nov/06/debate-on-the-address, accessed 16 November 2018
4. Shuckburgh, Evelyn, *Descent to Suez: Diaries 1951-56*, Weidenfeld and Nicholson, 1986, p27
5. Gilbert, *Never Despair,* p489
6. Shuckburgh, p31
7. Thorpe, p440
8. Shuckburgh, p32
9. Ibid.
10. Horne, A., *Macmillan 1894-1957*, Macmillan, 1988, p347
11. McMahon, Robert, J., *Dean Acheson and the Creation of an American World Order*, Potomac Books, 2009, p34
12. Shuckburgh, p27

13. Dutton, p331
14. Secretary of State for Foreign Affairs (Anthony Eden), House of Commons, Hansard, Egypt (Terrorist Activities), 29 January 1952, https://api.parliament.uk/historic-hansard/commons/1952/jan/29/egypt-terrorist-activities, accessed 20 November 2018
15. Gilbert, *Never Despair,* p504

Chapter 35: Commitments

1. Eden, Anthony, Memorandum for Cabinet, 'Britain's overseas obligations', 18 June 1952, CAB 129/53
2. Eden, Anthony, India, 30 October 1952, FO 800/798
3. Soames, p568
4. Thorpe, p450
5. Gilbert, *Never Despair,* p554
6. Thorpe, p448
7. Shuckburgh, p66
8. Toye, p287
9. Dutton, p329
10. Eden, Anthony, 'Egypt: the Alternatives', 16 February 1953, CAB 129/59
11. Dutton, p361
12. Shuckburgh, p76
13. Ibid., p77
14. Prime Minister to Sec. of State for War, 9 December 1953, FO 800/750
15. Toye, p299
16. Gilbert, *Never Despair,* p579
17. Dutton, p336
18. Ferrel, R.H., (Ed.), *The Eisenhower Diaries*, W.W. Norton & Company, 1981, p223

Chapter 36: Frailties

1. Eden, Anthony, *Full Circle*, Cassell, 1960, p50
3. Gilbert, *Never Despair,* p590
4. Shuckburgh, p83
5. Lovell, Mary S., *The Churchills: In Love and War*, W.W. Norton & Company, 2012, p511
6. Churchill, Winston, House of Commons, Foreign Affairs, 11 May 1953, https://api.parliament.uk/historic-hansard/commons/1953/may/11/foreign-affairs, accessed 7 December 2018
7. Gilbert, *Never Despair,* p610
8. Thorpe, p461
9. Gilbert, p620

10. Thorpe, p463
11. Byroade to Matthews, Proposal to Organise a Coup d'état in Iran, Department of State, 26 November 1952
12. Lomas, Daniel, 'Iran, Britain and Operation Boot', *History Matters*, August 2013, https://www.historytoday.com/daniel-wb-lomas/iran-britain-and-operation-boot, accessed 2 October 2019
13. De Bellaigue, Christopher, *Patriot of Persia: Muhammad Mossadegh and a Very British Coup*, Random House, 2013, p274
14. 318. Memorandum From the Chief of the Iran Branch, Near East and Africa Division, Directorate of Plans (Waller) to Director of Central Intelligence Dulles, 16 September 1953, Foreign Relations of the United States, 1952–1954, IRAN, 1951–1954, United States Government Publishing Office Washington, 2017, p759
15. Shuckburgh, p91

Chapter 37: Bermuda and Berlin

1. Gilbert, *Never Despair,* p652
2. Shuckburgh, p107
3. Gilbert, *Never Despair,* p654
4. Moran, Lord, *Churchill: Taken from the Diaries of Lord Moran: The Struggle for Survival*, H. Mifflin, 1976, pp482-483
5. Gilbert, *Never Despair,* p658
6. Churchill to Eisenhower, 5 November 1953, Foreign Relations of The United States, 1952–1954, Western European Security, Volume V, Part 2, Conference files, lot 60 D 627, CP 187, https://history.state.gov/historicaldocuments/frus1952-54v05p2/d320, accessed 7 December 2018
7. Shuckburgh, p112
8. Dutton, p243
9. Gilbert, *Never Despair,* pp673-674
10. Dutton, p340
11. Shuckburgh, p118
12. Eden, *Full Circle*, p74

Chapter 38: Eden's finest hour

1. Ho Chi Minh to President Harry, S. Truman, Washington and Pacific Coast Field Station Files 1942-1945, 28 February 1946, https://research.archives.gov/id/305263, accessed 14 December 2018
2. Cable, James, *The Geneva Conference of 1954 on Indochina*, Macmillan Press, 2000, p10
3. Moran, p423

4. Eden, *Full Circle*, p91
5. Sullivan, Marianna P., 'France's Vietnam Policy, A study on French-American relations', *Contributions in Political Science*, Number 12, Greenwood Press, p45
6. Gilbert, *Never Despair*, p674
7. Hastings, Max, *Vietnam: An Epic History of a Divisive War 1945-1975*, William Collins, 2018, p66
8. Gilbert, *Never Despair*, p709
9. Hastings, *Vietnam: An Epic History of a Divisive War 1945-1975*, p65
10. Eden, *Full Circle*, p101
11. Cable, James, *The Geneva Conference of 1954 on Indochina*, Macmillan, 1986, p67
12. Hastings, *Vietnam: An Epic History of a Divisive War 1945-1975*, p42
13. Thorpe, p484
14. Eden, *Full Circle*, p117
15. Dutton, p346
16. Churchill, Winston, S., House of Commons, Hansard 17 and 20 May 1954, South-East Asia (Defence) and United States-French Discussions. https://api.parliament.uk/historic-hansard/commons/1954/may/17/south-east-asia-defence-1 and https://api.parliament.uk/historic-hansard/commons/1954/may/20/united-states-french-discussions, accessed 21 December 2018
17. Shuckburgh, p187
18. Gilbert, *Never Despair*, p714
19. Eden, *Full Circle*, p127
20. Cable, pp91-92
21. Van Dang, Nong, *Churchill, Eden and Indo-China, 1951-1955*, Anthem Press, 2011, p161
22. Dutton, p346
23. Sullivan, p51

Chapter 39: The end of the road

1. Gilbert, *Never Despair*, p719
2. Ibid., pp719-720
3. Thorpe, p494
4. Lloyd, Selwyn, Memorandum in Selwyn Lloyd papers, Churchill College, Cambridge, SELO 313 (1), quoted Thorpe, p500
5. Gilbert, *Never Despair*, pp757-758
6. Ibid., pp764-765
7. Gilbert, *Churchill: A Life*, p932
8. Gilbert, *Never Despair*, p773
9. Ibid., p776

Chapter 40: 'I am going'

1. Dutton, p352
2. Shuckburgh, p155
3. Gilbert, *Never Despair,* p812
4. Colville, John Rupert, *Winston Churchill and His Inner Circle*, Wyndham Books, 1981, p287
5. Wesley, F.C., *The Spectator*, Volume 193, 1954, A Spectator's Notebook, 17 September, p328
6. Eden, *Full Circle*, p260
7. Shuckburgh, p249
8. Mohammed, H. Heikal, *Cutting the Lion's Tail: Suez through Egyptian Eyes*, Andrew Deutsch, 1986, p84
9. Dutton, p363
10. Gilbert, *Churchill: A Life,* p936
11. Thorpe, p507
12. Soames, p589-590
13. Shuckburgh, p254
14. Gilbert, *Churchill: A Life,* p939
15. Coleville, John, *The Churchillians*, Weidenfeld & Nicholson, 1981, p.171; Rothwell, Victor, *Anthony Eden: A Political Biography, 1931-1957*, Manchester University Press, 1992, p164

Chapter 41: Flying solo

1. Gilbert, *Never Despair,* p830
2. Lamb, Richard, *The Failure of the Eden Government*, Sidgwick and Jackson, 1987, p7
3. Gilbert, *Churchill: A Life,* p943
4. Eden, Anthony, Talks with the Soviet Union, 26 March 1955, CAB 129/74/33
5. Gilbert, *Never Despair,* p842
6. Dutton, p276
7. Dutton, p259
8. Carlton, p376

Chapter 42: Dark horizons

1. Thorpe, p529
2. Churchill, Winston, House of Commons, Hansard, 1 March 1955, Defence
3. Gilbert, *Never Despair,* p848
4. Ibid., p617
5. 'Princess Margaret: recently unearthed letter sheds new light on decision not to marry', Roya Nikkhah, *Daily Telegraph*, 7 November 2009

6. Lamb, p45
7. Eden, *Full Circle*, p354
8. Gilbert, *Never Despair,* p860
9. Eden, *Full Circle*, p358
10. Gilbert, *Churchill: A Life,* p947
11. Eden, *Full Circle*, p363

Chapter 43: Suez

1. Soames, p605
2. Tunzelman, Alex Von, *Blood and Sand: Suez, Hungary and the Crisis that Shook the World*, Simon and Schuster, 2016, p1
3. Mr Peyton, House of Commons, Hansard, Suez Canal, 7 May 1956
4. Churchill, Winston, S., *The Unwritten Alliance*, Rosetta Books, 2014
5. Eden, Anthony, Cabinet meeting 4 October 1955, CAB 128/29
6. Gilbert, *Never Despair,* p877
7. Dutton, p360
8. Eden, *Full Circle*, p422
9. Nationalization of Suez Canal: text of speech by Col Nasser in Alexandria, 26 July 1956, FO 371/119080/14211/108
10. Thorpe, p570
11. Soames, p609
12. Moran, Lord, *Winston Churchill: The Struggle for Survival, 1940-1965*, Sphere books, 1968, p735

Chapter 44: 'A slow bleeding to death'

1. Thorpe, p593
2. Gilbert, *Churchill: A Life,* p948
3. Eden, *Full Circle*, p430
4. Ibid., p433
5. Gilbert, *Never Despair,* p885
6. Eden, *Full Circle*, p433
7. Thorpe, p599
8. Soames, p612
9. Thorpe, p605
10. Kyle, Keith, *Suez: Britain's End of Empire in the Middle East*, I.B. Tauris, 2003, p298, 497
11. Cabinet Minutes and Conclusions, 23 October 1956, CAB 128/30
12. Gatskill, Hugh, House of Commons, Hansard, Middle East Situation, 31 October 1956
13. Gilbert, *Churchill: A Life,* p949

Chapter 45: A premature end

1. Thorpe, p627
2. Eden, *Full Circle*, p552
3. Zelikow, Philip and Ernest R. May, *Suez Deconstructed: An Interactive Study In Crisis, War and Peacemaking*, Brookings Institution Press, 2019
4. Kunz, Diane, B., *The Economic Diplomacy of the Suez Crisis*, University of North Carolina Press, 2000, p148
5. Eden, *Full Circle*, p557
6. Eden, Anthony, House of Commons, Hansard, 20 December 1956, Israel and Egypt Anglo-French ultimatum
7. Kyle, Keith, *Suez: Britain's End of Empire in the Middle East*, I.B. Tauris, 2003, p497
8. Rhodes, p597
9. Carlton, p464
10. Thorpe, p644
11. Lamb, Richard, *The Failure of the Eden Government*, Sidgwick and Jackson, 1987, p305

Chapter 46: Out of office

1. Thorpe, p653
2. Ibid, p648
3. Carlton, p466
4. Gilbert, *Never Despair,* p907
5. Gilbert, Martin, *Winston S. Churchill, VII, 1945-1965*, pp618-619
6. Gilbert, *Never Despair*, p912
7. Ibid., p913
8. Dowty, Alan, *Middle East Crisis: US Decision-Making in 1958, 1970 and 1973*, University of California Press, 1985, p50
9. Gilbert, *Churchill: A Life,* p953
10. Thorpe, p661

Chapter 47: Old men

1. Gilbert, *Never Despair*, p921
2. Thorpe, p677
3. Kennedy, John, F. to Winston Churchill, 6 July 1962, https://www.loc.gov/exhibits/churchill/interactive/_html/wc0307.html, accessed 4 February 2019
4. Thorpe, p681
5. Gilbert, *Winston S. Churchill, VII, 1945-1965*, p636
6. Gilbert, *Never Despair*, p969

Endnotes

7. Earl of Avon, House of Lords, International situation, Hansard, 26 June 1963
8. Soames, Mary, *Clementine Churchill*, p478
9. Earl of Avon, House of Lords, Motion for an humble address and tributes, Hansard, 25 January 1965
10. Eden, Anthony, Remembering Winston Churchill: tributes to a legendary statesman and a wartime hero, Broadcast BBC 2, 5 December 1974, http://www.bbc.co.uk/archive/churchill/11017.shtml, accessed 4 February 2019

Epilogue

1. Thorpe, p657
2. Jenkins, Roy, *Churchill*, Pan Macmillan, 2002, p513
3. Eden, *The Reckoning*, p534

Select Bibliography

Writing anything about Winston Churchill is a problematic task, as there can be few people in history whose lives have been so closely researched. As with every historian writing about Churchill, I owe a great debt to the lifetime of scholarship conducted by Martin Gilbert. Anthony Eden's life is less well documented, but for much of it he carefully kept a diary, which is now held along with almost all of his political and personal correspondence in the Avon Papers at the University of Birmingham. The collections of the National Archives, the Avalon Project, the Truman Library, Hansard, British Pathé and BBC Television archives were also of great assistance in the completion of this book.

In the interests of brevity, especially when it comes to sources relating to Churchill, I have only included in this bibliography works specifically referenced within the text.

Adams, R., *British Politics and Foreign Policy in the Age of Appeasement,1935-39*, Springer, 1993

Barker, Elizabeth, *Churchill and Eden at War*, Macmillan, 1978

Barnes and Nicholson (ed.), *The Empire at Bay: The Leo Amery Diaries 1929-1945*, Hutchinson, 1988

Beitzell, Robert (ed.), *Tehran, Yalta, Potsdam: The Soviet Protocols*, Academic International, 1970

Boyle, Peter, *The Eden-Eisenhower Correspondence, 1955-1957*, University of North Carolina Press, 2006

Brendon, Piers, *The Decline and Fall of the British Empire*, Random House, 2010

Buchanan, Patrick, J., *Churchill, Hitler, and "The Unnecessary War": How Britain Lost Its Empire and the West Lost the World*, Crown, 2007

Cable, James, *The Geneva Conference of 1954 on Indochina*, Macmillan Press, 2000

Carlton, David, *Anthony Eden: A Biography*, Allen Lane, 1981

Churchill, Winston, *The Second World War, Volume 1: The Gathering Storm*, Cassell & Company Ltd, 1948

Churchill, Winston, *The Second World War, Volume V: Closing the Ring*, Cassel & Co Ltd., 1951

Churchill, Winston, *The Second World War*, Random House, 2002

Churchill, Winston, *The Grand Alliance*, Cassell & Co., 1949

Churchill, Winston, S., *The Hinge of Fate: The Second World War, Volume 4*, Rosetta Books, 2010

Churchill, Winston, *Triumph and Tragedy*, Houghton Mifflin Company Boston, 1953

Churchill, Winston, S., *The Unwritten Alliance*, Rosetta Books, 2014

Clark, M., *Mussolini*, Routledge, 2014

Clemens, Diane Shaver, *Yalta*, Oxford University Press, 1970

Cohen, Michael J., *Churchill and the Jews, 1900-1948*, Routledge, 2013

Coleville, John Rupert, *Winston Churchill and His Inner Circle*, Wyndham Books, 1981

Coleville, John, *The Churchillians*, Weidenfeld & Nicholson, 1981

Cooper, Artemis and Beevor, Anthony, *Paris After the Liberation: 1944-1949*, Penguin, 2007

Danchev and Todman (ed.), *War Diaries 1939-1945: Field Marshall Lord Alanbrooke*, Weidenfeld & Nicolson, 2001

Davies, Norman, *Rising '44: The Battle for Warsaw*, Macmillan, 2003

De Bellaigue, Christopher, *Patriot of Persia: Muhammad Mossadegh and a Very British Coup*, Random House, 2013

Dietrich, John, *The Morgenthau Plan: Soviet Influence on American Postwar Policy*, Algora Publishing, 2013

Dilks, David, (ed.), *The Diaries of Sir Alexander Cadogan, 1938-1945*, Cassell, 1971

Dowty, Alan, *Middle East Crisis: US Decision-Making in 1958, 1970 and 1973*, University of California, 1984

Dutton, David, *Anthony Eden: A Life and Reputation*, Hodder, 1997

Eden, Anthony, *The Eden Memoirs: Facing the Dictators*, Cassell & Company, 1962

Eden, Anthony, *The Reckoning*, Cassell, 1965

Eden, Anthony, *Full Circle*, Cassell, 1960

Faber, David, *Munich, 1938: Appeasement and World War II*, Simon & Schuster, 2009

Farrell, Brian, *Churchill and the Lion City: Shaping Modern Singapore*, NUS Press, 2011

Fenby, Jonathan, *Alliance: The Inside Story of how Roosevelt, Stalin and Churchill Won One War and Began Another*, Simon and Schuster, 2015

Ferrel, R.H., (ed.), *The Eisenhower Diaries*, W.W. Norton & Company, 1981

Ford, Douglas, *Britain's Secret War against Japan, 1937-1945*, Routledge, 2001

Gilbert, Martin, *Churchill: A Life*, Random House, 2000

Gilbert, Martin, *Road to Victory: Winston, S. Churchill 1941-1945*, Heinemann, 1986

Gilbert, Martin, *Churchill and America*, Simon and Schuster, 2008

Gilbert, Martin, *Churchill and the Jews: A Lifelong Friendship*, Henry Holt and Company, 2007

Gilbert, Martin, *The Holocaust: A History of the Jews of Europe during the Second World War*, Henry Holt and Company, 1985

Gorodetsky, Gabriel (ed.), *The Maisky Diaries: Red Ambassador to the Court of St James's 1932-1943*, Yale University Press, 2015

Gutman, Israel and Berenbaum, Michael, *Anatomy of the Auschwitz Death Camp*, Indiana University Press, 1998

Harbutt, Fraser J., *The Iron Curtain: Churchill, America, and the Origins of the Cold War*, Oxford University Press, 1988

Harvey, Oliver, *The Diplomatic Diaries of Oliver Harvey, 1937-1940*, Harper Collins, 1970

Hastings, Max, *Armageddon*, Macmillan, 2004

Hastings, Max, *Finest Years: Churchill as Warlord 1940-45*, Harper Press, 2009

Hastings, Max, *Vietnam: An Epic History of a Divisive War 1945-1975*, William Collins, 2018

Holmes, Richard, *The World at War: The Landmark Oral History from the Previously Unpublished Archives*, Random House, 2008

Horne, A., *Macmillan 1894-1957*, Macmillan, 1988

James, Robert Rhodes, *Anthony Eden*, Papermac, 1987

Janam, Mukherjee, *Hungry Bengal: War, Famine and the End of Empire*, Oxford University Press, 2015

Jenkins, Roy, *Churchill*, Pan Macmillan, 2002

Kennedy, Ludovic, *Pursuit, The Chase and Sinking of the Bismarck*, Book Club Associates, Collins Sons & Co Ltd, 1975

Kunz, Diane B., *The Economic Diplomacy of the Suez Crisis*, University of North Carolina Press, 2000

Kyle, Keith, *Suez: Britain's End of Empire in the Middle East*, I.B. Tauris, 2003

Lamb, Richard, *The Failure of the Eden Government*, Sidgwick and Jackson, 1987

Lehrman, Lewis E., *Churchill, Roosevelt & Company: Studies in Character and Statecraft*, Rowman & Littlefield, 2017

Lomas, Daniel W.B., *Intelligence, Security and the Attlee Governments, 1945-1951: An Uneasy Relationship?*, Oxford University Press, 2017

Lovell, Mary S., *The Churchills: In Love and War*, W.W. Norton & Company, 2012

MacDonogh, Giles, *1938: Hitler's Gamble*, Constable, 2009

Maisky, Ivan, *Memoirs of a Soviet Ambassador: The War 1939-1943*, Hutchinson, 1967

Maler, Thomas, *When Lions Roar: the Churchills and the Kennedys*, Crown, 2014

Mangold, Peter, *Britain and the Defeated French: From Occupation to Liberation, 1940-1944*, I.B.Tauris, 2011

Materski, Wojciech, *Katyn: A Crime without Punishment*, Yale University Press, 2008

McMahon, Robert J., *Dean Acheson and the Creation of an American World Order*, Potomac Books, 2009

McGowan, Norman, *My Years with Churchill*, Souvenir Press, 1958

McCrea, John L., *Captain McCrea's War: The World War II Memoir of Franklin D. Roosevelt's Naval Aide and USS Iowa's First Commanding Officer*, Skyhorse Publishing Inc., 2016

Michael, Robert Marrus, *The End of the Holocaust*, Walter de Gruyter, 1989

Mohammed, H. Heikal, *Cutting the Lion's Tail: Suez through Egyptian Eyes*, Andrew Deutsch, 1986

Moran, C., *Winston Churchill: The Struggle for Survival*, Constable & Company, 1966

Moran, Lord, *Churchill: Taken from the Diaries of Lord Moran: The Struggle for Survival*, H. Mifflin, 1976

Muller, James W., *Churchill's "Iron Curtain" Speech Fifty Years Later*, University of Missouri Press, 1999

Murfett M., *Shaping British Foreign and Defence Policy in the Twentieth Century: A Tough Ask in Turbulent Times*, Springer, 2014

Neiberg, Michael, *Potsdam: The End of World War II and the Remaking of Europe*, Hachette, 2015

Nicolson, Sir Harry, *Diaries and Letters: 1939-1945*, Collins, 1967

Peters, A.R., *Anthony Eden at the Foreign Office 1931-1938*, Gower Publishing Ltd., 1986

Plokhy, S.M., *Yalta: The Price of Peace*, Penguin, 2010

Pottle, Mark (ed.), *Daring to Hope – The Diaries and Letters of Violet Bonham Carter, 1946-1969*, Orion, 2000

Roberts, Andrew, *Churchill: Walking with Destiny,* Penguin, 2018

Robin, Anthony and Kushner, Jeremy, *The Persistence of Prejudice: Antisemitism in British Society during the Second World War*, Manchester University Press, 1989

Rothwell, Victor, *Anthony Eden: A Political Biography, 1931-1957*, Manchester University Press, 1992

Shuckburgh, Evelyn, *Descent to Suez: Diaries 1951-56*, Weidenfeld and Nicholson, 1986

Soames, Mary (ed.), *Speaking for Themselves, the Personal Letters of Winston and Clementine Churchill*, Transworld Publishers, 1998

Soames, Mary, *Clementine Churchill,* Doubleday, 2002

Stettinius, *Roosevelt and the Russians: The Yalta Conference*, Greenwood Press, 1970

Simpson, John, *A Mad World, My Masters: Tales from a Traveller's Life*, Pan Macmillan, 2001

Smith, T.O., *Britain and the Origins of the Vietnam War: UK Policy in Indo-China, 1943-50*, Palgrave, 2007

Sullivan, Marianna P., 'France's Vietnam Policy, A study on French-American relations', *Contributions in Political Science*, Number 12, Greenwood Press

Taylor, Frederick, *Coventry: November 14, 1940*, Bloomsbury, 2015

Telford, Taylor, *Munich: the Price of Peace*, Vintage Books, 1979

Thorpe, D.R., *Eden: The Life and Times of Anthony Eden First Earl of Avon, 1897-1977*, Random House, 2011

Toland, John, *Hitler: the Definitive Biography*, Knopf Doubleday, 2014

Toye, Richard, *Churchill's Empire*, Macmillan, 2010

Tunzelman, Alex Von, *Blood and Sand: Suez, Hungary and the Crisis that Shook the World*, Simon and Schuster, 2016

Van Dang, Nong, *Churchill, Eden and Indo-China, 1951-1955*, Anthem Press, 2011

Zelikow, Philip and May, Ernest R., *Suez Deconstructed: An Interactive Study In Crisis, War and Peacemaking*, Brookings Institution Press, 2019

Index

Abyssinia 3, 5, 9, 10, 13, 16
Arctic convoys 38, 54, 56, 57, 88
   convoy PQ17 56
Athens 37, 38, 123, 124, 125
   Churchill and Eden's visit to 123
atom bomb 71, 150, 192, 215
   Hiroshima 150, 215, 245
   Nagasaki 150, 215
   see also Cold War
Attlee, Clement 81, 96, 102, 105,
   141, 142, 144, 146, 148, 149,
   150, 152, 152, 154, 158, 159,
   163, 164, 165, 166, 167, 168,
   174, 186, 212, 247
Austria 3, 14, 15, 16, 139, 166, 202
   see also Schuschnigg, Kurt von

Baldwin, Stanley 6
Barbarossa 41
Battle of Britain 25, 29
Bermuda Conference 189, 190,
   194, 196
Bengal famine 119, 120, 156
Ben Gurion, David 228, 243
Bevin, Ernest 102, 148, 149, 154,
   159, 165, 168
Bismarck 38, 39, 40, 56
Bletchley Park 34, 42, 45
Blitz 26, 34, 36

British Empire viii, 42, 50, 79, 93,
   119, 122, 131, 132, 154, 155,
   161, 173, 225
Brooke, General Alan 85, 95, 105
Bulganin, Nikolai 211, 216, 218,
   230, 231
Burma 119, 121, 122, 124, 134,
   143, 158, 159, 218
Butler, Rab 208, 211, 217

Canada 83, 84, 85, 86, 110
   Churchill and Eden holiday 86
Casablanca Conference 62, 68,
   69, 70, 71, 72, 81
Chamberlain, Neville 5, 8, 9, 10,
   11, 12, 13, 16, 17, 19, 20, 22,
   33, 178
   peace for our time 17
Chamberlain, Lady Ivy 11
Chartwell 27, 77, 149, 185, 212,
   238, 239
Chequers 9, 25, 35, 41, 43, 46,
   177, 185, 198, 207, 225, 227
China 26, 50, 75, 76, 132, 158,
   161, 162, 172, 193, 199, 250
Churchill, Clarissa
   see Eden, Clarissa
Churchill, Clementine 27, 29, 30,
   49, 58, 68, 96, 113, 125, 128,

146, 149, 152, 158, 162, 170,
176, 184, 189, 198, 202, 208,
210, 223, 227, 240, 248
Churchill, Randolph 28, 29
Churchill, Winston
  birthdays 35, 94, 203,
    205, 246
  Coventry air raid 33, 34
  crisis over leadership 53
  disagreements with Eden
    63, 68, 69, 82, 102,
    111, 247
  funeral 247
  ill health 27, 95, 96, 185,
    187, 189, 228, 243, 246
  strokes 185, 187, 189,
    228, 243, 246
  Iron Curtain 145, 153, 154
  on Indian independence 79,
    155, 156
  on Singapore 26, 121
  painting 6, 30, 72, 149,
    239, 243
  Sutherland portrait
    204, 205
  praise for Mussolini 4
  relationship with Roosevelt 23,
    26, 39, 44, 46, 48, 49, 68, 72,
    84, 85, 95, 96, 111, 128, 137
  relationship with Queen
    Elizabeth 174, 208, 210
  resignation 6, 79, 146, 205,
    206, 207, 208
  speaking style 7, 15
  talks at Harrow 203
  visit to Moscow 58, 59, 60
  visits to the United States 49,
    81, 85, 86, 153, 154, 243

Ciano, Count 11
Cold War viii, 89, 114, 139,
  158, 165, 171, 175, 193, 212,
  215, 217, 218, 219, 220, 221,
  245, 250
  Marshall Plan 160
  Mutually Assured
    Destruction 245
Congress of Europe 160
Conservatives 7, 17, 19, 146, 164,
  168, 170, 177, 211, 212
Czechoslovakia 3, 8, 17, 18, 114,
  139, 153, 158, 220

Darlan, Francois 62, 63, 68
De Gaulle, Charles viii, 23,
  25, 62, 63, 69, 70, 71, 81,
  82, 85, 86, 96, 97, 101,
  102, 103, 113, 115, 116,
  117, 118, 122, 123, 132, 134,
  145, 249
  Churchill and Eden
    disagreement over 63, 81,
    82, 102, 122, 249
D-Day 65, 101, 102, 104, 122
  Churchill visit 103, 104
  Eden visit 104
Dulles, John Foster 188, 189, 191,
  194, 195, 196, 197, 198, 199,
  208, 221, 222, 226, 227
Dunkirk 24, 82

Eden, Anthony
  affairs 27, 30, 155
  art collecting 30
  affirmation from Dale
    Carnegie 31
  and Mussolini 3, 4, 83

difficulties working with
   Churchill travelling 49,
   50, 141
drug use 234
first meeting with Churchill 2, 3
First World War record 2
flying experiences 32, 37, 61, 87
frustrations with politics 80,
   141, 142, 186
   Viceroyship 79, 80
   UN Secretary General
      role 142
ill health 92, 182, 183, 242, 243
   botched operation 182, 183
   holiday in Jamaica 233
memoirs 54, 75, 130, 131, 151,
   182, 206, 218, 222, 232,
   239, 244, 248
Shakespeare 30, 145, 174, 243
speaking style 7
visits to Moscow 45, 47, 60,
   87, 88, 89
visits to the United States 74,
   97, 171, 172
Eden, Beatrice 27, 29, 30, 61, 79,
   80, 81, 142, 143, 145, 155,
   157, 239
   affairs 27, 142
Eden, Clarissa 176, 185, 186, 190,
   198, 201, 210, 226, 238, 239
Eden, Simon 27, 28, 30, 61, 121,
   124, 143, 145, 146
Egypt 6, 32, 33, 34, 54, 123, 167,
   168, 172, 173, 175, 177, 178,
   180, 189, 191, 198, 201, 205,
   206, 220, 221, 222, 224, 225,
   226, 227, 228, 230, 232, 233,
   235, 240

Eisenhower, Dwight D. viii, 62,
   63, 69, 95, 96, 102, 115, 136,
   138, 139, 144, 178, 179, 180,
   181, 182, 184, 186, 188, 189,
   190, 191, 194, 195, 196, 199,
   202, 207, 20-8, 211, 212, 213,
   215, 216, 221, 223, 225, 226,
   230, 233, 240, 243
El Alamein, battle of 61
Ethiopia
   see Abyssinia
elections 124, 135, 136, 142, 145,
   191, 192, 199, 221, 230

Fascism 3, 4, 14, 224
flying bomb 104, 105
France vii, 4, 9, 11, 17, 18, 23, 24,
   25, 39, 43, 45, 58, 62, 63, 69,
   70, 74, 81, 85, 86, 93, 96, 97,
   98, 100, 101, 102, 103, 104,
   105, 116, 117, 118, 122, 123,
   132, 133, 142, 194, 203, 223,
   227, 228, 230, 231, 233, 249
French Algiers Committee 85

Gallipoli Campaign 6, 30
Geneva Conference 193, 194,
   195, 196, 197, 198, 201
Gold Standard 6
Grandi, Dino 11
Greece 33, 37, 38, 112, 123, 124,
   125, 126

Hemingway, Ernest 4, 115
Hitler, Adolf vii, 3, 4, 6, 7, 8, 9,
   12, 14, 15, 16, 17, 18, 19, 22,
   25, 26, 31, 34, 36, 37, 38, 41,
   42, 43, 47, 49, 51, 52, 59, 65,

66, 67, 71, 72, 73, 83, 89, 90,
100, 105, 106, 115, 116, 117,
139, 140, 148, 150, 157, 192,
196, 225, 227
Hood, HMS 39, 40
Holocaust 64, 65
Home Guard 23
Hopkins, Harry 44, 75, 94, 130,
133, 137
Hull, Cordell 68, 85, 86, 87, 88,
89, 111, 128

India viii, 6, 44, 79, 80, 93, 98,
105, 119, 120, 121, 122, 155,
156, 158, 159, 178, 194, 218
independence 6, 79, 93, 155,
156, 157, 158, 159, 194
see also Bengal famine
Indochina 26, 75, 93, 97, 98, 122,
132, 133, 192, 193, 194, 195,
196, 197, 190, 199, 205, 245, 250
Dien Bien Phu 194, 195, 197
see also Geneva Conference
invasion of Soviet Union
see Barbarossa
Italy 3, 5, 9, 10, 11, 12, 14, 24,
26, 59, 70, 74, 83, 88, 90, 96,
98, 106, 149
entry into Second World War 24
see also Mussolini

Japan 26, 46, 70, 71, 91, 97, 98,
111, 132, 141, 148, 150, 193
see also Pearl Harbor

Kai-shek, Chiang 75, 91, 162
see also China
Katyn Massacre 77, 78

Kennedy, President 242
Khrushchev, Nikita 211, 213, 218,
219, 231

Labour Party 240
see also Attlee, Clement
Liberals 169
Lloyd George, David 2, 4, 5, 26,
35, 65

Macmillan, Harold 201, 202, 203,
210, 123, 238, 240, 243, 244
Maisky, Ivan 42, 43, 45, 47, 52,
56, 57, 64, 71, 72, 73, 74, 77
Mao, Zedong 75, 158, 162
see also China
Mongomery, Bernard 60, 61,
76, 103, 104, 105, 138, 140,
193, 194
see also North Africa
Mountbatten, Admiral 86
Molotov, Vyacheslav 51, 52, 58,
60, 86, 87, 88, 89, 112, 131,
133, 134, 144, 160, 182, 191,
192, 197, 199, 201, 202, 250
Moscow 42, 45, 47, 48, 50, 58,
60, 86, 87, 88, 89, 90, 91, 92,
93, 106, 107, 108, 112, 113,
114, 117, 118, 133, 136, 153,
170, 181, 218, 230, 231
Mussolini, Benito 3, 4, 5, 7, 8, 9,
11, 12, 13, 14, 15, 16, 18, 24,
77, 83, 178, 223, 225, 230
Myanmer
see Burma

Nasser, Gamal Abdel viii, 205,
206, 220, 221, 222, 223, 224,

225, 226, 227, 228, 230, 240, 241, 242
NATO 158, 161, 170, 175, 190, 191, 192
North Africa 32, 37, 38, 40, 49, 53, 54, 58, 60, 61, 62, 68, 69, 70, 72, 81, 83, 90, 96, 119, 249
  Torch landings 62
  see also Western Desert

Overlord
  see D-Day

Pacific War 60, 121
  see also Singapore, Churchill, Winston on
Paris 9, 23, 24, 68, 115, 116, 117, 118, 122, 171, 199, 207, 228
  liberation of 115, 116, 117
Pearl Harbor 46
Petain, Marshall 23, 25, 68
Poland 19, 20, 22, 43, 48, 49, 50, 51, 64, 75, 87, 89, 91, 93, 97, 106, 113, 127, 130, 134, 135, 136, 139, 144, 145
  see also Warsaw Rising
Polish government 43, 48, 51, 64, 77, 78, 97, 106, 107, 108, 113, 114, 135, 136
  see also Katyn massacre
Potsdam Conference 143, 148, 149, 153, 181

Quebec Conference 85
  see also Canada, Churchill and Eden visit
Queen Mary 101, 171, 172, 179

Royal Air Force 24, 25, 34, 61, 65, 100, 106, 121, 244, 245, 247
Royal Navy 22, 39, 40, 76, 111, 128
Rommel, Erwin 37, 38, 40, 53, 60, 61
Roosevelt, Franklin Delano viii, 9, 10, 11, 23, 26, 36, 39, 40, 44, 46, 48, 49, 50, 51, 52, 53, 58, 62, 68, 69, 70, 71, 72, 74, 75, 76, 81, 83, 84, 85, 86, 91, 92, 93, 94, 95, 96, 97, 98, 101, 201, 103, 107, 108, 101, 111, 115, 116, 118, 122, 124, 126, 127, 128, 130, 131, 132, 133, 134, 136, 137, 143, 144, 161, 171, 173, 187, 193, 249
  Eden jealousy over relationship with Churchill 85

Schuschnigg, Kurt von 14, 16
Spanish Civil War 4, 18
  Churchill and Eden discussion over lunch 4
Stalin, Joseph viii, 41, 43, 45, 47, 48, 49, 50, 51, 53, 57, 58, 59, 60, 68, 73, 74, 75, 77, 78, 83, 87, 88, 91, 92, 93, 94, 96, 97, 100, 103, 106, 107, 108, 111, 112, 113, 114, 115, 117, 118, 126, 127, 129, 130, 131, 132, 133, 134, 135, 136, 139, 143, 144, 145, 150, 152, 153, 160, 171, 176, 179, 181, 182, 187, 190, 202, 207, 250
  see also visit to Moscow, Churchill, Winston *and* visits to Moscow, Eden, Anthony

Stalingrad 60, 73, 74, 87, 90, 108
    debate over how to honour
      citizens 73, 74
Sudetenland 8, 17
Suez Canal 146, 168, 180, 184,
    189, 205, 206, 220, 222, 226,
    227, 228, 232, 235, 242
    see also Suez Crisis
Suez Crisis viii, 223, 225, 233, 235

Tehran Conference 92, 94, 96
Tobruk 35, 38, 53
Tripartite Pact 26
Truman, Harry 137, 143, 144,
    145, 148, 150, 152, 153, 154,
    160, 165, 171, 172, 173, 186,
    193, 250

U-boats 38, 56, 88, 90, 91
unconditional surrender 70, 71,
    133, 139, 140

United Nations 76, 131, 135, 137,
    141, 151, 165, 167, 198, 226,
    230, 232, 239

V1 bomb
    see flying bomb
VE Day 251
Vichy France 25, 26, 62
    see also Petain, Marshall
Vietnam
    see Indochina

Warsaw Rising 106, 107, 108,
    118, 110, 112, 115
Western Desert 32, 33, 35

Yalta Conference 127, 131, 132,
    133, 135